Feminist Edges of t

Feminist Edges
of the Qur'an

AYSHA A. HIDAYATULLAH

OXFORD
UNIVERSITY PRESS

OXFORD
UNIVERSITY PRESS

Oxford University Press is a department of the University of Oxford.
It furthers the University's objective of excellence in research, scholarship,
and education by publishing worldwide.

Oxford   New York
Auckland   Cape Town   Dar es Salaam   Hong Kong   Karachi
Kuala Lumpur   Madrid   Melbourne   Mexico City   Nairobi
New Delhi   Shanghai   Taipei   Toronto

With offices in
Argentina   Austria   Brazil   Chile   Czech Republic   France   Greece
Guatemala   Hungary   Italy   Japan   Poland   Portugal   Singapore
South Korea   Switzerland   Thailand   Turkey   Ukraine   Vietnam

Oxford is a registered trade mark of Oxford University Press
in the UK and certain other countries.

Published in the United States of America by
Oxford University Press
198 Madison Avenue, New York, NY 10016

© Oxford University Press 2014

All rights reserved. No part of this publication may be reproduced,
stored in a retrieval system, or transmitted, in any form or by any means,
without the prior permission in writing of Oxford University Press,
or as expressly permitted by law, by license, or under terms agreed with the
appropriate reproduction rights organization. Inquiries concerning reproduction
outside the scope of the above should be sent to the Rights Department,
Oxford University Press, at the address above.

You must not circulate this work in any other form
and you must impose this same condition on any acquirer.

Library of Congress Cataloging-in-Publication Data
Hidayatullah, Aysha A.
Feminist edges of the qur'an / Aysha A. Hidayatullah.
p. cm.
ISBN 978-0-19-935956-1 (hardcover : alk. paper) — ISBN 978-0-19-935957-8
(pbk. : alk. paper) — ISBN 978-0-19-935958-5 (ebook) — ISBN 978-0-19-935959-2
(ebook) 1. Qur'an—Feminist criticism. 2. Qur'an—Hermeneutics.
3. Feminist criticism. I. Title.
BP130.2.H53 2014
297.1'226082—dc23
2013033495

1 3 5 7 9 8 6 4 2
Printed in the United States of America on acid-free paper

Contents

Preface vii

Acknowledgments xi

Note on Transliteration and Translation xiii

Introduction 1

PART I: *Historical Emergence of Feminist Qur'anic Interpretation*

1. History of Tafsir 23
2. The Frames of Feminism 37
3. Relationships to Feminist Theologies and the State 46

PART II: *Three Methods of Feminist Qur'anic Interpretation*

4. Historical Contextualization Method 65
5. Intratextual Method 87
6. The Tawhidic Paradigm 110

PART III: *Critiques of Feminist Qur'anic Interpretation*

7. Initial Conclusions 125
8. A Critical Reassessment 146

9. Confronting Feminist Edges 178

Appendix: Select Qur'anic Verses 197
Notes 199
Bibliography 241
Index 255

Preface

MORE THAN TWENTY years have passed since the initial publication of *Qur'an and Woman*, Amina Wadud's now classic work that brought worldwide attention to an emerging revolution in women's readings of the Qur'an.[1] I marvel now as I look back at how that far-reaching revolution unfolded in my own small world. As a college student in the United States in the late 1990s struggling with my identifications as both a feminist and a Muslim, I was electrified by my first encounters with the works of Wadud, as well as those of Leila Ahmed, Riffat Hassan, and Azizah al-Hibri. Their works opened a new world of possibilities for me in relating to the Qur'an, as they did for countless other Muslim women, lending me hope for something beyond the painful experiences of feeling alienated as a woman by a religious tradition to which I was deeply devoted.

I discovered that Wadud, Hassan, and al-Hibri challenged patriarchal and sexist interpretations of the Qur'an and men's exclusive authority to interpret it, and they clarified the flaws and biases of traditional male interpretations, which, they argued, had obscured the liberating content of God's word. Uplifted and inspired by their works, I came to believe that the Qur'an itself was just to women, but that alternative interpretations were necessary to uncovering the text's egalitarian ethos. Directly after college, I began my graduate studies of Islam in a rush of excitement and optimism, confident that the critical study of the Islamic tradition would help me absolve the Qur'an of any blame for abuses of Muslim women and prove that it was Muslims, rather than God or the Prophet Muhammad, who were responsible for injustices perpetrated against them. I pursued my studies in search of a coherent picture of the "real" Islam perfectly aligned with my feminist values. I set out on the journey already sure of what was waiting for me at the end, equipped with a brand of certainty possible only in one's youth.

As it should be with any good education, by the time I began my dissertation, a number of things I learned had begun to chip away at that certainty, not the least of which was the discovery that the Prophet Muhammad kept at least one female slave. My study of the life of Mariyah the Copt first challenged my confidence that the Prophet had led a life, ahead of his time, commensurate with contemporary feminist values.[2] The discovery of unflattering practices and attitudes regarding women in the historical record of early Islam, though, did not shake my confidence that the Qur'an, as the divine word of God, still set the ultimate standards of feminist justice, even if Muslim understandings and applications of those divine standards often fell short throughout history. As planned, I set out to write my dissertation about the works of Amina Wadud, Riffat Hassan, Azizah al-Hibri, Asma Barlas, Fatima Mernissi, Sa'diyya Shaikh, and Kecia Ali—arguing that collectively they signaled the development of a coherent new field of feminist Qur'anic interpretation.

In 2009, I finished the dissertation I had set out to write, but its completion produced a paradoxical outcome. My study had the unsettling effect of unraveling for me the convictions that had initially guided me through that work, and the receipt of my doctorate left me with more questions than answers. My work had left me with the nagging suspicion that the text of the Qur'an could not in the end be coherently read through the techniques of feminist exegesis nor fully absolved of all blame for its sexist interpretations. By the end of the first year of my faculty appointment at the University of San Francisco (USF), I began to see that, as Raja Rhouni has put it, perhaps "Islamic feminist theory based on the postulate of the normativity of gender equality in the Qur'an has reached a theoretical dead end," though it was on that very postulate that most of the works analyzed in my dissertation were based.[3] In the time that has passed since then, I have become only further convinced that if Muslim women are to come fully to terms with cases in which the Qur'anic text lends itself to meanings that are detrimental to them, we must begin to confront those meanings more honestly, without resorting to apologetic explanations for them, or engaging in interpretive manipulations to force egalitarian meanings from the text. Furthermore, I have also come to believe firmly that we must begin to radically reimagine the nature of the Qur'an's revelation and divinity.

This new turn in my thinking, though, presented the problem of what should be done with my original work. With so much of it "undone" by the new directions of my intellectual trajectory, one option was to toss my earlier work into the dustbin of a past life. The other possibility was to publish it as a necessary documentation of revolutionary works of feminist Qur'anic exegesis at the end of the twentieth and beginning of the twenty-first century. No matter how much my positions have changed and are no longer mirrored in their assumptions, such a turn in my thinking would not have been possible in the first place had it not been for those courageous and groundbreaking works. I came to the decision that the story of those pioneering works deserves to be told with the same care with which they nurtured my development and the journeys of countless other Muslim women.

Had it not been for the observations of my editors and anonymous reviewers, this book would likely have stopped there—attempting nothing more than the worthwhile task of telling the story of groundbreaking Muslim feminist exegetical works and summarizing their findings. The astute readers of my prepublication manuscript, however, prompted me to articulate and forefront my newer insights despite my hesitations and reservations. I am all too aware of the tremendous risks associated with airing my critiques of feminist Qur'anic interpretation: creating the impression of undermining the work that has lent hope to so many Muslim women, and betraying the thinkers to whom I am deeply indebted for my intellectual framing;[4] undercutting the courageous work of activists all over the world who have fought for real-life gender reform on the basis of feminist interpretations of the Qur'an, using them to create urgent and vital improvement in the everyday realities of Muslim women; and supplying bigoted opponents of Islam with more fodder to fuel anti-Islam propaganda based on the ideological premise that Islam is irreconcilably misogynistic—making available to them criticisms they may twist into weapons to further their racist assault on Muslims, buttressed by the imperialist campaigns of American and European state actors capitalizing on widespread fears of Islam.[5] During the course of revising my manuscript, I feared that there were more reasons not to publish my critical insights than reasons in favor of proceeding.

In the end, only one reason to publish my criticisms outweighed all the reasons not to: the conviction that only complete intellectual honesty can ensure the long-term survival of feminist Qur'anic interpretation—even if it is called something entirely different one day; even if it transforms into something unrecognizable to us. If, as I have found, feminist Qur'anic interpretation has the tools of its own destruction already built into it, I am convinced that the way to keep moving forward is to trace the trajectory of its own undoing to its logical end, to understand its undoing in order to forge another path, and to examine the nature of its weaknesses in order to rebuild it in stronger ways. To make matters more complicated in pursuing this reinvestigation, it was not only the Qur'an that I began to see differently. I also began to observe the aporias of many of the ideas that the exegetes inherited from feminist thought; their often uncritical adoption seemed to make some of the foundational claims of feminist Qur'anic interpretation all the more untenable. The problems doubled in scope, as did the urgency of a candid revisiting of fundamental assumptions about both the Qur'an and feminist justice.

I have narrated the journey of this book to exhume the struggles that may have become buried in the course of editing and disciplining it into a publishable state (even though I am wary of the lucrative market for my very personal reflections and the voyeurism they might facilitate—given that a segment of readers, as Juliane Hammer has observed, are likely to enjoy consuming them out of a patronizing enthusiasm for stories of Muslim women's struggles to seek "liberation"[6]). There are many scholars who derive pleasure in pointing out the faults of others' work, gleefully measuring their success by how often they prove others wrong. My experience in writing the critical portions of this book could not have been further from pleasurable. The criticism of ideas I have long held most dear, often developed by scholars whom I hold in the highest esteem, came with much loss and anguish. If this process sometimes caused me great pain, it is likely that some personally invested readers may experience some measure of the same grief I did. It is primarily for this reason that some statement of my intentions seems appropriate here: If I have undercut or irreparably damaged something in the course of my critiques, I have done so only because I have valued that something more than to let it be diminished by denial. If I have undermined anything, I have done so in accordance with my conscience, with a deep respect for my predecessors and the gravity of the endeavor, and ultimately, with the enduring hope for something better.

And in the very end, as Muslims say, God knows best.

Aysha A. Hidayatullah
June 2013
Oakland, California

Acknowledgments

I HAVE MANY people to thank for their support in writing this book. First, I owe a special debt of gratitude to Kimberly Rae Connor, Kecia Ali, Judith Plaskow, Juliane Hammer, Peter Matthews Wright, and Caleb Elfenbein for reading and commenting on my manuscript at various stages. I must also thank Cynthia Read at Oxford University Press for her support of this book, as well as my manuscript's two anonymous reviewers: whoever you are, know that your critical feedback was central to improving this work. I am deeply grateful to all of you for your invaluable insights—acknowledging, of course, that all shortcomings in this book are my own.

I owe many other debts of gratitude for things beyond the immediate demands of the manuscript itself, particularly my parents, Anjum and Anwer Hidayatullah, and brother, Asim Anwer, for encouraging my education, and my cousins, aunts, and uncles for their heartening affection and backing. I am also especially grateful to Dwight Reynolds, Juan Campo, and Rudy Busto of University of California, Santa Barbara (the committee for the dissertation this book is based on) for their patience and guidance; Kim Connor for prompting me to find my voice after I arrived at University of San Francisco (USF); Juliane Hammer for her devoted encouragement; Laury Silvers for her bold authenticity; Sa'diyya Shaikh for her grace and spiritual discernment; Amina Wadud for reminding me when I stood on the edge of the abyss that I need not fall; Susan Abraham for her fortitude and example; Fatima Seedat for her sharp vision and testimony; Kecia Ali for her generous and formidable insights; Zayn Kassam for her disarming sincerity; Judith Plaskow for her wisdom and mentorship; my colleagues in the Theology and Religious Studies department at USF for making USF a wonderful home for me; Jake Nagasawa for his luminosity and unfailing help in surviving the everyday of the university; my former students Carolynne Andersen (who along with Jake scanned several thousand pages of my reading materials), Monica Doblado, Nicole Moore,

Caroline Fruth, and Sarah Wells, all of whom have lent me the hope and strength to keep teaching with an open heart; Vincent Pizzuto for his inspiring generosity; Lois Lorentzen for the true gift of her mentorship; the Leadership Team of the University of San Francisco for their tremendous support of my work (especially the Dean of the College of Arts and Sciences Marcelo Camperi, Vice Provost for Diversity Engagement and Community Outreach Mary Wardell-Ghirarduzzi, and Provost Jennifer Turpin); all the organizers, leaders, and fellow participants in the 2011–2012 Wabash Workshop for Pre-Tenure Asian and Asian American Religion and Theology Faculty, who provided the crucial push to bring this book to fruition; Mark Miller, a true man for others, for his uncommon kindness; Aaron Hahn Tapper for his long-standing encouragement; Patricia Kubala for her loving support the long route from UC Santa Barbra to Oakland; C. Thaler for her saving brilliance; Kristen Brustad and Mahmoud Al-Batal for their immeasurable support during my undergraduate years; Sophia Pandya for her sisterhood and mentorship in Santa Barbara; Taymiya Zaman for her wicked humor and relentless honesty; Jawziya Zaman for bringing me back to earth; Susan Henry-Crowe for nurturing my voice before I even knew I had one; both her and Chuck Hayes for their loving embrace each time I have returned to where I started; Alta Schwartz and Richard Gale for always providing a place to think about possibilities; Reema Ali for saving my life in more ways than one; Zahra Ayubi for her camaraderie in the struggle; Amanullah De Sondy for his charisma and joyousness; Zahra Noorbakhsh for the medicine of laughter; Annalise Glauz-Todrank for her boundless devotion and care; Caleb Elfenbein for his calm witness for so many years; Harley Augustino for helping me to see beyond every horizon; Jeremy Soh for his life-giving wisdom throughout this book's trials; Michael Jerryson for his familial kindness and belief in me; Sienna and Parker Jerryson for their bright-eyed precocity and healing presence; and Fawn Jerryson for the gift of a sisterhood beyond space and time. Finally, hearty thanks are due to all the other teachers and friends who have touched my life and had a hand in making the writing of this book possible.

Note on Transliteration and Translation

I HAVE UTILIZED a simplified Arabic-to-English transliteration method that is based on the *International Journal of Middle East Studies* system but excludes most diacritical marks—both for the ease of readers unfamiliar with Arabic and because readers of Arabic will easily identify terms without requiring diacriticals. Though I do not employ underdots for Arabic consonants or macrons for long vowels, I do employ the symbols of (') for the medial-position and final-position letter *hamza* and (') for the letter *'ayn*. To make words easier to recognize, my transliterations of Qur'anic excerpts do not reflect the assimilation of the definite article by sun letters, and they reflect elisions of *hamza* only in the case of preceding inseparable prepositions, conjunctions, and prefixes. I have also standardized several recurring Arabic terms that do not appear in italics due to their commonality and increasing recognition in English, including Qur'an, sura, Hadith(s), Sunna, ijtihad, tafsir, shaykh, ulama, Sunni, and Shi'i. In addition, I frequently use a few anglicized adjectival terms derived from Arabic words, namely Qur'anic and tawhidic.

All English translations of portions of the Qur'an appearing throughout the book are my own unless otherwise indicated.

Feminist Edges of the Qur'an

Introduction

> *This movement seeks to take the Western "hermeneutic" methodology and apply it to the Noble Qur'an and Islamic religious texts in general, with complete indifference to the principles of Qur'anic exegesis and rules of interpretation established in our Arabic-Islamic heritage . . . The dangers of this phenomenon may not be obvious today; but as this "intellectual" output continues, the cultural environment will become polluted by its by-products until future generations are left unable to breathe clean air . . . I ask Allah—Most High—to bring these bright minds back to the vastness of their culture and heritage, and the origins and reality of their existence.*
>
> —HASAN MAHMUD ʿABD AL-LATIF AL-SHAFIʿI, "The Movement for Feminist Interpretation of the Qur'an and Religion and Its Threat to the Arabic Language and Tradition."[1]

IT MAY SEEM odd to begin a book about the rise of feminist exegesis of the Qur'an with a statement that seeks so passionately to discredit it, but the inadvertent admission found between the lines of the shaykh's entreaty gives plenty of cause to celebrate the advancement of feminist Qur'anic interpretation. These words published in 2010 by a scholar of the Qur'an at the University of Cairo firmly attest to the growing recognition of a marked movement for feminist interpretation of the Qur'an, even among its staunchest opponents. That al-Shafiʿi takes it upon himself to address these works and that he refers to them as constitutive of a "movement" or "phenomenon" furnish powerful evidence that feminist scholarship of the Qur'an consists not merely of a few scattered and obscure works with a scant readership but rather has grown by now into an identifiable field of Qur'anic interpretation with which increasing numbers of Muslims are beginning to grapple. In other words, even those who remain unconvinced by the arguments of Muslim feminist scholars are at the very least forced to take note of what al-Shafi'i inadvertently admits: that feminist scholarship of the Qur'an—whatever one's views of it may be—has now emerged as a force with which Muslims must reckon.

Al-Shafi'i's alert to the "threat" posed by this scholarship is also an indication of how high the stakes are in feminist interpretation of the Qur'an, which often takes on a civilizational importance in discourses about Islam; these stakes are far more than symbolic. The battle over Muslim women, since the time of European colonial rule in the Muslim world, has recurrently treated them as pawns in a territorial contest between the West and Muslims over "culture" and modern "progress." Against the backdrop of the colonial history in which Europeans framed their conquests of Muslim lands as civilizing missions that would save Muslim women from Muslim men, Muslim defensiveness against Euro-American onslaughts on Muslim cultures has resulted in the casting of Muslim women in the perpetual role of cultural gatekeepers, rendering them the repositories for Muslims' most deeply held values, and transforming debates on gender into contests over cultural authenticity whereby many Muslims have come to associate feminism with imperialist violence. In recent times, a powerful manifestation of this discourse surfaced in the justification of the U.S. invasion of Afghanistan in 2001 with reference to the "plight" of Muslim women; today Muslim women's behaviors and appearances continue to serve as barometers for Muslim communities' acclimation to Western democratic values. In the confines of this restrictive discourse, Muslim women's efforts at developing feminist exegesis of the Qur'an are often reduced, as we see in the position of al-Shafi'i, to their internalization of "Western" modes of thinking and the betrayal of the foundations of Muslim religio-cultural heritage.

The accusation that feminist Qur'anic interpretation is contaminated by Western modes of thought enlists the charge that it transgresses the boundaries of Islamic tradition. Thus, skepticism of the credibility of feminist Qur'anic interpretation also results from what many scholars have commonly referred to as the modern "crisis" of Islamic authority, one which has broken the "monopoly" of the ulama (an elite class of religious scholars often viewed as the custodians of Islamic tradition) on the production of authoritative religious knowledge.[2] This historical development laid the Qur'an open to the interpretations of other thinkers in the service of numerous reform platforms. However, as Juliane Hammer has argued, "the very crisis of authority that provided an opening" for feminist Qur'anic interpretation is also its "greatest obstacle," as interpretive authority becomes increasingly disputed, diffuse, and difficult to consolidate.[3] This contestation over authority, in fact, directly informs my reference to "edges" in *Feminist Edges of the Qur'an*, whose title draws on the work of Richard Bulliet in *Islam: The View from the Edge* (1994) and *The Case for Islamo-Christian Civilization* (2004).[4]

As Bulliet points out, Islamic history repeatedly features elite religious authorities' attempts to eliminate what they perceive as unacceptable, nonnegotiable aberrations to their views of Islam.[5] Such authorities draw lines around an inviolable "center" of Islamic tradition, attempting to seal it off from deviations in thought and practice outside of its imagined "edge" as a way to secure compliance with their religious authority.[6] However, as Bulliet demonstrates, Muslim thought and practice on the "edge" have persisted steadily throughout the course of Islamic history; various groups of Muslims have always practiced Islam in ways that do not conform to the regulations of the "center."[7] Moreover, he argues that the "impetus for change in Islam has more often come from . . . the edge than from the center."[8] I see feminist Qur'anic interpretation as residing precisely at such an edge, a place of animated change and the avowal and disavowal of tradition—a place home to many "Muslims in spiritual quandary," including, but not only, Muslim feminists.[9] My location of feminist Qur'anic exegesis at this edge, however, should not be read as its relegation to the permanent margins of Islamic tradition. As Bulliet aptly points out, "Several major developments that are now considered integral to the Islam of the center originally formed on the edge"; that is, the edge of Islam has periodically moved, holding the possibility for a new location in relation to the "center."[10] Thus, the title of *Feminist Edges of the Qur'an* connotes that feminist Qur'anic exegesis is located at the feminist edge of contemporary notions of Islamic tradition—a place of increased encounter and confrontation, as observed in the epigraph of this chapter. The feminist edge of Qur'anic interpretation, then, is the site of dynamic challenges to the boundaries of Islamic tradition.

The objective of this book is to synthesize and critically respond to the works of late twentieth-century and early twenty-first-century scholars engaged in feminist interpretations of the Qur'an. My purpose is twofold: to read the works side by side as forming a nascent field of Qur'anic tafsir (i.e., exegesis or interpretation), and to provide a critical assessment of their methods and conclusions. With the aim of clarifying overall trends in the most significant feminist scholarship on the Qur'an for the benefit of readers hoping to understand the field as a whole, I outline the works' common terms, themes, and concepts, and I outline their collective trajectory. I then move on to offer an in-depth critical response to the works, assessing the theoretical viability of many of their fundamental tenets and offering some of my own contributions and conclusions.

But first we might ask, what is feminist interpretation of the Qur'an, and why refer to it as such? Feminist exegesis of the Qur'an is a strand of contemporary Qur'anic tafsir (whose general history is the subject of chapter 1) that, in contrast to premodern tafsir works, explicates the Qur'an not by proceeding systematically through the entirety of the text but rather selects verses according to their applicability to the themes of interest to the exegete, who interprets the selected verses in conjunction with one another to shed light on the Qur'an's broader treatment of the chosen themes.[11] As Hammer points out, the "application of the term *tafsir*" to these works points to the expansion of "the ways in which Muslims, especially modern and contemporary, have approached their sacred text."[12] The feminist exegetical works I examine share the aim of advocating the full personhood and moral agency of Muslim women *within* the parameters of the Qur'an, which they all treat as the divine word of God, and to which they attribute the principle of the equality of all human beings, male and female.

Some readers will likely object to my classification of these works as feminist, as some of their authors disavow or, at the very least, are ambivalent toward feminist terms and vocabulary. Such ambivalence or rejection of feminist terminology derives from unresolved disputes over the appropriateness or openness of a term embroiled in the history of Western colonialism and sometimes treated as contradictory to religious subjectivities. However, I use the signifier "feminist" in classifying these works to emphasize their pointed challenge to male power and interpretive privilege—which vitally links them, for better or for worse, to feminist thought regardless of authorial intention or self-identification. While it is, of course, essential to consider authors' self-identifications carefully, I do not uphold the premise that scholars are the final authorities on what we can call their work. I reject the ideological limitations that such a notion places upon critical thought and historiography, which effectively sections off areas of critical inquiry and grants others a peculiar immunity from scrutiny—a move that is often undergirded by a spoken or unspoken claim to sacrosanct notions of individuality and self-knowledge. Moreover, despite the very real problems with employing the term "feminist" in describing these works (detailed in chapter 2), I also maintain my use of the term as a much needed alternative to calling these works women's tafsir or gender sensitive (or "gender just") tafsir. The former attaches a dangerous essentialism to women's ways of reading the Qur'an (or worse, to "the Muslim woman" altogether[13]), as if all women have the same views of the Qur'an. The latter incorrectly suggests that these works centrally participate in a critical interrogation of gender; while the works do in fact take on gender as a category of analysis, for the most part, they take the existence of gender and sex binaries for granted (as examined in chapters 7 and 8). Finally, I employ the term cognizant of the dangers of "ghettoizing" feminist interpretations (reinforcing their "otherness" and marginality) by calling them feminist; we might hold out hope that there will come a time when feminist perspectives will become widely integrated enough into mainstream thought that they will no longer require this distinguishing qualifier, even though at present this is not the case.

I have chosen to focus on the works of scholars who, through the publication of full-length monographs or a substantial repertoire of works consistently and primarily focused on feminist Qur'anic exegesis, have engaged in feminist interpretation of the Qur'an in a sustained manner by applying a common set of identifiable textual approaches to the Qur'an. Therefore, my focus does not include the works of pioneering scholars such as Fatima Mernissi, Ziba Mir-Hosseini, Leila Ahmed, Zayn Kassam, Ghazala Anwar, Amira Sonbol, Gwendolyn Zoharah Simmons, Maysam al-Faruqi, Aminah McCloud or Nimat Barazangi, and many others too numerous to name, who are not primarily engaged in Qur'anic exegesis or in the case of Barazangi, not concerned with gender as a category of analysis. My examination also does not include Laleh Bakhtiar's recent translation of the Qur'an; although her translation is in part inspired by an interest in the Qur'an's treatment of women (particularly the so-called wife-beating verse) and thus is informed by an interpretive perspective somewhat relatable to the works studied here, it is not, however, a work of tafsir whose interpretive techniques are made explicit.[14] It is also important to state that a focus on the works of the chosen exegetes may inadvertently contribute to the obscuring of Shi'i perspectives in feminist Qur'anic interpretation. This result reflects the current tendency of the field of feminist Qur'anic interpretation not to incorporate explicitly Shi'i perspectives and to treat Sunni perspectives as an unnamed "default." This bias is thus also present in this book, and though it is inadvertent, it is an important one to bear in mind.

For a number of reasons related to both the history of Islam in the United States and the structure and trends of U.S. academia that have resulted in somewhat unique opportunities for Muslim women to conduct and publish their feminist Qur'anic interpretations, all but one of the scholars whose works this book examines are located in the United States. This is probably one of the many underlying reasons why the works exhibit the similar and overlapping interpretive strategies in which I am interested, and it means that the scope of this study is not global. The American focus of this book follows from a thorough familiarity with the U.S. context that best positions me to analyze these works. This also means that the works examined here have been published initially in English (though sometimes later translated from English into other languages). Due to trends in the U.S. academic publishing market and its international reach, along with the domination of English as a global language, Margot Badran has observed that "English is the common language of Islamic feminism."[15] The language of the works and location of their authors have the twin effects, in Hammer's words, of both "privileging and discrediting them in the Muslim world"; this is the result of the view held by many Muslims in Muslim-majority countries of American Islam's lack of authenticity, concurrent with the "role of the United States as a soft power which produces and distributes knowledge and information on a global scale."[16] Bearing in mind the causes and effects of this soft power, even as I acknowledge the U.S.-centric focus of my work and justify it as a matter of scope, as Sadia Abbas might point out, doing so does not absolve my work of its inevitable "complicity with the institutions of empire."[17] Such complicity allows my focus to take on the misleading appearance of somehow resulting benignly from a mere accident of history or an apolitical methodological decision, when in reality it is shaped by a U.S. hegemony that both creates conditions for the emergence of feminist Qur'anic exegesis in the United States and contributes to the limitation of the possibilities for its production (and the recognition of that production) elsewhere.

But, for a moment, if it is possible to find some quiet in the midst of the politicized and sensational commotion around feminist Qur'anic interpretation, we might be able to make out a story that is often drowned out by all the background noise. The story of the emergence of feminist Qur'anic interpretation beginning in the late 1970s and early 1980s has by now been told in different ways and to different degrees by numerous scholars, including Zayn Kassam,[18] Roxanne Marcotte,[19] Nelly van

Doorn-Harder,[20] Juliane Hammer,[21] and many others. Here I focus on the U.S.-based scholars Riffat Hassan, Azizah al-Hibri (a scholar of Islamic law who has nonetheless devoted much of her attention to the Qur'an), Amina Wadud, and Asma Barlas; in addition, I also include Saʿdiyya Shaikh (located in South Africa rather than the United States, and although often associated with her work on Sufism, she has published works that are vitally related to the work of the aforementioned scholars) and U.S.-based scholar Kecia Ali (who, although reputed for her work on Islamic jurisprudence and ethics, has responded in crucial ways to their discussions). In general, this book pays the most attention to Wadud and Barlas due to their publishing full-length books whose primary undertaking is Qur'anic exegesis, as well as to Kecia Ali due to her influence on my critical treatment of the works. The story of these works' emergence, which is followed by short biographical profiles of each scholar, begins with a first generation of scholars consisting of Riffat Hassan, Azizah al-Hibri, and Amina Wadud, with Hassan starting her work in the 1970s and the latter two beginning theirs in the 1980s. In telling the story, I respond directly to Juliane Hammer's call to understand the works of pioneering scholars of feminist exegesis in light of their historical context and activist engagements.[22]

The historical backdrop of the works of the first generation is the rise of the "Islamic revival" and Islamism in many parts of the Muslim-majority world. For Hassan, this backdrop is located specifically in Pakistan and for Wadud in her temporary home in Malaysia;[23] for Wadud, Hassan, and al-Hibri, the backdrop also consists of American reactions to these events when they are at home in the United States, where the three relocated while pursuing their careers in the academy. The emergence of their work is thus also marked by Muslim women's increased involvement worldwide in international human rights initiatives and local grassroots NGO work beginning in the 1980s (leading to the founding of groups such as Women Living Under Muslim Laws and Malaysia-based Sisters in Islam), especially the historic 1995 U.N. World Conference on Women in Beijing, and the escalation in discussions among Muslim women there about the U.N.'s CEDAW (Convention on the Elimination of All Forms of Discrimination Against Women) document.[24] During this time, a growing number of Muslim women interested in women and Islam also began their studies in the U.S. academy, leading to the rise of a second generation of scholars beginning in the late 1990s and early 2000s, represented here by Saʿdiyya Shaikh (who pursued her doctorate in the United States despite working largely from a South African perspective that grounded her efforts in a response to apartheid) and Kecia Ali (who has worked entirely in the United States). These women (among whom I include myself) are the direct beneficiaries of the enormous ground covered by the first generation, though a marked generation gap, which I will explain below, emerged between the first and second group.[25] Although chronologically speaking, Asma Barlas would belong to the second generation, given that her participation in the field of feminist Qur'anic exegesis does not commence until much later than that of Hassan, al-Hibri, and Wadud, nevertheless, she is more closely related to the first generation of scholars because her approach resembles the first-generation characteristics I identify below. The story of the second generation is still unfolding and rapidly expanding, and it is too early to tell much of it; therefore, I will draw fewer conclusions about it.

While the first generation worked as "trailblazers" under tremendous pragmatic pressures to address an aggressive wave of oppressive restrictions on Muslim women, the second generation builds upon on their exegetical work in ways that are shaped markedly less by such pragmatic pressures.[26] Though second-generation scholars are clearly also engaged in significant activist projects in their own times, their work is far less driven by the immediate demands of the activism that the Islamic revival required of the first generation, which I would argue accounts for the far greater degree of apologia about "true" Islam's nonoppressive treatment of women in works of the first generation, due to its pragmatic value in combating interpretations of Islam that were extremely damaging to women. The first generation also experienced with particular brutality the male domination of Islamic scholarship, as well as sexism, racism, and Orientalist attitudes within the U.S. academy, including the particularly condescending and exclusionary tendencies of feminists in the U.S. academy in the 1980s and 1990s.[27] Although such dynamics remain prevalent today, the first generation arguably experienced a more intense brand of alienation, hostility, and vicious attacks on their credibility as pioneering Muslim women scholars within Muslim communities and the academy. This is perhaps also why it may not be mere coincidence that the scholars of the first generation studied here have all published deeply personal writings about the intimate details of their lives, which is not characteristic of the second generation of scholars. I suspect that first-generation scholars experienced a kind of isolation and a desire for the recognition of their mistreatment that may have, in part, inspired the narration of their personal journeys. Without reducing their eloquent writings to these factors, here I am thinking mainly of Riffat Hassan's candid "Jihad Fi Sabil Allah," Azizah al-Hibri's "Hagar on My Mind," and Wadud's "On Belonging as a Muslim Woman" in addition to many portions of her *Inside the Gender Jihad*.[28]

The fortitude required to endure the hostile environments in which the pioneering scholars began their work is perhaps related to a defensive and self-protective quality sometimes observed in the approaches of the first generation. This quality may bear some relationship to the peculiar lack of collaboration between the scholars despite the obvious parallels in their works and the mutual affirmation they could have experienced by working together.[29] The fragmentation between their efforts is concretely demonstrated in the tendencies of Riffat Hassan, Azizah al-Hibri, and Amina Wadud not to refer to each other's writings in overlapping discussions. (This is despite the fact that all three scholars are included in Gisela Webb's anthology *Windows of Faith: Muslim Women Scholar-Activists in North America*.[30]) In Hassan's works on the creation story, to my knowledge she does not cite the other scholars; though she began her work before al-Hibri and Wadud, I have yet to locate references to their groundbreaking work in her later writings. Al-Hibri also does not cite the others in her discussions of the creation story or verse 4:34 to my knowledge (though she does, however, on one occasion cite a passage from Wadud on nonspecific notions of gender in the Qur'an[31]). In *Qur'an and Woman*, Wadud's work exhibits two rare instances of citing al-Hibri: one in which she excerpts two short passages from al-Hibri's very important work on verse 4:34, and another in which she cites a statement on patriarchal practice in Islam.[32] In her endnotes in *Qur'an and Woman*, Wadud also refers to a relatively obscure article by Riffat Hassan for its discussions of certain Hadith reports but does not cite or discuss Hassan's pioneering readings of the Qur'anic creation story.[33] Both Wadud and al-Hibri have employed the concept of "satanic logic," but neither has referenced the other, though Wadud may be vaguely referring to al-Hibri's use of the concept in a reference to monotheism being a focal point in Islamic reform in her recent *Inside the Gender Jihad*.[34] In this book, I have not located references to al-Hibri or Hassan in Wadud's retrospective reflections on the development of Muslim feminist scholarship. In pointing out the lack of mutual reference to one another, I do not claim that the first-generation scholars intentionally neglect each other's work or that it amounts to territorialism, as I cannot judge fully what accounts for this characteristic. However, it is still significant that they either did not or could not work in solidarity, since their work could have otherwise gained more momentum or taken different directions. In contrast, Asma Barlas credits Hassan, al-Hibri, and especially Wadud, whose work in particular she openly builds upon and who is also the subject of an entire article she authored;[35] this is despite the fact that Barlas tends not to engage the work of second-generation scholars to whom she is chronologically related. Meanwhile, Saʻdiyya Shaikh and Kecia Ali prominently acknowledge and discuss the works of both first-generation and second-generation scholars. Overall, the second generation already exhibits a much higher degree of collaboration and mutual support and engagement. In order to familiarize readers with other important aspects of these scholars' individual careers, I offer a short biographical sketch of each figure.

Riffat Hassan

Riffat Hassan has been a professor of Religious Studies at the University of Louisville, Kentucky since 1976. Born in Lahore, Pakistan, to an upper-class family and educated in English medium British schools in Pakistan, she attended university in England in the 1960s, earning a doctorate focused on the philosophy of Muhammad Iqbal.[36] She went on to teach at the University of Lahore in the late 1960s and then worked for Pakistan's Ministry of Information and Broadcasting until 1972. Shortly thereafter she emigrated to the United States and began teaching at Oklahoma State University, where, in her own words, she "began [her] career as a 'feminist theologian'" in 1974.[37] She recounts that prior to finally settling down in the United States, she had briefly returned to Pakistan but was resolved that the corrupt Pakistani government would not allow her to live and work there.[38] Her involvement in "an ongoing 'trialogue' of Jewish, Christian, and Muslim scholars" throughout 1979 to investigate "women-related issues in the three 'Abrahamic' faith traditions" (related, it seems, to a continuing interest in the deterioration of Pakistani women's rights under the administration of General Muhammad Zia-ul-Haq beginning in 1979) appears to have been formative to her work as a self-proclaimed feminist theologian.[39] Of all the scholars examined in this study, Hassan appears to be the only one to have expressly identified her work with feminist theology. In a 1991 essay, she wrote, "The importance of developing what the West calls 'feminist theology' in the context of Islam is paramount today with a view to liberating not only Muslim women but also

Muslim men from unjust structures and laws that make a peer relationship between men and women impossible."[40]

From 1974 to 1983, Hassan engaged in the "systematic study of the Qur'anic passages relating to women," aiming to interpret the Qur'an from a "non-patriarchal perspective."[41] During the mid-1980s and throughout the 1990s, she spent much of her time traveling internationally to participate in discussions on women's human rights throughout the Muslim-majority world, speaking at numerous U.N. conferences.[42] During this time, she renewed her activist dedication to women's rights in Pakistan, founding the International Network for the Rights of Female Victims of Violence in Pakistan (INRFVVP) in 1999.

In the mid-1980s, she developed a pioneering rereading of the Qur'anic creation story as a way to combat gender inequality in Muslim societies on theological grounds.[43] Hassan argues that in Islam, assumptions about men's superiority are all based upon three erroneous theological assumptions about the Adam and Eve story: that Eve was created from Adam's rib; that Eve was responsible for the Fall of man; and that woman was created for the benefit of man. Performing her own close readings of the Qur'anic verses, Hassan concludes that the Qur'an does not narrate any sort of Fall of humankind; both Adam and Eve commit a sin, both are equally responsible for its commission, and both are forgiven by God. She also asserts that both man and woman are created from the same substance in the same primordial moment and thus are equal partners of creation.

Azizah al-Hibri

Azizah al-Hibri is a professor emerita of the University of Richmond School of Law in Virginia, where she taught from 1992 to 2012; she was also a professor of Philosophy at Texas A&M University and Washington University from 1975 to 1983. Born to an affluent family of Islamic scholars in Lebanon, where she was taught the Qur'an and classical Arabic at home as a child, she received her B.A. in philosophy at the American University of Beirut.[44] She emigrated to the United States in 1966, at the height of the U.S. civil rights movement, to continue her education. During the year before her arrival in the United States, she apparently corresponded and met with Malcolm X, who she says, during his visit to the American University of Beirut, encouraged her to be a strong female leader.[45] At the University of Pennsylvania, she earned a doctorate in philosophy in 1975 and a law degree in 1985.[46]

An avowed secularist in her early life, she was inspired by the feminist movement in the United States in 1970s, as well as by Marxist and feminist philosophy (an interest reflected in her becoming the founding editor of the journal *Hypatia* in 1986).[47] However, beginning in the 1980s, al-Hibri became increasingly critical of U.S. feminism, which in her words had lost its "anti-establishment" focus, implicating itself in U.S. policies abroad plagued by cultural imperialism and resulting in a "new breed of American feminists" who were "using feminism to achieve patriarchal goals" and with whom she no longer identified.[48] Al-Hibri has sometimes employed the term "womanist" in labeling her approach to reinterpreting the Qur'an.[49] Some insights into her use of the term may be gleaned from a 1995 press release of Karamah (an organization for Muslim women lawyers she founded) that employed the term in addressing the Fourth U.N. World Conference on Women in Beijing, noting that "many Muslim women have felt silenced by the very western movement that claims to stand up for their rights."[50] The statement explains the history and relevance of the term womanist to Muslim women: "Alice Walker and other women of color have chosen to refer to themselves not as 'feminists' but rather as 'womanists.' The difference is that a 'womanist' is committed to survival and wholeness of an entire people, male *and* female . . . This tool is the point of view of Muslim women, and these women have begun to speak out in their own voice."[51]

Alongside the shift in her feminist identification, al-Hibri also experienced a shift in her religious identity. Believing that Islam was inherently patriarchal, she had left her faith as a young woman but she reaffirmed her faith, now understanding Islam as a religion opposed to gender hierarchies.[52] This shift is apparent in her contribution to the classic 1982 special issue of the journal *Women's Studies International Forum* on women in Islam, for which she also served as the guest editor.[53] Afterward, she began engaging in international women's and human rights advocacy through NGOs in various Muslim countries, calling for reform of Islamic family law based not on secular principles but on the principles of Islamic law itself.[54] In response, in the United States she founded the organization Karamah: Muslim Women Lawyers for Human Rights in 1993, with the aim of creating a new generation of women interpreters of Islamic law.[55]

Al-Hibri focuses on reform through the vehicle of marriage contracts and has written on Islam and democracy and the reclaiming of ijtihad in Islamic jurisprudence. She rereads Qur'anic verses concerned with inheritance, marital responsibilities, and divorce.[56] Many of her arguments involve a commitment to understanding specific pronouncements in the Qur'an within the context of what she regards as more general egalitarian principles espoused by it and within the context of the Prophet's commandments to treat spouses with dignity.

Amina Wadud

Amina Wadud has been a visiting scholar at the Starr King School for the Ministry since her retirement as a professor of Islamic studies at Virginia Commonwealth University in 2008; her position at VCU was preceded by a teaching post at the International Islamic University Malaysia from 1989 to 1992. Born into a Methodist Christian family in Maryland, she converted to Islam as a college student in 1972.[57] She received her B.S. in education from the University of Pennsylvania and earned her doctorate in Arabic and Islamic studies from the University of Michigan in 1988, studying classical Arabic and the Qur'an at various institutions of higher learning in Egypt. In a number of works, Wadud describes her life as powerfully marked by racism against African Americans, which has been formative to her identity, experience, and scholarship as an African-American Muslim woman.[58] She published her landmark book *Qur'an and Woman: Rereading the Sacred Text from a Woman's Perspective,* now considered a classic of feminist Qur'anic interpretation, in Malaysia in 1992; it was later published in the United States in 1999.[59] In her preface to *Qur'an and Woman*, she states that she began the research for the book in 1986; she recalls, "I approached this research as if my life depended on the understandings I gained from studying the Qur'an."[60] During her formative years in Malaysia, she became an active member of Sisters in Islam, a nonprofit research collective and activist organization of Muslim women, guiding the organization's readings of the Qur'an in the late 1980s as it developed its founding platforms.[61]

Wadud explicitly labels *Qur'an and Woman* a work of tafsir that uses gender as a category of thought and demonstrates the Qur'an's adaptability to modern women's concerns.[62] Her main concern is the methodology of Qur'anic interpretation; she applies principles taken from within the Qur'an to its interpretation, using a threefold hermeneutical model that examines the Qur'an's context, grammatical and linguistic composition, and its unity as a whole text.[63] Wadud examines verses on women in light of the entire Qur'an, studying the larger textual and contextual development of terms throughout the text, and reading the Qur'an in light of her observation of its continuing movement toward greater social justice. She asserts that the exegete's perception of woman and masculinity/femininity influences how the Qur'an is interpreted, which necessitates that clear distinctions be made between the text and its interpretation. She argues that the Qur'an must be continually reinterpreted because its general principles are eternal and newly applicable in changing contexts, and thus its interpretation can never be final.

In *Qur'an and Woman* she explicitly states that she never refers to herself as a feminist.[64] In her subsequent book, *Inside the Gender Jihad: Women's Reform in Islam* (2006), she describes herself as "pro-faith, pro-feminist"; thus, Wadud understands her work as "feminist" but "refuse[s] to self-designate as feminist, even with 'Muslim' put in front of it" because her personal "emphasis on faith and the sacred prioritize[s] [her] motivations in feminist methodologies," and because "as an African-American, the original feminist paradigms were not intended to include [her]."[65] In *Inside the Gender Jihad*, Wadud builds upon her interpretive work in *Qur'an and Woman*, and she also chronicles her experiences and broader reflections as a Muslim woman scholar, including her controversial leading of a congregational Friday prayer of men and women in New York City in March 2005. All of her papers and publications are archived at the DePaul University Archives.

Asma Barlas

Asma Barlas has been a professor of politics at Ithaca College in New York since 1991. In the late 1970s and early 1980s, she worked as a diplomat in the Ministry of Foreign Affairs of Pakistan under the administration of General Muhammad Zia-ul-Haq.[66] In 1982, the general removed her from her position because of her critical comments about him and his government; she also worked briefly as a journalist in Pakistan before she sought political asylum in the United States a year later for unspecified safety reasons.[67] She received her university education in journalism as well as literature and philosophy in Pakistan and received her doctorate in international studies from the University of Denver in 1990, and her interest turned to the Qur'an in the mid-1990s. In *"Believing Women" in Islam: Unreading Patriarchal Interpretations of the Qur'an*, Barlas advocates reading the Qur'an as a historically situated text.[68] Drawing heavily on Wadud's *Qur'an and Woman*, she emphasizes the thematic holism, textual polysemy, and interpretive openness of the Qur'an. Barlas's work seeks to demonstrate that the Qur'an is not only nonpatriarchal, but in fact deliberately antipatriarchal, pointing out the Qur'an's insistence that God is not to be imagined as a father or son of any kind, and its treatment of God as transcendent, unique, and incomparable, and thus beyond gendered representation; she also argues that the Qur'an refuses to sacrilize any of God's prophets as fathers.

Barlas claims that she approaches the Qur'an as "a 'believing woman.'"[69] She prefers to be called "a believer, rather than a feminist."[70] In her words, "the Qur'an's concern with equality and rights prefigures modern, Western, and feminist discourses," and it is "grounded in a very different ethics and epistemology" from them.[71] Furthermore, "'it is not necessary to use feminine hermeneutics to read the Qur'an as an antipatriarchal and egalitarian text.'"[72] Barlas aims not to "misrepresent the Qur'an as a feminist text," though she admits that she does "situate and assess the Qur'an's teachings in light of some modern, feminist theories," and that "the use of such terminology shows [her] own intellectual disposition and biases."[73]

Sa'diyya Shaikh

Sa'diyya Shaikh is a professor at the University of Cape Town in South Africa. Of Indian ancestry but born and raised in South Africa, Shaikh witnessed firsthand the anti-apartheid movement there, which has shaped her interests in reading the Qur'an for its liberating possibilities, especially in relationship to Sufism. These interests are central to the recent publication of her *Sufi Narratives of Intimacy: Ibn 'Arabi, Gender, and Sexuality* (2012), which explores the relationship between Sufi metaphysics and gendered selfhood and ethics.[74] Shaikh received her doctoral training in religion at Temple University in Philadelphia in the 1990s. An important segment of her work examines how gender has been constructed in medieval works of tafsir, treating women as irrational, carnal, and deficient in leadership, intellect, and knowledge, while treating men as superior creatures and even divine intermediaries for women.[75] Shaikh tracks how these constructions of gender have been used throughout medieval Qur'anic exegesis and connects them to the sanctioning of domestic violence and marital rape in local communities today; her interest in local communities of Muslim women has also led to her work on their reproductive choices. Though in one of her essays she examines the problematic history of the term in depth, Shaikh adopts the term "feminist" to describe her work.[76] She often freely identifies herself as "a Muslim feminist" and describes her work as guided by a "feminist hermeneutics."[77]

Kecia Ali

Kecia Ali is a professor of religion at Boston University. Ali converted to Islam at a young age, and she earned her doctorate in religion from Duke University in 2002. Her main interest in jurisprudence is reflected in her recent books *Imam Shafi'i: Scholar and Saint* (2011) and *Marriage and Slavery in Early Islam* (2010), which examines the parallel treatments of slavery and marriage in early Sunni jurisprudence.[78] In *Sexual Ethics and Islam: Feminist Reflections on Qur'an, Hadith, and Jurisprudence* (2006), Ali examines the gendered presumptions upon which concepts of marriage in Islamic law have been based.[79] Specifically, she investigates the jurisprudential construction of marriage as the contractual exchange of male financial support in return for sexual access to a woman's body. Ali examines this construction, based upon the gendered treatment of women as proprietary objects in the law, in relation to Qur'anic verses on sex that presume male control over women's bodies and in tension with the Qur'an's other statements on the spiritual equality of men and women. To my knowledge, Ali's work has not emphasized an explicit position on feminism, but the title of her book on sexual ethics implies at the very least a tacit acceptance of it.

Three Interpretive Approaches

A vital component of this book's attempt to tell the story of feminist Qur'anic interpretation is the argument that the works studied here, despite the fragmentation of the first generation's efforts noted earlier, constitute an interrelated body of work, based on a shared genealogy in the lineage of modernist approaches to the Qur'an and their common use of three identifiable textual strategies and interpretive devices: (1) historical contextualization, (2) intratextual reading, and (3) the tawhidic paradigm.

The first interpretive method, historical contextualization, entails researching the occasion of a verse's revelation (*sabab al-nuzul*); distinguishing between descriptive and prescriptive verses of the Qur'an (i.e., differentiating between verses that are describing the practices of the seventh-century Arabian audience to which it was directly addressed and verses that are prescribing practices); distinguishing between universal and particular verses (i.e., differentiating between Qur'anic verses that apply only to specific situations and those that apply to human beings generally); and locating the role of historical biases about gender and biological essentialism in the interpretive arguments of traditional exegetes of the Qur'an.

The second interpretive method, intratextual reading, treats the Qur'an holistically: tracing how linguistic terms are used across the text of the Qur'an; comparing Qur'anic verses to one another instead of reading them in isolation; and reading Qur'anic verses in light of the observation of the Qur'an's overall movement toward advocating justice for all human beings. The third interpretive method, the tawhidic paradigm, engages the Islamic concept of tawhid, that is, God's unity, indivisibility, and incomparability. In this scheme of God's oneness and omniscience, sexism is a form of idolatry, since it attributes God-like roles to men over women. In addition, human beings are understood as fallible creatures, who attempt to fulfill their role as God's trustees using only the imperfect capacities, knowledge, and means that are endowed to them; as such, they are subject to their own flawed understandings of the Qur'an in a particular time and space. Thus, they can only *attempt* to understand God's mandates and engage in an open-ended *process* of searching for understanding. They can never pronounce a final interpretation of the Qur'an, since to do so would be to claim to have God's knowledge and to place themselves in the role of God. Therefore, the Qur'an must be open to continual, dynamic interpretation as the context for interpretation evolves, and clear distinctions must be made between the text of the Qur'an and its interpretation.

Outline of Chapters

The chapters of this book are organized into three parts. Part I, Historical Emergence of Feminist Qur'anic Interpretation, consists of three short chapters designed to locate feminist Qur'anic interpretation contextually, acquainting newcomers to the topic with the historical and political developments that have shaped the emergence of feminist scholarship on the Qur'an. Chapter 1 provides background on the Islamic tradition of tafsir, discussing at length its transformation in the modern era in order to trace the influence of modernist approaches to the Qur'an on Muslim feminist interpretations of the Qur'an. Chapter 2 examines Muslim debates over "feminism," while chapter 3 contextualizes the development of feminist

Qur'anic exegesis in light of its engagement with Jewish and Christian feminist theologies, as well its confrontations with state apparatuses since 9/11.

Part II, Three Methods of Feminist Qur'anic Interpretation, attempts to draw out the overall architecture of feminist Qur'anic interpretations, clarifying the recurring interpretive techniques that methodologically link the works together. Part II consists of chapters 4, 5, and 6, each of which conducts close readings of feminist Qur'anic exegesis in the application of the three interpretive strategies. Chapter 4 traces the use of the historical contextualization method, performing in-depth readings of those portions of the works that are most illustrative of this method, and identifying emerging patterns in the formation of their arguments. Chapter 5 traces the method of intratextual reading in the works, while also providing close readings of exemplary passages that treat the Qur'an as a unified text whose meanings are best understood by analyzing the whole text. Chapter 6 traces the method of the tawhidic paradigm, again closely reading portions of the works that argue for an ongoing interpretation of the Qur'an, based on God's supreme authority and human beings' temporal and limited understanding of the text.

Part III, Critiques of Feminist Qur'anic Interpretation, comprises three evaluative chapters. Chapter 7 makes some initial critical observations, pointing to conceptual problems and limitations in feminist exegesis. I examine the problem of feminist "impasses" in the Qur'anic text as well as feminist tafsir's appeals to "equality" and "justice." Chapter 8 expands these initial critical observations into a much more detailed and radical critique of feminist approaches to the Qur'an, suggesting that the feminist interpretive endeavor has reached a point of irresolvable contradiction by making claims about the Qur'an that are not fully supported by the text; in that chapter I make a number of difficult admissions about the viability of current strands of feminist Qur'anic interpretation. In chapter 9, I discuss daunting challenges to the authority of feminist tafsir posed by the androcentrism of the exegetical tradition, and I revisit feminist tafsir's concepts of sexual difference. I end by asking where radical questioning of the foundational claims of feminist tafsir leaves us.

These concluding discussions, then, point to an additional connotation of the title of this book. I have discussed above that one feminist "edge" of the Qur'an is an edge of dynamic possibility with respect to the Islamic tradition (specifically Qur'anic interpretation). Another edge I have found, however, is an edge of incommensurability. Making claims about the Qur'an that are not, as it turns out, fully supported by the text takes us to an edge not only at the perceived borders of the interpretive tradition but also to the edge of how we relate to the Qur'an as the word of God and the nature of its revelation. In asking questions that push at the edges not only of the interpretive tradition but also of the Qur'anic text itself, we stand at a far more precarious frontier. The questions we might ask about the Qur'an's possible incommensurability with contemporary notions of feminist justice are questions asked, in the words of Judith Plaskow, "at the edge of a deep abyss."[80] These are questions asked at the frontier of faith by way of deeply destabilizing theological wrestling. Although the pursuit of such questions requires some significant departures in thought, my hope is to contribute to the genesis of new possibilities for feminist interpretation of the Qur'an, possibilities which—I might add—are imaginable only because of the pathbreaking work of pioneering scholars of feminist tafsir. My objectives in this book are to build upon rather than invalidate previous work and reanimate rather than silence conversation.

PART I

Historical Emergence of Feminist Qur'anic Interpretation

I
History of Tafsir

Qur'an and Woman contributes a gender inclusive reading to one of those most fundamental disciplines in Islamic thought: tafsir, or Qur'anic exegesis.
—AMINA WADUD, Qur'an and Woman[1]

Muslim scholars have laid down certain basic conditions for sound tafsir. Any tafsir which disregards these principles must be viewed with great caution, if not rejected altogether.
—AHMAD VON DENFFER, 'Ulum al-Qur'an[2]

IN ONE DECEIVINGLY simple sentence in her preface to *Qur'an and Woman*, Amina Wadud locates her work squarely within the revered tradition of Qur'anic tafsir (exegesis)—a central source of knowledge in Islamic thought. In doing so, she unflinchingly draws upon the authority of the Islamic interpretive tradition dating all the way back to the time of the Prophet Muhammad himself. This summoning of the tafsir tradition invokes the weighty conventions and standards developed over the course of Islamic history to distinguish sound understandings of the Qur'an from distorted human projections of the text. In order to contextualize feminist readings of the Qur'an as contributions to the field of tafsir, this chapter provides a basic background on the history of that tradition's development from its early classical origins to its modern and contemporary manifestations.

Development of the Premodern Tafsir Tradition

The Arabic term tafsir (pl. *tafasir*) most commonly refers to a commentary on the Qur'an or an interpretation of it. For Muslims, the first *mufassir* (interpreter; pl. *mufassirun*) of the Qur'an was the Prophet Muhammad. Following his death, the Prophet's Qur'anic interpretations were transmitted and augmented by those of his Companions (*ashab*), which were in turn transmitted and augmented by their Successors (*tabi'un*). Perhaps most renowned among these first transmitters of tafsir is 'Abd Allah ibn 'Abbas (d. 688 C.E.), the companion of the Prophet who was given the epithet "*tarjuman al-Qur'an*, 'the interpreter of the Qur'an.'"[3] Historians are unsure of precisely how or when the tafsir tradition emerged as a cohesive genre; they even disagree about whether the Prophet permitted the practice of tafsir by others, or if he simply discouraged exegesis of *mutashabihat* (ambiguous) verses of the Qur'an.[4] In any case, classical proponents of the permissibility of tafsir were ultimately successful in defending its practice by pointing to certain Qur'anic verses that they read as encouraging it.[5]

Tafsir works relying on traditions leading back to the Prophet and his Companions are known by the roughly synonymous terms *al-tafsir bi-l-ma'thur* (tafsir by tradition) and *al-tafsir bi-l-riwayah* (tafsir by transmission). Premodern exegetes define such works in contradistinction to *al-tafsir bi-l-ra'y*, or interpretation that centers on the individual reasoning of the interpreter; this type of tafsir relies not only upon Hadith but also upon reason as a necessary vehicle for understanding the Qur'an. However, premodern proponents of *al-tafsir bi-l-riwayah* often criticized the reliance upon reason in *al-tafsir bi-l-ra'y*, condemning the method for what they viewed as its propensity for haphazard meanings derived from unsubstantiated speculation.

Initially, the handing down of the earliest *tafsir bi-l-riwayah* occurred by way of oral transmission only, a process that was only much later deemed authoritative through the science of Hadith authentication (during the ninth and tenth centuries C.E.). Because tafsir at this stage was largely interwoven within the rest of Hadith transmissions, it is unclear when exactly it became distinguished from the larger body of Hadith.[6] It was not until the early eighth century C.E. that the first known written works of tafsir most likely emerged.[7] The formative period of written Qur'anic tafsir production extended into the early ninth century C.E., although tafsir works of the first Islamic century did not yet take on "the unified character" of the tafsir of subsequent centuries.[8] The works of this early period consist mostly of the paraphrasing of Qur'anic verses and explanatory narratives about them based upon *isra'iliyat*, Jewish and Christian texts and reports. Other tafsir works of this period tend to discuss largely legalistic verses of the Qur'an, such as those concerned with inheritance, debt, charity, fasting, and prayer.[9]

An intermediate stage of tafsir works is often attributed roughly to the ninth century C.E.; works of this period add to previous works by applying newly emerging grammatical and linguistic sciences of the Arabic language to the Qur'anic text.[10] A late developmental stage of tafsir can be traced roughly to the tenth century C.E., continuing through the end of the premodern era.[11] This stage is known for the emergence of the tafsir model that marks an authoritative high point in traditional tafsir, that of the "comprehensive, hadith-based" format that parses through the entire Qur'an, moving successively verse by verse.[12] The landmark work of this late period is *Jami' al-bayan 'an ta'wil ay al-qur'an* of Abu Ja'far Muhammad ibn Jarir al-Tabari (d. 923 C.E.). Relying mostly on the *al-tafsir bi-l-riwayah* approach, Tabari's tafsir is celebrated as the "summative repository of the first two and one half centuries of Muslim exegetical endeavor."[13] This work was highly influential and authoritative in the subsequent development of the exegetical tradition, as a large number of *mufassirun* succeeding Tabari would come to rely on it. A number of other works were also significant to the development of the tafsir tradition: *Al-kashshaf 'an haqa'iq ghawamid al-tanzil*, authored by the Mu'tazilite grammarian and philologist Abu al-Qasim Mahmud ibn 'Umar al-Zamakhshari (d. 1144);[14] *Mafatih al-ghayb* (or *Al-tafsir al-kabir*) of the Ash'arite theologian Fakhr al-Din al-Razi (d. 1209);[15] *Al-jami' li-ahkam al-qur'an* of Abu 'Abd Allah Muhammad ibn Ahmad al-Ansari al-Qurtubi (d. 1272); and *Tafsir al-Jalalayn*, by Jalal al-Din ibn Ahmad al-Mahalli (d. 1459) and his student Jalal al-Din 'Abd al-Rahman ibn Abi Bakr al-Suyuti (d. 1505).

Of special note is also *Tafsir al-qur'an al-'azim* of 'Imad al-Din Abi al-Fida Isma'il ibn Kathir (d. 1373), whose teacher was Taqi al-Din Ahmad ibn Taymiyah (d. 1328).[16] Ibn Kathir was heavily influenced by Ibn Taymiyah's suspicion of the use of *isra'iliyat* to interpret the Qur'an, his condemnation of *al-tafsir bi-l-ra'y*, and his strict adherence to the traditions of the Prophet and the Companions.[17] Therefore, Ibn Kathir's tafsir assigns virtually absolute authority to the example of the Prophet and his Companions, calling for a "radical return" to early Islam and discounting much of the exegetical tradition since then, in particular any works "'infected' by biblical narratives or other non-Muslim literary sources."[18] In sharp contrast to the tafsir works of his predecessors, Ibn Kathir disregards the notion of "exegetical diversity (*ikhtilaf*)," as well as the possibility of multiple interpretive meanings characteristic of the tafsir tradition leading up to him.[19]

Among the most important Shi'ite commentaries are *Tafsir al-qur'an* of 'Ali ibn Ibrahim al-Qummi (d. 919); *Majma' al-bayan li-'ulum al-qur'an* of Abu 'Ali al-Fadl al-Tabarsi (d. 1153); and *Al-tibyan fi tafsir al-qur'an* of Abu Ja'far Muhammad ibn al-Hasan al-Tusi (d. 1067). On the whole, Shi'ite commentaries treat the guidance of the Shi'ite Imams as a necessary component of Qur'anic tafsir. They sometimes criticized the compilation of the 'Uthmanic codex of the Qur'an deemed authoritative by Sunnis, holding that it lacked certain statements supporting Shi'ite doctrine.[20] Shi'ite commentators also tend to engage more in allegorical interpretation, seeking esoteric nuances and more multilayered meanings than is generally characteristic of Sunni tafsir.

Among the most well known tafsir works by Sufi commentators are *Tafsir al-qur'an al-'azim* of Sahl ibn 'Abd Allah al-Tustari (d. 896) and the commentary of 'Abd al-Razzaq al-Kashani (d. 1330), called the *Tafsir Ibn al-'Arabi* (erroneously attributed to his teacher Muhyi al-Din ibn al-'Arabi).[21] Tafsir works focusing on mystical themes and meanings of the Qur'an are generally called *al-tafsir bi-l-isharah*, which refers to seeking indicators of the inner meanings of the Qur'an. This kind of tafsir is sometimes also denoted by the term *ta'wil*, a term that in early Islam was used interchangeably with *tafsir* but which later came to mean the interpretation of allegorical Qur'anic meanings, in contrast to the term *tafsir*, which generally referred to interpretation of more apparent Qur'anic meanings.[22] Sufi commentators are known for their use of intuition to cull mystically oriented meanings from the Qur'an about human existence and reality. Sunni commentators are often averse to these Sufi interpretive methods, frequently using the term *ta'wil* in a negative sense to refer to attempts to force obscure, convoluted meanings from the Qur'an.

'Ulum al-Qur'an and Cumulative Authority in Tafsir

Tafasir derive Qur'anic meanings by performing a number of important functions, some of the most significant of which include identifying the time or circumstances in the career of the Prophet during which a verse may have been revealed; closely studying a verse's linguistic terms and grammatical structures; determining the scope of a verse's meanings; deducing its legal implications, if any; and determining whether a verse is abrogated by another verse.[23] As a result, the tradition of tafsir relies on a number of elaborate sciences of the study of the Qur'an, called *'ulum al-qur'an*. Some of the most significant of these sciences cover *asbab al-nuzul* (the occasions of revelation), *ahkam* (legal applications), *i'rab* (grammar), *al-lughah* (language), *al-'amm* (general verses) and *al-khass* (specific verses), *muhkamat* (straightforward verses) and *mutashabihat* (ambiguous verses), and *al-nasikh wa-l-mansukh* (abrogating and abrogated verses).[24] Works of tafsir are deemed authoritative according to estimations of their competent execution of the *'ulum al-qur'an*, distinguishing them from unsound interpretations of the Qur'an.

In addition, the most celebrated works of traditional tafsir (particularly the *Tafsir* of Tabari) derive their authority and authenticity from the adoption of the transmissions of the Prophet and his Companions. On the whole, *al-tafsir bi-l-riwayah* emerged as "the bedrock of what is viewed as orthodox exegesis and represents the most commonly accepted mode of interpretation" among Muslims, even in the present time.[25] Authority within the tafsir tradition is also established through its self-referential, repetitive, and cumulative tendencies, principally exhibited through frequent and lengthy citation of earlier works and "a continual building upon the past."[26] A number of oversights, however, have been noted in the ascription of authority to traditional tafsir works in this manner. For example, Andrew Rippin and Farid Esack have questioned the legitimacy of the oppositional distinction traditionally drawn between *al-tafsir bi-l-riwayah* and *al-tafsir bi-l-ra'y*, since all tafsir works are subject to the preferences and decisions of the *mufassir*. Rippin observes that although the *Tafsir* of Tabari is considered the preeminent work of *al-tafsir bi-l-riwayah*, Tabari clearly "provides his own personal interpretation, both implicitly by his editorial selection of material and explicitly by stating his opinion where different trends of interpretation exist."[27] Similarly, Esack notes, "While it may be argued that Tabari's exegesis is entirely based on Hadith, the concomitant assumption that Tabari as a person, editor, philologist, and jurist and his social milieu played no role in his own selection or mediating process is clearly a dubious one."[28] Likewise, cumulative references to previous *tafasir* are also mediated by the personal preferences of the *mufassir*. As Rippin notes, the citation of previous works occurs "within a certain framework of the author, his concerns and allegiances . . . The citations are always subject to choice, the authorities subject to selection. Time, location, sectarian and popular beliefs will all have affected the selections and choices."[29] Such observations point to the particular constructedness of the standards of authority ascribed to certain works of tafsir over the course of Islamic history.

Modern Developments in Tafsir

Major developments in the field of tafsir during the modern era were shaped definitively by the Islamic modernist movements. Islamic modernism was an intellectual trend of the late nineteenth and twentieth centuries that aimed at creating "a synthesis between modern values and systems on the one hand, and what were seen to be eternal Islamic values and systems on the other."[30] Its proponents, often called Muslim modernists, attempted to reconcile Islam with "modern" values of rationality, science, and democracy, concepts that Muslims debated with increased urgency as a result of colonialism and charged interactions with the Western world.[31] In contrast to premodern Muslim perspectives that were ostensibly intolerant of a reliance on reason and led to the treatment of innovation (*bidʿah*) as heresy, Muslim modernists welcomed and engaged with the changes brought on by a reliance on reason.[32] In fact, they argued that Islam was compatible with the notions of rationality upheld by the European Enlightenment and modern science and was in no way fundamentally opposed to modern visions of progress.[33] In addition, modernists advocated "rational" interpretation of Islamic texts. Central to the modernist perspective was ensuring that their approaches were authentic to Islam. Modernists viewed the Islamic heritage as the embodiment of all "precursors to modernity" and considered themselves "authentic representatives of Islamic heritage."[34] Among the most influential modernist figures of the late eighteenth through mid-twentieth centuries were Sayyid Ahmad Khan (1817–1898) of India, Muhammad ʿAbduh (1849–1905) of Egypt, and Fazlur Rahman (1919–1988) of Pakistan and the United States; their works demonstrate key trends in modernist approaches to the Qurʾan.

The Egyptian intellectual Muhammad ʿAbduh, author of the theological treatise *Risalat al-tawhid* and the Qurʾanic commentary *Tafsir al-manar*, defined Islam as "the religion of reason and progress."[35] Like other Muslim modernists, he argued that the solution to the decline of Islamic society was to "link the principles of change to Islam," which already contained within it all the guidance necessary for "selecting what was good and necessary in modern life."[36] He and other modernists called for revisiting the Qurʾan and Sunna (the life example of the Prophet), using reason to address the debates of modernity.[37] Indian scholar Sayyid Ahmad Khan similarly advocated returning to the textual sources, primarily the Qurʾan, as a strategy for reforming Islam.[38] His *Tafsir al-qurʾan*, which has been called the "first major explicitly Modernist commentary," employs a "rationalist" approach in its aim to demonstrate the compatibility of modern natural science with the Qurʾan.[39]

For many modernists, such as the Pakistani scholar Fazlur Rahman, the decline of Muslim societies was due to "intellectual ossification and the replacement of scholarship based on original thought by one based on commentaries and super-commentaries" on Islam's fundamental texts.[40] This tendency, combined with a blindness to the Qur'an's historical context, had led to the establishment of "archaic laws" that contributed to Muslims' inability to address modern dilemmas and encumbered the "vibrancy" of Islam.[41] As a corrective, Rahman sought to distinguish between the Qur'an's legal and moral statements, and between its contingent and noncontingent aspects.[42] From the perspective of Rahman and other Muslim modernist thinkers, premodern jurists and exegetes of the Qur'an had neglected "the moral ideal behind the text" and erroneously treated the language of the text as "literal legal enactments."[43]

Modernist exegetes also sought specifically to establish the compatibility of the Qur'an with modern scientific findings and promoted the use of scientific reason to interpret the Qur'an.[44] In fact, for both 'Abduh and Khan, science was crucial to understanding the Qur'an.[45] Other modernists went so far to suggest that the Qur'an anticipated the findings of modern science before their discovery by human beings, another indication of the Qur'an's veracity and inimitability (i'jaz).[46] Both Khan and 'Abduh also rejected interpretations of the Qur'an that resorted to projecting "miraculous events" and "supernatural phenomena" onto the text, as such interpretations were antithetical to science.[47] This position reflected the overall modernist trend toward dissociating the Qur'an from any "legendary traits, primitive ideas, fantastic stories, magic, fables, and superstitions."[48] According to Muslim modernist interpreters, in the case of any seeming contradictions between scientific rationality and the Qur'an, one must read the text metaphorically and allegorically, which would immediately resolve any apparent contradiction due to human misreading.[49] Khan argued that *ta'wil* (allegorical interpretation) directly aided in deriving the Qur'an's intended meaning, since God had employed some language deliberately intended to be read metaphorically.[50]

Since the Qur'an was discernible through reason, a capacity possessed by every human being, modernist scholars held that the Qur'an's meanings could be intelligible to anyone.[51] Therefore, modernists often claimed that the technical mechanics of tafsir with which only the ulama were familiar were unnecessary for interpreting the Qur'an.[52] 'Abduh, for instance, stressed the need for the accessibility of tafsir to all people.[53] Therefore, his *Tafsir al-manar* deliberately excluded "the theological speculations, the detailed grammatical discussions, and the obtuse scholarship which characterized the commentaries of the past."[54] What was most important for 'Abduh was to make the moral and legal norms of the text and the "didactic aim" of each passage intelligible to all Muslims, rather than engaging in meticulous linguistic discussions about "single words and phrases" within it.[55]

An understanding of the Qur'an's historical context (*siyaq*) was also central to the tafsir of modernists.[56] According to 'Abduh, for example, the Qur'an must be read in light of what it meant for the first Muslim community, its original audience.[57] For Khan, historical context was especially crucial in cases in which the Qur'an used figurative language that conveyed meanings distinct to the immediate audience of its revelation in seventh-century Arabia. Such textual cases of metaphor must be understood in line with "their currency ... in the Arabic usage of the Prophet's day, making them comprehensible to his contemporaries."[58] Khan, therefore, sought to understand the meanings that would have been experienced by the Qur'an's first audience.[59] Khan's and 'Abduh's emphasis on the historical context of the Qur'an coincides, however, with a noted skepticism toward the Hadith. 'Abduh called for rejecting any Hadith reports that were not verifiable as genuinely originating with the Prophet or not universally accepted by Muslims; Khan went as far as to reject the Hadith entirely.[60] Though this extreme view of the Hadith was not shared by all modernists, on the whole, they tend to exhibit some margin of skepticism with respect to the historicity of the Hadith (discussed further in chapter 4).

Finally, another characteristic of many modernist interpretations of the Qur'an is the last-resort appeal to the notion of "the limits of human knowledge."[61] In cases in which the meaning of the Qur'an continues to be evasive or contradictory even after the application of reason and allegorical interpretation, modernist scholars often cite the limitations of human awareness as an explanation, acknowledging the possibility of Qur'anic meanings that cannot be accessed by human creatures.[62] 'Abduh, for example, insists that in these cases the "unknown should be left unknown."[63] Therefore, he argues, commentators must avoid reading certain statements as "definite where they have been left indefinite (*mubham*) in the text itself" or using *isra'iliyat* texts (which 'Abduh treated as historically suspect external sources) to supplement the Qur'an's accounts without proper justification for doing so.[64] As far as modernists are concerned, since the ultimate arbiter of the Qur'an's meaning is God, the admission of the human inability to understand certain passages of the Qur'an does not pose a threat to the larger project of Qur'anic interpretation. In fact, as 'Abduh observes, the existence of some evasive meanings is likely an intentional characteristic of the text, since "any ambiguity which exists in the Qur'an . . . is there for a reason: in order to divert attention away from the material world toward the spiritual."[65] Thus, the meanings of some passages of the Qur'an may be deliberately elusive and perform a special function.

To summarize, the main tenets of modernist approaches to the Qur'an consist of the call for a modern revisiting of the Qur'an using scientific and rational interpretation, particularly as a way to combat the attachment of superstitious meanings to the text; the use of metaphorical interpretation; an emphasis on the Qur'an's historical context; the accessibility of Qur'anic interpretation to all Muslims, not just the ulama; and attributing difficulties in understanding the Qur'an to human limitations, rather than to the text, which remains without flaw.

The Work of Fazlur Rahman

The modernist work of Fazlur Rahman deserves particular attention; it became highly influential in the development of feminist Qur'anic interpretation, particularly by providing a model for distinguishing the Qur'an's universal moral values from its more specific pronouncements aimed at its immediate seventh-century audience of revelation. For Rahman, traditional modes of Islamic thought had hindered Muslim thought's entrance into the modern era.[66] Most damaging was the fact that the fields of Islamic law, *kalam* (disputative theology), and tafsir had disregarded the historical limitations of the "socio-legal content" of the Qur'an.[67] In "reinforcing the total 'otherness' of the revelation," Hanbali traditionalists and Ash'arites had treated the Qur'an as "ahistorical" and "beyond the reach of humankind."[68] This had also confined the tafsir tradition to a "decontextualized approach that treated the Qur'an as a series of isolated verses," failing to comprehend the "'underlying unity'" of the Qur'an.[69] The problem was reinforced by the exclusive authority attached to "super-commentaries" of the Qur'an.[70] In addition, Muslim scholars, including his modernist colleagues, had failed to develop an organized method and hermeneutics for interpreting the Qur'an.[71]

Rahman agreed with other modernists that all of the Qur'an's principles spoke to contemporary needs.[72] In any instance in which those principles appeared incompatible with a contemporary situation, the interpretive method was to blame.[73] Also, like many of his modernist contemporaries, Rahman aimed to draw out the Qur'an's enduring principles and "recast them in terms of a modern intellectual outlook," though "without abandoning the belief in the divine origin of every single word of the qur'anic text."[74]

Rahman's unique contribution in this vein, however, was his historical approach to differentiate "the ideal from the contingent" within the Qur'an.[75] For Rahman, it was vital to identify precisely the historical contexts of verses since the Qur'an's "concerns, interests and guidance were directly connected with and organically related to the linguistic, cultural, political, economic and religious life" of the seventh-century Arabs to which it was initially revealed.[76] Thus, the linguistic form of the Qur'an's language was necessarily contingent upon its context, as it needed to directly "address problems of the time in *their* specific circumstances."[77] Rahman boldly asserts, therefore, that "'the actual legislation of the Qur'an cannot have been meant to be literally eternal by the Qur'an itself.'"[78] When interpreted properly, the contingent form of these verses need not obscure the Qur'an's timeless ideals.[79] Hence, Rahman developed his "double movement" method for distilling the intent and universal principles of the Qur'an from its historically specific contents. In the first step of this method, "one must move from the concrete case treatments of the Qur'an—taking the necessary and relevant social conditions of that time into account—to the general principles upon which the entire teaching converges."[80] In the second step, one applies that general meaning to one's own socio-historical context of understanding in the present.[81] This method would enable Muslims to properly revise laws derived erroneously from legal portions of the Qur'an that were pronounced in a specific manner for the first Muslim community.[82] This revision should take place by first drawing out the Qur'an's moral principles and subsequently using those moral principles to derive laws.[83]

Rahman aimed at highlighting in the Qur'an what, to him, was an "obvious direction toward the progressive embodiment of the fundamental human values of freedom and responsibility," which it was necessary to distill from the "actual legislation of the Qur'an" that had to "accept the then existing society as a term of reference."[84] Rahman acknowledges that the Qur'an had to speak formally in the terms of the possibilities and constraints of the context of its immediate audience of address.[85] This, however, did not detract from the Qur'an's clearly identifiable objectives toward social justice, including human equality.[86] Thus, in a sense, Rahman's work is an attempt to derive an ethics from the Qur'an based on principles made visible by reading the text in light of its historical context.[87]

Two other contributions of Rahman's are worthy of special attention. First, he argued that in all cases in which the Qur'an conflicted with the Hadith, the Qur'an had to be privileged over the Hadith categorically, since the Qur'an was the direct and preeminent source of God's guidance.[88] Second, for Rahman there could not be only one authoritative set of meanings derived from the Qur'an.[89] This was the case not only because multiple interpretations are essential to the Qur'an's continuing relevancy; multiple interpretations are also inevitable since "immutability" and "sacredness" are qualities that belong solely to the Qur'an and not to human interpretation.[90] Rahman maintained that the "socio-moral" values derived from the Qur'an according to his method would protect against any "unnecessary arbitrariness, or unprincipled and forced readings of the text" that could result from an allowance for multiple interpretations.[91]

Modern Shifts in Interpretive Authority

Muslim modernist movements had the effect of challenging the authority of the professional class of scholars in Muslim societies known as the ulama, who represent the vanguard of the Islamic scholarly tradition. Modernists challenged the power of the ulama by criticizing what they viewed as "the closing of the gates of *ijtihad*" (the use of independent reasoning in jurisprudence to confront new contemporary situations not directly addressed by the Qur'an and Sunna) in the course of Islamic thought by the tenth century C.E.; modernists viewed this as the cause of the stunting of a once dynamic jurisprudential interpretive tradition that had become irrelevant for Muslims in the modern era. Modernists therefore sought to revitalize the notion of ijtihad and reappropriate it. Though ijtihad had long been understood as the purview of traditionally trained scholars, modernists broadened the concept to mean rational interpretation undertaken by any educated Muslim.[92]

Interestingly, two of the most important premodern thinkers who paved the way for the subversion of traditional religious authorities were Ibn Taymiyah, the early fourteenth-century figure discussed earlier in relation to authoritative works of tafsir, and Muhammad ibn 'Abd al-Wahhab (d. 1787), whose followers are called Wahhabis or Muwahiddun ("believers in divine unity").[93] Both Ibn Taymiyah and 'Abd al-Wahhab located the primary authority of Islam within the Sunna of the Prophet, Companions, and Successors, rather than within the long tradition of Islamic scholarship by the ulama.[94] The critique of traditional authority leveled by Ibn Taymiyah and 'Abd al-Wahhab was in turn taken up by modern Muslim thinkers. This subversion of traditional authority "effectively liberated Muslims from the need for specialist expertise" to understand Islam's fundamental texts and "weakened the assumption of 'ulamatic' training as the necessary credentials for speaking on behalf of Islam."[95]

The modern subversion of the ulama's exclusive claim to interpretive authority within Islam was compounded by the development of modern nation-state structures within Muslim countries, creating governing bodies with which the ulama would also have to contend for authority.[96] Moreover, modern educational systems and the advent of print culture broadened access to texts and knowledge that had been previously inaccessible to laypersons; this further threatened the "monopoly" of the ulama on Islamic knowledge.[97] Altogether, these modern developments granted a new class of intellectuals direct access to sacred texts and commentaries, allowing them to engage in Qur'anic interpretation without the intermediaries of traditional scholarly authorities.

Modernity and Women

In the midst of Muslim confrontations with modernity, among the most charged debates were those that addressed the changing roles of women. Beginning in the late nineteenth century, growing numbers of urban, literate, upper-class Muslim women, particularly in the Middle East, entered conversations on male-female relations.[98] As part of the growth of modernist movements and anticolonial nationalist struggles, a critical mass of Muslim women initiated public discussions of their evolving roles and identities in modern Muslim societies.[99] In this endeavor they received the support of a number of male modernist thinkers, such as Muhammad 'Abduh, who called for women's education and entrance into the public sphere; modernist thinkers often treated educated and publicly active Muslim women as "symbols of the nation's newly founded vigour and modernity."[100] Margot Badran, Nadje al-Ali, and Leila Ahmed have documented in great detail the rich history of both secular and religious women's movements in the Muslim world, which boast an impressive array of social organizations and outspoken female leaders who struggled to redefine notions of modern yet "authentic" Muslim womanhood in the late-nineteenth and twentieth centuries.[101] These movements called for women's equal rights in the public sphere, particularly in the areas of education, work, politics, and nationalist movements, as well as reform in personal status laws regarding roles in the family.

The Emergence of Tafsir by Women

In the midst of modern efforts to reevaluate women's roles, some Muslim intellectuals focused their attention specifically on questions of women in the Qur'anic text. This scholarly inquiry was focused on "gender equality and social justice as basic and intersecting principles enshrined in the Qur'an."[102] Reflecting the modernist tendency to subvert traditional religious authorities who had monopolized the fields of Islamic knowledge, some female scholars and their allied male colleagues increasingly turned to the Qur'an as the primary source for deriving their claims to male–female equality, thus ushering in a new era of what some have retrospectively called a "Qur'an-based Islamic feminism" (discussed further in chapter 2).[103] In this case, however, what is challenged is not only traditional authority in general, but specifically men's exclusive authority to interpret the Qur'an. One of the earliest women associated with this trend is Nazira Zain al-Din, who published *Al-sufur wa-l-hijab* (*Unveiling and Veiling*) in Beirut in 1928. In this bold work, she claims her own authority to interpret the Qur'an; based on her reading of the Qur'an, she argues against segregation of the sexes and notions of women's inferiority to men.[104] Such scholars thus "point out that classical, and also much postclassical, interpretation" is based on "men's experiences" and "male-centered questions," to which the perspectives of women must be added.[105]

The successors to these women interpreters of the Qur'an (and their male supporters) emerged in the later twentieth century with the rise of Islamist and Islamic revivalist movements throughout the Muslim world (discussed in the introduction). Many of their readings were associated with the collective efforts of organizations and multiauthor publications, such as Women Living Under Muslim Laws (an international network), Sisters in Islam (Malaysia), and *Zanan* magazine (Iran);[106] they also emerged in the works of individual scholars studied in this book. Their efforts draw to varying degrees upon modernist attitudes toward the Qur'an. Like Muslim modernists, these interpreters defend the legitimacy of multiple, independent readings of the Qur'an through their claim to ijtihad.[107] In attending to the historically contingent aspects of the text, and by distinguishing between universal and particular elements of the Qur'an, they follow "in the footsteps of modernist scholars who have characteristically sought reform based on the value system of the Qur'an as a whole in order to derive new guidance consonant with the present."[108] Like modernists, they also "ask questions of scripture as a timeless text"; however they do so "from the vantage point of their own experience, knowledge, and observation" as women.[109] They claim that in interpreting the Qur'an from their own perspectives they are doing what *mufassirun* have always done.

Hibba Abugideiri has noted that Qur'anic interpretation undertaken by women in the United States in particular has been characterized by "a critique of traditional exegesis that situates itself within a legacy of Qur'anic exegesis."[110] At the same time that these works criticize the tradition of Qur'anic interpretation, they also claim their own place in its lineage. They also exhibit a critical transition in the understanding of woman's identity from "relational" to "independent vicegerent" of God.[111] This new set of readings "emphasizes individual agency," proclaiming "women's right to a direct relationship with God with no human (cleric) mediators."[112] Abugideiri argues that these interpretations are thus "shaking the very foundations of knowledge, of what constitutes 'truth'" in Islam, insofar as they "shift the [interpretive] lens from viewing religious knowledge as authoritative and incontestable to viewing it instead as constructed, value-laden and context-specific."[113] In the following chapter, I turn to the understandings of "Islamic feminism" that frame the emergence of these works.

2

The Frames of Feminism

> *It is important to focus on the content of Islamic feminism, on its goals, and not to get bogged down with distracting issues about who has the right to think/analyse and to speak. It is important not to be too defensive or proprietary about Islamic feminism. The way I see it, Islamic feminism is for all.*
>
> —MARGOT BADRAN, "Islamic Feminism: What's in a Name?"[1]

> *One can't avoid being called a feminist any time one speaks about women's liberation or equality, no matter what sort of language one speaks in . . . Even if we believe that reality exists independently of how we choose to define it, as we know, the very process of defining it also gives it a particular shape.*
>
> —ASMA BARLAS, "Engaging Islamic Feminism: Provincializing Feminism as a Master Narrative"[2]

ACCORDING TO MARGOT Badran, a leading historian of "Islamic feminist" movements, the terminology of Islamic feminism provides a common, inclusive language to describe the wide variety of Muslim women's profaith work against sexism and male domination. Although some activists and scholars avoid or even explicitly reject this term (as she points out, it "was bestowed not by its creators but by witnesses to something new underway"), for Badran it remains useful for resisting assertions that "Islam" and "feminism" are inherently opposed to one another, as well as for challenging the notion of any one group's exclusive ownership of feminism.[3] For her "feminism" qualified by the term "Islamic" provides a common language for all. In contrast, for Asma Barlas, an exegete of the Qur'an who advocates its antipatriarchal ethos, it is the very inclusivity of the term feminism—its openness to being claimed for vastly different aims—that prompts her "to resist it in *all* its forms," even when it is qualified as "Islamic."[4] Divergent claims about the appropriateness of the term "feminism" point to a series of contentious debates that form the backdrop for the emergence of feminist tafsir.

Late nineteenth-century and early twentieth-century Muslim debates on modernity may have opened the door for a new era in Muslim women's activism, but they also reduced Muslim women to pawns in the clashes between nationalist Muslim movements and European colonial powers.[5] Raging debates about the place of Muslim women in modern society treated them as territorial objects vied for by Western colonizers and Muslims on the defense, reducing them to repositories of Islam's cultural "essence."[6] As Leila Ahmed has argued, the restrictive terms of these debates can be traced to European colonial administrators' use of feminist discourse as ethnocentric justification for the occupation of Muslim countries.[7] Deeming Muslim societies' gender-segregated treatment of women backward and barbaric, European missionaries and officials characterized Muslim peoples as inferior and in need of civilizing. Thus they justified their "attacks on Islam and Muslim cultures by suggesting that their colonial 'civilizing' mission was . . . intended to free the poor oppressed women in Islam."[8] In their defensive responses, Muslim nationalists touted that Islam "had unequivocally empowered Muslim women" long before the feminist movements in the West, which provided nothing of value that Islam had not already given to women in granting them marriage and property rights.[9] Some Muslim reformists resisted women's entrance into the public sphere in the modern era, viewing it as the product of Western contamination of Muslim culture, while others promoted the education and political participation of Muslim women as components of a modern yet authentic Islam.[10] No matter the position taken, these debates repeatedly configured the struggle over women's rights as a "contest over culture," a framing that would continue to structure Muslim debates over feminism and women's roles throughout the twentieth century.[11]

The anticolonial struggles of the Muslim world later in the twentieth century gave rise to various national projects around the Muslim world in which women's rights were "symbolically foregrounded and then pragmatically relegated to the political margins."[12] Subsequently, the rise of the Islamic revival and Islamism in many Muslim-majority countries beginning in the late 1970s incorporated a vision of women's roles that insisted on "the return of women to a 'purer' and more 'authentic' domestic life away from the public scene."[13] These political developments were often inspired by the desire to recuperate an indigenous self felt to be violated or lost through the West's prolonged assaults upon the Muslim world; the recovery of a pure Islam thus became central to the recovery of this self.[14] Islam, then, became the "site of resistance" to violently imposed "Western notions of 'progress.'"[15] The search for the pure origins of Islam reinitiated by the Islamic revival replayed the modern strategy of returning to scripture as the uncontaminated vessel of true Islam.[16] In seizing upon women as the foremost emblems of Islamic purity, revivalists and Islamists justified the restrictions on women's freedoms through their treatment of Islam's foundational texts, particularly the Qur'an. Since it was the foundational texts of Islam that served as the justification for such measures against women, these texts, in turn, became the medium for women's resistance to their repressive treatment. As Ziba Mir-Hosseini has argued, Islamism thus inadvertently served as the catalyst for the formation of women's movements based on counter-readings of foundational Islamic texts that held that the Qur'an guarantees the equality of men and women; this movement came to be identified retrospectively in the 1990s as "Islamic feminism" by some observers and participants in these developments.[17] Employing the tools of ijtihad and tafsir, women grounded their calls for gender equality in a claim to authenticity sought in the Qur'an.[18] Significantly, in this process of returning to the same sources as the Islamists, those who would later be called Islamic feminists reinforced the discourse of pure origins and the excavation of a "true" Islam.

The flurry of heated debates over the definition of "Islamic feminism" is captured in an extensive body of writings that includes the contributions of Ziba Mir-Hosseini, Valentine Moghadam, miriam cooke, Sa'diyya Shaikh, Omaima Abou-Bakr, and especially Margot Badran, among many others.[19] Such writings track a wide range of responses to Islamic feminism, ranging from the assertion that feminism is indigenous to Islam to the position that Islam and feminism are mutually irreconcilable entities. The latter position is one shared by various critics of Islam who allege that Islam is uniquely oppressive of women, secular feminists who view religion as fundamentally incompatible with women's liberation, and Muslim conservatives who renounce feminism as a foreign ideology at odds with Islamic morality. The last of these groups often associates feminism with assumptions about the moral laxity of the West, insisting that it sanctions immoral sexual behavior and endangers family structures; proponents of this position may also associate feminism with secularism and separatism, holding that feminism disavows religion and promotes rivalry with, or dissociation from, men.

In opposition to the claim that feminism is exclusively Western, Saʻdiyya Shaikh has argued: "To accept feminism as a Western concept is ... to concede the most visible discourses around women's rights and gender justice as the property of the West and to marginalize the indigenous histories of protest and resistance to patriarchy by non-Western women."[20] Margot Badran has also maintained that treating feminism as a Western concept "serves to perpetuate the notion" that Muslim societies are "incapable of generating critiques of patriarchy and female subordination."[21] Badran argues that the view of Islam and feminism as mutually opposed to one another is due to ignorance about Islam and/or feminism and utilized by Muslims threatened by gender reform to discredit the activist and scholarly efforts of Muslim women.[22] She posits that there is nothing inherently contradictory within the notion of an Islam-inspired feminism.[23] In disputing claims about the incompatibility of Islam and feminism, Shaikh notes that advocates of Islamic feminism must "navigate the terrain between being critical of sexist interpretations of Islam and patriarchy in their communities while simultaneously criticizing neocolonial feminist discourses on Islam."[24] Refusing to surrender definitions of feminism to neocolonial or secular agendas, an increasing number of Muslim women since the 1990s have begun to affirm their feminist and Muslim identities as part of one another; Badran documents the increased adoption of the term "Islamic feminism" by activists in Egypt, Iran, Turkey, South Africa, Malaysia, and the United States in the 1990s.[25] In the years since, internet technology has contributed to the rapid global dissemination of this terminology, leading to its use worldwide.[26]

As Shaikh notes, for a growing number of Muslim women, Islamic feminism is based upon an insistence that both identifications are constitutive of one another and that feminism "[emerges] organically out of their faith commitment."[27] Shaikh has noted that Islamic feminists view their feminism as "integral to Islam and responsive to the core Qur'anic call to justice."[28] With women's greater access to higher education, including the Islamic sciences, a growing number of Muslim women scholars aimed to resolve the "dissonance between the ideals of Islam which are premised on an ontology of radical human equality and the fact that in varying social contexts Muslim women experience injustice in the name of religion."[29] Badran similarly describes these scholars' efforts as stemming from a feminism that "derives its understanding and mandate from the Qur'an and seeks rights and justice within the framework of the equality of women and men in the totality of their existence."[30]

Given the widely divergent views of Islamic feminism and its viability, as well as the diversity of Muslim women's contexts and projects, one is unable to control the meanings attached to Islamic feminism, no matter how one chooses to relate to it or define it. As Ziba Mir-Hosseini has recently pointed out, Islamic feminism cannot be nailed down to any one meaning; there exists no fixed, consensus-based meaning for it. To begin with, she notes, its meaning depends first and foremost on one's definitions of "Islam" and "feminism."[31] In addition, Mir-Hosseini has observed that the positions of Islamic feminism's advocates are so "local, diverse, multiple and evolving" that she feels it is "futile and even counter-productive to try to put these diverse voices into neat categories and generate definitions."[32] For her, the terminology of Islamic feminism is "so loaded with disputed meanings and implications, so enmeshed in local and global political struggles, that it is no longer useful in any kind of descriptive or analytical sense."[33] Even if one does not adopt the position that the term is useless, it is clear that the terminology of Islamic feminism is likely to remain contested and no one coherent meaning will be agreed upon.

In the case of the works of Qur'anic exegesis that are examined in this book, their authors may avoid and even disavow feminist terminology in identifying both themselves and their work. (See individual profiles in the introduction for information on each scholar's position on the matter.) They state some of these reasons themselves, and we can infer others. These reasons might include their or their audiences' views of feminism as an ideology that is external to the Islamic tradition; feminism's colonial history, and its associations with imperialism and violent incursions against Muslims based on the claim that Islam oppresses women; and feminism as an exclusionary discourse that universalizes the perspectives of non-Muslim European and American women. For example, in her reflections on feminism, Asma Barlas resists the identification of her work with feminism, citing feminism's hegemonic subsuming of all efforts toward women's equality (effectively making the language of feminism the only language with which one can talk about equality);[34] the problem of feminism "flattening out important differences" between women, including among Muslim women;[35] and the violence committed against Muslims in its name.[36] Those persuaded by Badran and Shaikh might argue that Barlas's stance closes off the possibilities of feminism, reducing it to, and thereby handing it over to, only one version of feminism whose dominance must be resisted. However, for Barlas, the assertion of feminism's diversity is precisely the problem, leaving it open to appropriation for agendas that are so widely divergent as to be absurdly contradictory to one another; granting feminism this openness means that positions that are offensive and even dangerous to the proponents of other positions are called by the same name.[37] Barlas, then, finds it unacceptable to adopt a term that can be used in a manner that is (literally) violently opposed to her work. Thus, for her, "if feminism in *any* form is complicit with . . . violence" against Muslims, she cannot accept any form of it.[38] Even if it is just one form of feminism that is complicit with such violence, she must "resist it in *all* its forms."[39]

However, other reflections by Barlas take us back to the issue that is most central to the "feminism" of the exegetical works studied in this book: the concern for credibility and authority. Even when other factors are at work, the adoption of the qualifier "Islamic," as well as the avoidance of the term "feminism," is frequently traced to the exegetes' awareness of how an association with feminism might impact the authority of their work within Muslim communities. For example, Barlas states that her problems with feminism are related not only to "an existential anxiety but also a practical issue"; she writes, "I think that many of us who are working on the Qur'an are trying to speak mainly, though not of course exclusively, to our own Muslim communities. And the fact is that most Muslims do not make such fine distinctions between feminisms" (presumably between feminisms that are compatible or at odds with Islam).[40] In my study of these exegetical works and their framing, it seems to me that the most significant factor in the exegetes' use or avoidance of the term has been their ability to persuade Muslim communities of their views on the Qur'an; the exegetes are aware that the legitimacy of their readings may be undercut by Muslims' negative associations with feminism. Facing the possibility of their work being labeled un-Islamic, it has been essential to the exegetes' credibility to claim that their approaches are firmly internal to Islam. They strive to show that their readings derive from "Islam" itself—that it is "Islam" that has birthed their (feminist) readings of the Qur'an rather than feminism birthing their approach to Islam; in other words, they assert that their readings are "prior" to feminism. Thus, we find numerous statements by the exegetes, particularly by Barlas and Amina Wadud, to the effect that their readings of the Qur'an are originally rooted in Islam rather than in feminism.[41]

However, I would argue that in the very act of avoiding or qualifying the terms of feminism, these works still remain firmly embedded in its discourses. Due to the colonial history cited earlier, even when the exegetes resist the term feminism, their stances continue to be shaped by feminism, since their opposition to it is still a response to it that is connected to an irrevocable history. In other words, feminist discourse still sets the terms of those who resist it. Thus, referring to this field of Qur'anic interpretation as something other than "feminist" does not isolate it from feminist discourse, as it is inescapably impacted by it. In my view one cannot escape the terms of feminism even as one resists them; there can be no return to a "pure" prefeminist past in talking about women and the Qur'an. Even when readings of the Qur'an are seen as arising organically out of "Islam" and indigenous to it, contemporary Muslim conversations about women are inextricably connected to the vexed history of how Muslims encountered feminism in the modern era. Even when one claims that her reading of the Qur'an derives purely from the Qur'an and not from feminism, that reading is still connected to the history of such a claim's emergence in relation to Western imperialism and feminism.[42] One cannot simply divorce this claim from its historical origins and neatly avoid its associations. This violent past, however painful or strategically damaging, can never be erased. As I have argued elsewhere, Muslim women have "never had the luxury of developing their ideas free of the discursive operations of colonial and neocolonial powers."[43] The exegetical works studied here cannot be sealed off from this history by disavowing the term feminism. I agree with Barlas that feminism possesses a hegemonic power to claim all efforts against male domination as its own, but I believe that it sets the terms not only because of present engagements that may or may not shift, but primarily also because of a history of colonial feminism that cannot be escaped whenever feminism is invoked, whether it be in the positive or the negative. Therefore, one reason I have elected—albeit with serious reservations—to use the term feminist to describe the exegetical works examined here is that not doing so will not prevent feminism's association with them.[44]

At the same time, I admit that my reference to these tafsir works as "feminist" may very well reinforce the hegemonic and even violent claims of feminism. Barlas's point is well taken: "When we call something Islamic feminism we close off the possibility of seeing it as anything else and it is this closure that I find problematic. When we ignore how people choose to name themselves, their work, and their struggles, we necessarily do some epistemic violence to them."[45] Out of respect for such considerations, throughout this book I have taken care to refer only to the exegetical works, but not their authors, as feminist—as an attempt to avoid disregarding what are often very personal identifications, while acknowledging that one can never fully separate a scholar's identity from her work. However, as stated in the introduction, I do not maintain that scholars should always have the exclusive right to name their work, and it seems to me most urgent and paramount to capture the radical critique of power that is at the center of the works studied here. These exegetes of the Qur'an boldly claim the right to interpret the Qur'an in opposition to the vanguard of authoritative Qur'anic interpreters who have repeatedly done violence to women by presenting their sexist biases as the mandate of God; the authors of these works radically challenge the treatment of human beings in Islam as normatively male. Therefore, referring to these works simply as "women's" interpretations of the Qur'an goes nowhere near capturing the subversion of entrenched power that animates these works, and it is my priority to do exactly that. As I have previously stated, referring to these works as simply "women's" works is to essentialize women's relationships to the Qur'an, many of whom may very well be uninterested in a critique of male power. In addition, employing the term "gender" as a descriptor is also unsuitable, since these works, even as they may treat gender as a category of thought, do not question the concept of gender and rather take its existence for granted (the problems of which are discussed in chapters 7 and 8).

The works examined in this book offer no suitable common identifier or cohesive terminology of their own with which to describe them, despite the fact that something crucial holds them together. Asma Barlas has observed: "Cumulatively . . . women's and feminist readings pose a challenge to dominant (and androcentric) modes of knowledge-construction and we can view them as comprising a single body of work."[46] Some might argue that the lack of a common descriptive term is an indication to the contrary or that the attempt to find a common term for them functions to cover over the differences between the works. Even so, I have resolved to use the term "feminist" to describe these works—however complicated it is by divergent views of the term and its history—in order to emphasize the modes of critical thought that they employ as part of a collective epistemological project; these works are feminist because they use a set of analytical tools to criticize male power and normativity.[47] Thus, I use "feminist" to refer to an evolving set of analytical tools utilized by these works for this purpose rather than to indicate some quality of an imagined static self. Raja Rhouni has observed that thinkers associated with Islamic feminism are often "overconcerned with the question of (fixed) identity,"[48] and, like her, I think it best to avoid thinking of feminism as a stable state of being or identity. We can never control the meanings attached to the term "feminist," particularly because of the fervent historical contentions over Islamic feminisms. Though I cannot avoid the attribution of other meanings to it, my reference to "feminist" exegesis of the Qur'an is informed by the view that what makes them feminist, and thus what holds them together crucially, is their shared use of dynamic epistemological tools to challenge the abuse of male power in the interpretation of the Qur'an. I have held this consideration above all others in framing this study.

3
Relationships to Feminist Theologies and the State

> *We can advocate as women of diverse faiths who refuse to allow those faiths to be used against us or against outsiders. We work for the full humanity of all women, men, and children and for the integrity and goodness of God's creation. Advocacy compels us to expose dualistic structures of domination and subordination, of mastery and oppression, that warp individual lives and relationships among us.*
>
> —PHYLLIS TRIBLE AND LETTY RUSSELL, Hagar, Sarah, and Their Children: Jewish, Christian, and Muslim Perspectives[1]

> *The United States has embarked upon an ambitious theological campaign aimed at shaping the sensibilities of ordinary Muslims whom the State Department deems to be too dangerously inclined toward fundamentalist interpretations of Islam . . . A cornerstone of this strategy is to convince Muslims that they must learn to historicize the Quran, not unlike what Christians did with the Bible . . . The recalcitrant Muslim is faulted for his inability to recognize that the truth of Qur'anic scripture is grounded not in its theological claims but in culture and history.*
>
> —SABA MAHMOOD, "Secularism, Hermeneutics, and Empire: The Politics of Islamic Reformation"[2]

GIVEN WHAT SABA Mahmood observes, it is no wonder that scholars of feminist tafsir have avoided attracting attention to how their works overlap with the efforts of Jewish and Christian feminist theologies. The exegetes have good reason to skirt such discussions since Muslim critics may view those parallels as indicators of feminist tafsir's supposed methodological foreignness and lack of credibility. Resemblances to Jewish and Christian feminist theologies may also be seen as inroads that facilitate efforts of neo-imperialists to force aspects of Jewish and Christian feminist theologies and Western ideology on Muslims. Nonetheless, Jewish and Christian feminisms form at least some part of the scholarly context for the emergence of feminist Qur'anic exegesis, and that context has some important implications, even if it is strategically inconvenient and perhaps even dangerous to associate feminist Qur'anic interpretation with Jewish and Christian feminist thought. To continue the objective of part I, that is, to explain the historical and political contexts of feminist tafsir's emergence, in this chapter I discuss feminist Qur'anic interpretation's engagement with Jewish and Christian feminist theologies, as well as its vulnerability to co-optation by U.S.-led efforts to "liberalize" Muslims.

Daughters of Abrahamic Religions

The recent emergence of "Abrahamic religions" as an interfaith category provides an important context for understanding the relationship between Jewish and Christian feminist theologies and feminist Qur'anic interpretation. The term "Abrahamic religions" emerged in the last decades of the twentieth century as a way to refer collectively to Judaism, Christianity, and Islam in the place of older terms such as "Semitic," "monotheistic," "prophetic," or "religions of the book."[3] This new reference prioritizes the lineage of the patriarch Abraham in all three religions as a unifying point of commonality between the faiths, emphasized as a feature that distinguishes them from other religions.[4] Pim Valkenberg has observed the paradox of using "Abrahamic" as a term to connote convergences among these religions when it also points to the divergences and conflicts among the three due to competing interpretations of each tradition's relationship to Abraham.[5] Proponents of each of the three religions have often thought their own religion to be the "genuine heir" of true revelation.[6]

In the study of women and religion since the 1990s, Amina Wadud has observed "a pragmatic trend . . . to draw attention to shared aspects of history and ideology between women of Judaism, Christianity, and Islam."[7] As Wadud points out, scholars began focusing on the shared experiences of the "daughters of Sarah and Hagar," aiming at the development of "epistemological relationships between women, in place of patriarchal conceptualizations of the Abrahamic tradition."[8] The recent publication of two edited collections of Jewish, Christian, and Muslim women's scholarship point to a growing interest in dialogue among women of the Abrahamic faiths. In *Hagar, Sarah, and Their Children: Jewish, Christian, and Muslim Perspectives* (2006), Phyllis Trible and Letty Russell, both pioneering Christian feminist theologians, highlight Sarah and Hagar "as the founding members" of the three faiths who have been ignored in discussions of the Abrahamic religions that focus only on the male figures of Abraham and his sons Isaac and Ishmael as the common ancestors of Jews, Christians, and Muslims.[9] In *Daughters of Abraham: Feminist Thought in Judaism, Christianity, and Islam* (2001), edited by Yvonne Haddad and John Esposito, Karen Armstrong's foreword praises the collection for providing valuable evidence of "Jewish, Christian, and Muslim women cooperating together to correct the abuses of the past."[10] Armstrong reads the volume as a challenge to "the old chauvinisms" of men from the three faiths, who have traditionally seen each other as "rivals, pretenders, heretics, or infidels," resulting in a long history of interreligious violence.[11] One contributor notes that, as partners in healing these tensions, the "daughters of Sarah and Hagar" have the ability to "[respect] each other's cultures and beliefs" while also being "responsible to their own community's concerns;" thus, they "may yet bring peace to the family of Abraham."[12] Women scholars from all three faiths resolve to work together in confronting the "patriarchal religious traditions" that have "systematically excluded women from contributing to traditionally accepted interpretations of the sacred texts."[13] As Nayereh Tohidi writes, they stand to benefit from "each other's experience in 'reclaiming' their faith and spirituality from the clergy-centered patriarchal monopoly of religious authorities."[14]

Development of Jewish and Christian Feminist Theologies

A close look at the footnotes and bibliographies of the works of feminist Qur'anic interpretation indicates an awareness of Christian and Jewish feminist writings; they often feature arguments and neologisms that are strikingly similar to those developed by Jewish and Christian feminist thinkers. Indeed, they share a common goal that is akin to the aims of other traditions of feminist theology: the criticism of sexism and male normativity in the interpretation of sacred texts. In light of this parallelism, a short history of Jewish and Christian feminist theologies is in order.

Jewish and Christian feminist theologies emerged in the United States and Europe in the late 1960s and 1970s. Reimagining God and reclaiming female voices in the Bible, feminist theologians argued for women's full access to religious learning, interpretation, and leadership. Feminist theology was based upon the fundamental observation that all understandings of the Bible are "unavoidably influenced by human subjectivity," always shaped by the experiences and biases of its interpreters, and "never objective and value-neutral."[15] Feminist theology thus claims that traditional theology has been guided exclusively by the narrow perspectives and interests of privileged white men, who have been influenced by the "culturally determined gender roles and attitudes" of their socio-historical contexts.[16]

Most feminist theologians argue that not only biblical interpretations but also biblical texts themselves have been shaped by patriarchal and androcentric assumptions. Such assumptions are revealed in "how biblical texts treat women in stories and laws, and neglect women's experiences."[17] Thus the field has also been primarily concerned with unmasking the scriptural treatment of man as the normative recipient of revelation and woman as wholly other to this male recipient. Feminist theologians examine the authorship, oral and written transmission, and collection of the Bible, studying how and by whom the text was put together, ordered, and amended. They approach the Bible as a compilation of texts authored within various historical and socio-cultural contexts and organized through a process of canonization undertaken by male authorities.[18]

Feminist theologians also criticize the portrayal of God as a male patriarchal figure. In *Sexism and God-Talk* (1983), Rosemary Radford Ruether argues that the use of language to portray God as male contradicts the understanding of God as beyond human gender. The use of male pronouns and the attribution of male qualities to God amounts to a kind of idolatry, or worship of the human male. In Christianity, it has led to the assumption that Christ was necessarily male "in order to both incarnate God and to possess full and normative humanness;" as a result "only men can be ordained because only men can represent Christ."[19] As a corrective, references to God must be understood as limited by human language and thus treated metaphorically and figuratively rather than taken literally.

Ruether's *Sexism and God-Talk* is also significant for its reclamation of the prophetic-liberating norm of traditional Christian theology, a central belief that human beings receive the word of God in order to guide them to the prophetic end of establishing the justice and equity at the heart of Jesus' message that recognizes the dignity of all human beings.[20] In re-adopting this norm, feminist theologians argue that "patriarchy and androcentrism in their many forms conflict with faith in a God whom Christian revelation proclaims to be love itself."[21] In this sense, they claim, "theologians and church authorities failed to bring the gospel to bear on the subjugation of women."[22] Thus patriarchy and sexism figure as "a kind of idolatry and blasphemy";[23] they result in the sinful "distortion of human rationality into domination and subordination, corrupting the humanity of both men and women."[24] Feminist theologians seek to reestablish "a vision of the church" as a "prophetic community" working toward "liberation from personal and social evil" and "exodus from oppressive social systems, such as patriarchy."[25]

In *The Church and the Second Sex* (1968), a classic in the field, Mary Daly examines hostile and misogynistic statements about women prevalent throughout Christian theology since its beginnings. Daly argues that such treatment of women is not merely "idiosyncratic" but rather "an integral part of the theological system itself."[26] In these representations, "woman is intrinsically subordinate in the order of creation, and hence in the family and society"; she is "the cause of sin entering the world by rejecting this ordained place."[27] In *Beyond God the Father* (1973), Daly criticizes the effective deification of patriarchal methods of knowing the Bible; this "methodolatry," as she calls it, results in the treatment of women's experiences and concerns as "nondata" and maintains an "invisible tyranny" that places women's questions outside the realm of recognizable queries.[28]

In *Texts of Terror* (1984), Phyllis Trible reinterprets the creation story of Adam and Eve, criticizing androcentric interpretations of the story that have been used to justify the treatment of women as inferior and subordinate to men. Such interpretations portray Adam/man as God's first and primary creation and Eve/woman as created second, from the rib of man. In this scheme, woman is derivative of and dependent on man, and she is created for the utility of man. In the narration of the Fall, woman is the temptress and responsible for the human pair's original sin; thereafter, man rules over her, and woman suffers the curse of painful childbirth. However, in revisiting Genesis, Trible argues that the creation of man and woman in the Bible is simultaneous.[29] "Adam" does not always function as a proper noun and often refers to a gender-neutral creature.[30] The human pair is originally created to live in mutual companionship, and a gender hierarchy between the two is apparent only after the sin of eating the tree. It is only after the Fall that such division appears.[31] It is only then that the human pair experiences "the discord and alienation of patriarchy."[32]

In her numerous works, Elisabeth Schüssler Fiorenza addresses patriarchal oppression as "not identical with androcentrism or sexism," or some kind of uniform dualistic oppression exercised by all men over all women.[33] Rather, she refers to *kyriarchy*, a term she introduces to denote a set of multidirectional, intersecting structures "of graded subjugations and oppressions."[34] As a corrective to kyriarchal/patriarchal operations of power in Catholicism, Schüssler Fiorenza has insisted that the center of biblical interpretation "must be women-church," or the "*ekklesia* of women as . . . the discipleship of equals."[35] Schüssler Fiorenza is among the theologians who argue that the Bible still contains elements that may be liberating for women despite the patriarchal culture in which it emerged.[36] Placing women's experience at the center of biblical interpretation, she outlines four kinds of feminist hermeneutics of the Bible: hermeneutics of suspicion (reading texts for male interests), hermeneutics of reclamation (locating texts suitable for feminist liturgy), hermeneutics of remembrance (recovering the stories of powerful woman figures), and hermeneutics of actualization (creating new rituals and forms of religious expression and art).[37]

In her *Standing Again at Sinai* (1990), Judith Plaskow views the Torah as an incomplete medium of God's revelation, limited by human language and the fallibility of its human transmitters and interpreters. It is merely the "partial record of the 'Godwrestling' of part of the Jewish people," restricted by their humanness and the times and places in which they lived.[38] According to Plaskow, the Torah is only an approximation of part of the primordial Torah that lies with God; it is an expression of a particular people's understanding of the divine.[39] As such, the Torah is incomplete; it is only a piece of God's revelation, since revelation is never final but ongoing. As such, the content of the Torah is not only adaptable and flexible to rereadings and applications by subsequent generations, but it also may be supplemented with new texts created by these subsequent generations. New readers may recover and compose parts of revelation that have not been transmitted. To this end, feminist theologians have reappropriated the practice of *midrash*, or the "imaginative development of a thought or theme suggested by Scripture."[40] Used traditionally used by Jews to "broaden or alter the meanings of texts" and "[elaborate] on the sources in response to questions" raised by readers in different contexts, feminist theologians have readopted *midrash* as a way to expand the biblical canon to include the experiences of women.[41]

In a similar manner, a hermeneutics of remembrance has been employed by a number of Christian feminist theologians as a way to locate inspirational female figures and liberating stories in the Bible, and to reclaim the suffering of oppressed women (and men) throughout Christian history.[42] As part of the process of rejecting androcentric biblical texts and favoring liberating portions of scripture, feminist theologians have attempted to recover the voices of women marginalized or excluded by the Bible but referenced in texts outside the traditional biblical cannon. Thus, they have called for the creation of an "'open canon' that includes texts written by women or reflecting women's experiences," often prompting the composition of new supplementary texts.[43]

One of the unifying claims of Jewish and Christian feminist theologies is that theology is an ongoing, dynamic, and open-ended process. "There is no final 'objective' or 'right' reading of biblical passages," and "no unified perspective on particular biblical texts is possible."[44] In fact, any attempt to forge a kind of "uniformity in the interpretation of biblical texts" is an extension of the structures of "patriarchal control of biblical interpretation."[45] In light of this resistance to uniformity, it was crucial for the first generation of (white) Jewish and Christian feminist theologians to recognize that their work had often universalized the experiences of white women.[46] Beginning in the 1980s, a critical mass of women-of-color theologians began to point out the "parochial assumptions of this first wave of feminist theology."[47] Often times, the work of feminist theologians of color was influenced by liberation theology, which first arose in Latin America in the 1960s. Liberation theology revised traditional Christian theologies from the perspective of the poor, focusing on their everyday life experiences of hardship and survival. Drawing on many of the same principles, women-of-color theologians formulated a number of critical responses to the universalisms implied by white feminist theologians, addressing the multiple oppressions of sexism, racism, colonialism, and poverty.

Womanist theologians, for instance, call for the application of African-American women's particular experiences to the interpretation of the Bible. They forgo the term "feminist" and replace it with the term "womanist" to signal their distinctive critical lens. Two signal works of womanist theology are Katie Cannon's *Black Womanist Ethics* (1988)[48] and Delores Williams' *Sisters in the Wilderness* (1993).[49] These works point to the centrality of the history and legacy of slavery to African-American women's identities, as well as their daily lived experiences of racist, sexist, and classist oppression. In reading the Bible through the particular experience of black women in America, womanist theologians speak to their struggles for survival and liberation from multiple forms of oppression.[50] Womanists also emphasize the social dimensions of sin and their responsibility to the larger community.[51] They are concerned with the realities of everyday life and everyday people (i.e., "ordinary"/"lived" theology),[52] and they advocate the importance of "God-walk" (i.e., praxis), not only "God-talk."[53] Additionally, womanist theology calls for dynamic dialogue and revision as part of its ongoing development.[54]

Latina and Chicana women have likewise emphasized the particularity of their experiences in cultivating their own *mujerista*, Chicana, and Latina feminist theologies. In *Mujerista Theology: A Theology for the Twenty-First Century*, Ada María Isasi-Díaz argues that the "daily struggle for survival" of Latina women is directly connected to their "religious understandings, sentiments, [and] beliefs; in other words religious knowledge is attained through real life experience."[55] Thus, "the community of Hispanic women is the real theologian" of *mujerista* theology.[56] Theirs is a praxis-oriented theology that holds itself accountable to the feedback and changing needs of the community of women. It is not merely a theology that scholars "read, study or write" but rather the "liberative action" of the whole community.[57] *Mujeristas* address "religious understandings and practices of Hispanas/Latinas" as "part of the on-going revelation of God."[58]

Other Latina theologians, such as María Pilar Aquino, have referred to themselves simply as Latina feminists. In the co-edited collection of works *A Reader in Latina Feminist Theology* (2002), Aquino and other Latina feminist theologians call for interpretations of the Bible from the point of view of everyday readers "in the flesh."[59] Like the *mujeristas*, they address the history of "conquest and colonization" of their societies as central to their identities in their home countries and in diaspora; they "challenge the dominant culture's devaluation of [their] culture, language, and indigenous intellectual legacy."[60] In contrast to Isasi-Díaz, however, Latina feminist theologians assert that feminism is not a foreign, imported concept but indigenous to their home countries. They oppose elitism in religious interpretation and embrace popular religion, asserting that all forms of women's knowledge are valid. Intent on social transformation, they call for theological solutions to everyday problems and for salvation and liberation in everyday life.

In the same vein, Asian and Asian-American women's theologies have also arisen as a corrective to the universalizing claims of white women theologians. Two signal works of this field are Chung Hyun Kyung's *Struggling to Be the Sun Again* (1990)[61] and Kwok Pui-lan's *Introducing*

54 EMERGENCE OF FEMINIST QUR'ANIC INTERPRETATION

Asian Feminist Theology (2000).[62] These works read the Bible through the lens of Asian and Asian-American women's concrete everyday experiences as shaped by the violent histories of Christian imperialism, missionary work in Asia, and the imposition of Eurocentric Christianity in their home countries and in diaspora communities. In light of their particular experiences, the aims of their theology include "the oral interpretation and retelling of biblical stories," the articulation of "scripture as performance," and postcolonial criticism of biblical traditions.[63] Like other women-of-color theologians, Asian women theologians critique myopic and elitist understandings of feminist liberation confined to the singular axis of gender. Because the term feminism "sometimes connotes a radicalism and separatism advocated by middle-class European and American women" and is thus rejected in some Asian communities, Asian women theologians adopt the label at times and forgo it at others.[64] Finally, they work to unmask the collusion of male authority and imperialism in dominant Christian theology, and they call for the broadening of the critical purview of theology to cover race, class, sexuality, and global capitalism.

Drawing on Jewish and Christian Feminist Theologies

As evidence of their shared influences, Muslim feminist exegetical works employ a number of terms, concepts, and strategies that converge with those of Jewish and Christian feminist theologies. I begin my observations of this with general references made by the exegetes to Jewish and Christian feminist theologies. First, Riffat Hassan has written of her dialogues with Jewish and Christian women beginning in 1979,[65] and she has expressed a desire for the development of "feminist theology" in Islam.[66] Hassan recalls of her early research: "As a result of my study and deliberation, I came to perceive that not only in the Islamic, but also in the Jewish and Christian, traditions, there are three theological assumptions [about the creation story] on which the superstructure of men's alleged superiority to women has been erected."[67] Thus, Hassan offers her rereading of the Qur'anic creation story in relation to feminist readings of the parallel story of the Bible. Similarly, Sa'diyya Shaikh notes that "there are a number of extremely valuable research tools developed in both secular and Christian feminist scholarship which may be utilized, albeit critically, in the examination of gender in Islam and Muslim societies."[68]

Muslim exegetes have also demonstrated their fluency with some of the basic terminologies and frameworks of Jewish and Christian theologies by citing a number of their fundamental concepts and key terms. For instance, Asma Barlas refers to Rosemary Radford Ruether to point to the inclusion of women as a category of the "oppressed" to which sacred texts speak,[69] Elisabeth Schüssler Fiorenza to argue that "gender dimorphism" is created by human beings rather than ordained by God,[70] and Mary Daly to refer to demeaning social constructions of the female gender.[71] Sa'diyya Shaikh refers to a work edited by Letty Russell to point to the androcentrism of medieval tafsir texts,[72] Ruether to refer to the polarized social construction of male and female gender,[73] and to Ruether again to examine how religion defines human beings through feminist analysis of "religious anthropology."[74]

In addition, the Muslim exegetes, like Jewish and Christian feminists, are interested in recovering the stories of female figures in early religious history. In particular, the exegetes frequently turn to Hagar (called Hajar in the Islamic tradition) as an empowering figure of "female struggle and liberation," who, in the courage and strength she displays during her trials in the wilderness with Ishmael, embodies an exemplary "active female role within Islam."[75] Al-Hibri, in fact, refers to herself as a "descendant of Hagar."[76] Likewise, Hassan calls Hagar her "foremother."[77] Wadud also refers to the trials of Hagar throughout a chapter of *Inside the Gender Jihad* titled "A New Hajar Paradigm: Motherhood and Family."[78] She discusses the story of Hagar, who struggled as a single parent, abandoned by Abraham and the larger community, to expose the neglect Wadud and other single mothers in the African-American Muslim community experience in relation to Islamic family law. Hagar's story, she argues, points to a serious "ethical aberration" and "legal invisibility" that has devastating consequences for single mothers who, like Hagar, "can only be considered deviant" within the Muslim community.[79]

The Muslim exegetes also call for the interpretation of the Qur'an in light of women's life experiences. Shaikh cites Judith Plaskow and Carol Christ's *Weaving the Visions* (1989),[80] another feminist theology classic, among other texts that treat "women's experiences as a conceptual category to redress the historical gender imbalance."[81] In addition, Wadud observes, "men have proposed what it means to be Muslim on the presumption that the male experience is normative, essential, and universal to all humankind."[82] Thus, she argues, understandings of the Qur'an and Hadith have tended to be "predominantly articulated on the basis of male experiences and through the male psyche."[83] Citing from Schüssler Fiorenza's *Bread Not Stone*, Wadud defines patriarchy as not "merely an affirmation of men and men's experiences" but also "a hegemonic presumption of dominance and superiority" that "extend[s] humanity to women only in functional juxtaposition" to male norms.[84] For Wadud, "It is indispensable to women's empowerment that they apply their experiences to interpretations of the sources."[85] In describing the elision of women's experiences from the purview of traditional Qur'anic interpretation, Wadud has perhaps also drawn from Mary Daly in her recent use of the term "methodolatry."[86]

In addition, Muslim feminist scholars are in conversation with Jewish and Christian feminist theologians' articulations of patriarchal oppression. Wadud, for instance, refers to Schüssler Fiorenza, whose understanding of "patriarchy" brings nuance to the simplistic notion of "'all men dominating all women equally.'"[87] Just as Schüssler Fiorenza broadens definitions of patriarchal oppression to include power dynamics outside simple gender binaries (for which she coins the term *kyriarchy*), Wadud understands oppression based upon selective interpretations of the Qur'an as multidirectional and produced through multiple, intersecting structures of power. Her discussions of the particular forms of racism experienced by African-American Muslims, for example, demonstrate her attention to the intersection of racial, gender, and class-based oppressions experienced by Muslim women.[88] Also referring to Schüssler Fiorenza, Sa'diyya Shaikh draws upon her definition of feminist hermeneutics in *Bread Not Stone* as a "'theory, method or perspective for understanding and interpretation' that is sensitive to and critical of sexism."[89] Shaikh also draws upon Schüssler Fiorenza's "hermeneutic of suspicion" to criticize interpretations of the Qur'an that sanction domestic violence.[90]

Finally, Asma Barlas has referenced Ruether's work in *Sexism and God-Talk* to criticize the use of male imagery to refer to God in Qur'anic interpretation. Ruether has noted that under male-dominated Christian structures of authority, women "relate to man as he relates to God. A symbolic hierarchy is set up: God-male-female. Women no longer stand in direct relation to God; they are connected to God secondarily, through the male."[91] Crediting Ruether for coining the phrase "God-talk," Barlas analyzes in detail the "Qur'an's repudiation of the patriarchal imaginary of God-the-Father."[92] In her criticism of portrayals of God throughout the tafsir tradition as male (in violation of the Qur'an's own directive, she argues), Barlas observes: "Masculinizing God is the first step in positing a hierarchy in which males situate themselves beneath God and above women, implying that there is a symbolic (and sometimes literal) continuum between God's

Rule over humans and male rule over women."[93] Here, Barlas borrows from Ruether's notion of the symbolic hierarchy established between God, men, and women. Likewise, Shaikh has also cited Ruether in pointing to the idolatrous nature of depictions of God as male.[94]

Divergences from Jewish and Christian Feminist Scholarship

Despite their common concerns and overlaps, it is important to point to a number of significant tensions between Jewish, Christian, and Muslim feminist works. To begin with, the recent treatment of the Hagar-Sarah story as cause for mutual empowerment (discussed earlier) fails to address at length the undeniably divisive elements of the story. In the biblical tradition, it is Sarah's anger at Abraham's childbearing concubine that forces Hagar and Ishmael into the desert wilderness (though in the Islamic tradition, Hagar's removal to the wilderness is differently understood as resulting from God's commandment to Abraham). Sarah's harsh treatment of Hagar and her banishment of mother and son are acts of animosity at the center of the women's relationship. Though their story is open to reinterpretation and feminist reclaiming, the dynamics of exile in the relationship of Sarah and Hagar are not easily set aside.[95] Just as these elements of the story of Sarah and Hagar must not be overlooked, it is important to note that relationships between women of the three faiths (including scholars of Jewish, Christian, and Muslim feminist scholarship) may also be marked by a counterproductive divisiveness.[96] Perhaps it is not only men of the three religions who have been suspicious of one another and hurt and excluded each other.

Some tensions between Jewish, Christian, and Muslim women play out in their interactions in the academy. They are particularly evident in Christianity's dominance in the field of feminist theological studies and the exclusion (even if unintentional) of non-Christian religions. As Rita Gross has argued, "feminist theology" and "Christian feminist theology" are frequently used synonymously in the language of most scholarship, conferences, panels, and informal discussions on feminist theology, implying that feminist theology is at its core Christian, and that all non-Christian feminist theologies are simply derivatives of, or minor exceptions to, Christian feminist theology.[97] Thus, all other traditions of feminist theology must be named by qualifying their non-Christian character, as in the case of references to Jewish and Buddhist feminist theologies. Likewise, womanist theology continues to be dominated by the concerns of Christian African-American women, almost completely excluding Muslim women from womanist discourse.[98] Amina Wadud notes that to begin with, "in their discussions of the 'black religious experience,' Christian scholars and theologians continually ignore the history of Islam."[99] Furthermore, as Debra Majeed has observed, "the womanist agenda [has] often made normative the Christian experience of African American women."[100] Wadud adds, "Not only is there no space for Womanist Muslim women, but also the specifics of race and gender as addressed within Christianity are assumed to be generic racial-gender concerns for all religions."[101]

Muslim scholars have sometimes noted the token inclusion of Muslim perspectives (not unlike the token inclusion of other non-Christian perspectives) in the form of invitations extended to a single Muslim scholar to represent Islam in multifaith panel discussions at academic conferences. The tokenization of Muslim women's perspectives within feminist theological discussions, when they are included at all, may also be accompanied by a lack of understanding of Islam among others scholars (also not unlike the lack of understanding of other non-Christian perspectives). It is perhaps such ignorance about Islam that sparked the following harsh response by Wadud in 2000 about her experiences at the American Academy of Religion: "When I want to seriously challenge patriarchy from within my own faith tradition, I do not go to the Women and Religion section of the AAR. They accept anything I say in a tokenistic fashion. They do not know enough to challenge it."[102] Here, Wadud points to the frustrations still shared by many Muslim women in multifaith conversations who may feel marginalized and treated like native informants of a foreign religion rather than being stimulated and constructively challenged. I point to some of the frustrations of Muslim women in multifaith discussions not to discount or insult well-meaning efforts but rather to speak to one set of challenges in the cooperation of Jewish, Christian, and Muslim women.

To point to another set of challenges, I turn my attention to the previously mentioned edited volumes *Daughters of Abraham* (containing equal numbers of Jewish, Christian, and Muslim contributions) and *Hagar, Sarah, and Their Children* (containing only one Muslim and one Jewish contribution), as well as Rosemary Radford Ruether's recent compilation *Feminist Theologies: Legacy and Prospects* (with a clear emphasis on Christian contributions over Jewish, Muslim, and Buddhist perspectives).[103] None of these volumes' editors discuss how to confront any of the challenges and tensions central to interreligious relationships between women of the Abrahamic faiths. The editors of the first two books refer vaguely to the troubled history of the faiths, only to divert their discussions abruptly to the promise and hope for peacemaking, healing, and solidarity among the faiths through the work of women. Ruether's very short introduction draws no clear connections between the works included in her volume. The silences of these compilations' editors regarding interreligious challenges speak to how little attention has been paid to these issues to date, even in volumes and venues that claim to address diversity within feminist theology. Such volumes add one or two Muslim (and other non-Christian) contributions into the mix of mostly Christian feminist voices and lay claim to a multireligious purview while neglecting to study the complicated realities of such claims.

In addition, one particular divergence between Jewish, Christian, and Muslim feminist works points to a potential impasse in collaborations between the so-called daughters of Hagar and Sarah. Like some Muslim modernists who opposed the traditional use of *isra'iliyat* (Jewish and Christian sources) to interpret the Qur'an, scholars of feminist tafsir often seek to distance the Qur'an from certain biblical interpretations of parallel stories and statements. This tendency poses serious obstacles to alliances between Jewish, Christian, and Muslim women exegetes. For example, as examined in chapter 5, some Muslim exegetes reject readings of the Qur'anic creation story they see as overlaid by biblical influences, claiming that Muslims' sexist interpretations of the story originate in biblical texts and interpretations that are uniquely demeaning to women. The use of this strategy is an affront to interfaith cooperation between Jewish, Christian, and Muslim feminists.[104]

Finally, it is especially important to point out that unlike Jewish and Christian feminist theologians, scholars of feminist tafsir unequivocally treat the entire text of the Qur'an as the verbatim word of God. Because they regard the entire Qur'an as divine and authentic, they do not dispute the text in the manner that many Jewish and Christian feminist theologians do; therefore, they do not employ the strategy of attributing problematic portions of the Qur'anic text to human error.[105] As Anne Sofie Roald has observed, Jewish and Christian feminists "do not part too much from the established research tradition" of historical-critical approaches to the Bible that already assume that the Bible is the work of human beings.[106] For instance, "it is possible to regard Jesus as the 'son of God'" even while undercutting the divinity of the biblical texts.[107] However, an understanding of the Qur'an as the word of human beings is not plausible for Muslim exegetes since "Islam's theology is contingent on the belief that the Koran is the word of God (*kalam allah*)."[108] Therefore Muslim exegetes are unable to edit or add to the text or disregard any problematic portions of it as Jewish and Christian feminists might. As Wadud notes, they "cannot rewrite the Qur'an. As an historical record of the words revealed by Allah to the Prophet Muhammad, those words are unchangeable."[109] As a result, rather than "trying to change the immutable words" of the Qur'an, they must engage with the text as it is.[110] Such a relationship to the Qur'an means that there are clear limitations upon how Jews, Christians, and Muslims might collaborate in feminist scholarship; more conversations are likely to be had, however, if there are new developments in Muslim exegetes' views of the nature of God's speech in the Qur'an.

Muslim Women's Scholarship, Interfaith Engagement, and Imperial Interests

These interfaith convergences and differences also raise the issue of how comparisons between Muslim, Jewish, and Christian feminist readings of scripture might present an opportunity for the co-optation of feminist Qur'anic interpretation by U.S. state institutions. Thus, while observing the parallels between Jewish, Christian, and Muslim feminist scholarship, it is also vital to question how noting them may inadvertently serve state interests in disciplining Islam and Muslims. In drawing attention to the concerns they share with Jewish and Christian women, Muslim women run the risk of being roped into neoconservative state platforms aimed at promoting the spread of so-called moderate forms of Islam deemed least likely to challenge the United States' global ascendency and branding all other forms of Islam as "fundamentalist" and dangerous.

As Juliane Hammer has observed, in the post-9/11 world where Muslims have come under the close scrutiny of the U.S. government and broader American public, a renewed interest in Islam and Muslim women has meant that "Muslim women's voices are increasingly audible in the public sphere."[111] In this context, however, U.S. discourses on Islam place Muslim women in compromising positions by treating their appearances and attitudes as indicators of how successfully Muslims have adopted "American" values. They are thus especially vulnerable, in Hammer's words, to being "co-opted into the government's political project of identifying 'moderate' and 'liberal' Muslims, domestically and abroad" and thus feeding the discourse of "good" and "bad" Islam observed by Mahmood Mamdani.[112] In this discourse, "good" (so-called moderate) Islam, particularly when it appears to advance the rights of women, is touted as the form of Islam most amenable to democracy and American ideals, and those identified as its proponents are increasingly singled out as the preferred ambassadors of Islam in contradistinction to other Muslims whose thinking is deemed backward and threatening to American ideals. As Suha Taji-Farouki has observed, "Western enthusiasm" for such ambassadors of "moderate" Islam "expresses an underlying assumption that this is what Islam 'needs' to render it capable of existing cooperatively in the modern world."[113] (This powerful discourse is at work, for instance, in the celebration of sensational figures such as Irshad Manji, the author of the bestselling book *The Trouble with Islam Today*, who is regarded as a courageous innovator of Muslim reform, particularly as it concerns Muslim women.[114]) Not unlike its use in colonial discourses, feminism is invoked in support of these state interests. Rastegar observes: "Issues of gender relations have come to stand in as a standard for whether a particular version of Islam is in line with U.S. interests. In reading positions on gender issues as a litmus test for pro-Western or anti-Western Islam, gender struggles are further politicized in such a way that women working for change are increasingly at risk of being branded as supporters of U.S. imperial interests."[115] Thus, Muslims engaged in feminist scholarship may be deemed as "liberal" allies of the state and deployed by state agendas to promote the United States' brand of democracy in the Muslim world.

In particular, as Saba Mahmood has argued, since 9/11 the U.S. State Department has aggressively pursued the reform of Islam "along the lines of the Protestant Reformation" by endorsing the work of "moderate" Muslims engaged in historical readings of the Qur'an who properly resemble Christians who read the Bible from a historical-critical perspective.[116] Such projects might treat the feminist scholarship of Muslims as well as their interfaith cooperation with Jews and Christians as signs of their receptivity to nonliteral interpretations of the Qur'an; thus scholars of feminist Qur'anic interpretation, particularly when they engage in interfaith initiatives, are prime candidates for profiling as allies in the project of advancing "good" Islam. In its potential co-optation by state campaigns to demonize all other forms of Islam and civilize Muslims, feminist Qur'anic interpretation bears the potential to contribute to anti-Muslim violence, both epistemologically and practically.

In light of the dangers of feminist Qur'anic interpretation's co-optation, Barlas's position on feminism discussed in the previous chapter takes on additional significance. In a time marked, she notes, by the justification of the U.S. invasion of Afghanistan as the liberation of Muslim women and the hypervisibility of Muslim women since 9/11, Barlas is acutely aware of the "captivity" of Muslim women by enduring Western discourses on Islam and Muslim women with grave consequences for the well-being of Muslims.[117] Her question about the terminological positioning of Islamic feminist work bears a particular relevance here: "How do we change something by calling it Islamic, or Qur'anic, or feminist?"[118] Another version of this question might be, in what ways does comparing feminist Qur'anic interpretation with Jewish and Christian feminist theologies become counterproductive to attempts to increase the self-determination of Muslim women? Whatever the answers to these questions, it is apparent that feminist interpretations of the Qur'an can be invoked for contradictory aims, and it remains for scholars of feminist Qur'anic interpretation to clarify their shared and divergent interests in relation to both the state and feminist theologies of other religious traditions.

PART II
Three Methods of Feminist Qur'anic Interpretation

4
Historical Contextualization Method

> *Today, however, people's desires for the sciences of the Qur'an are false and restrained, as they are turned away from them. And no amount of censure could prevent this from happening. As a result, we have ended up benefiting the beginners in the sciences of the Book, by expounding the occasions for which it was revealed. This is because it is the best that one ought to know and the most appropriate thing to which one should direct one's attention, since it is not possible to know the interpretation of a given verse or the meaning it alludes to without knowing its story and the occasion of its revelation.*
>
> —'ALI IBN AHMAD AL-WAHIDI,
> Asbab al-Nuzul[1]

AS EARLY AS the eleventh century C.E., the Persian exegete al-Wahidi pointed to the necessity of correctly understanding the circumstances of the Qur'an's revelation in order to understand its meanings, indicating that the issue of context was a significant exegetical concern long before modern Muslims' interest in the topic. In this chapter, I trace feminist tafsir's methodological use of the historical context of the Qur'an's revelations, an approach I have called the historical contextualization method. In works of feminist exegesis, this method entails researching the occasion of a verse's revelation (*sabab al-nuzul*); distinguishing between descriptive and prescriptive verses of the Qur'an (i.e., differentiating between verses that describe the practices of the seventh-century Arabian audience to which it was directly addressed and verses that prescribe practices to all audiences); distinguishing between universal and particular verses (i.e., differentiating between verses that apply only to specific situations and those that apply to human beings generally); and identifying historical situations that shaped the context of revelation in seventh-century Arabia and subsequent exegesis of the Qur'an.

Historical Method and the Qur'an

In her *"Believing Women" in Islam: Unreading Patriarchal Interpretations of the Qur'an*, Asma Barlas explains why many contemporary Qur'anic exegetes have been largely resistant to the method of reading the Qur'an in its historical context: "Conservatives theorize the Qur'an's universalism (transhistoricity) by *de*historicizing the Qur'an itself, and/or by viewing its teachings ahistorically. This is because they believe that historicizing the Qur'an's *contexts* means also historicizing its *contents*, thereby undermining its sacred and universal character."[2] In other words, interpreters of the Qur'an have avoided reading verses in relation to the context of their revelation for fear that this approach would imply that the Qur'an is meaningful only within certain historical contexts but not others. If the Qur'an is thus relevant only to certain times and places and peoples, it thereby ceases to be a universal revelation addressed to all humanity, which undermines the notion of its divine authorship by an omniscient and omnipresent God. As Barbara Stowasser has put it, the danger is that "Scripture may 'be dissolved into mere history that no longer sounds a divine voice.'"[3] Scholars of feminist tafsir, however, defend the practice of reading the Qur'an historically against the claim that this approach diminishes its universality. Barlas posits that "critical scholars who argue for a historicizing understanding of revelation are not rejecting the doctrine of its universalism. On the contrary, they reject the opposite: the view that the sacred can be temporalized only within a specific context."[4] For Barlas, reading the Qur'an historically does not limit its meaning to the context of revelation; rather, reading the Qur'an historically allows the Qur'an to be read in light of changing historical circumstances, thus making it relevant and applicable universally. In other words, to read the Qur'an in historical context is to uphold the Qur'an's universality.

According to exegetes of feminist tafsir, a historically contextualized reading of the Qur'an not only gives credence to its universality. It also helps to produce more precise readings by aiding readers in determining whether the Qur'an is making particular or universal evaluations. They point out that, by ignoring the role of a verse's historical context in constructing its meaning, exegetes have erroneously attributed general or universal meanings to verses that address only particular, limited, or conditional circumstances. According to the principles of classical Qur'anic exegesis, verses of the Qur'an may be categorized as either *'amm* (general) or *khass* (specific). However, the exegetes argue that when Qur'anic interpreters have ignored verses' historical contexts, they have often failed to distinguish between *'amm* and *khass* verses. As a result, "the tendency [has been] to universalize particulars, rather than see them as pointers to a precise context from which [exegetes] must derive universal principles."[5] Amina Wadud asserts that the meanings of *khass* Qur'anic pronouncements must not be taken at face value; their historical contexts must be understood in order to deduce their intents and thereby derive their universal meanings. To fail to do so, Barlas argues, is to "subvert [the verses'] openly stated intent and purpose," producing distorted understandings of them.[6]

As Amina Wadud observes in her *Qur'an and Woman: Rereading the Sacred Text from a Woman's Perspective*, when there are particular practices referred to in the Qur'an, they are often "restricted to that society which practised them . . . Therefore, each new Islamic society must understand the principles intended by the particulars. Those principles are eternal and can be applied in various social contexts."[7] This is especially important in regard to instances in which the Qur'an is referring to gendered practices: "The attitudes towards women at the time and place of the revelation helped to shape the particular expressions in the Qur'an. The concerns it addressed were particular to that circumstance. These particulars are not meant as the entire Qur'anic intent, but are the means for determining that intent provided we have appropriate historical information."[8] Wadud insists that the Qur'an be read with the understanding that its pronouncements were framed by the terms of the context of the seventh-century Arabian audience to which it was immediately addressed; in order for the text to have broader meaning outside that immediate context, that particular historical context must be acknowledged, taken into account, and examined.[9] To fail to do so would place limitations on the Qur'an's power to provide universal guidance in all times and places.

Before continuing, it is necessary to point out the ways in which the feminist method of historical contextualization relates to the early genre of *asbab al-nuzul*. *Asbab al-nuzul* (sing. *sabab al-nuzul*) may be defined as "reports, transmitted generally from the Companions of Muhammad, detailing the cause, time and place of the revelation of a portion (usually a verse) of the Qur'an."[10] As an outgrowth of the common practice of referring to the Prophet Muhammad's *sirah* (his biography based on the Sunna) to clarify the meanings of the Qur'an, collections of *asbab al-nuzul* began to appear as a genre around the eleventh century.[11] Exegetes relied on *asbab al-nuzul* to understand the circumstances in which a verse was revealed in order to gain a more precise understanding of a verse's direct meaning. The views of the exegete al-Suyuti (d. 1505) on the term *sabab* indicate the significance of *asbab al-nuzul* reports in the exegetical tradition. Andrew Rippin notes that for al-Suyuti, "The *sabab* reveals God's concern with His creation through His action;" it is "the metaphorical 'tent rope' connecting heaven and earth."[12] In other words, the *asbab al-nuzul* are evidence of God's interest and intervention in the affairs of human beings at particular historical moments in response to particular human experiences. As Rippin argues, "The *sabab* acts in a historical-theological way, acting as the guarantor of the veracity of God's revelation to man and His concern for His creation."[13] Thus, the *asbab al-nuzul* not only provide the mundane contexts for Qur'anic pronouncements but also point to God's intimate involvement in human history through the language of the Qur'an.

In Sunni works of Qur'anic exegesis from the eighth to fifteenth century C.E., the *asbab al-nuzul* provide "an authoritative interpretational context" and identify "the limits of each narrative pericope" for a given set of verses.[14] According to scholars of *'ulum al-Qur'an* (sciences of the Qur'an), the *sabab* of a verse helps distinguish between the portion of a verse "attached solely to the historical event and that part, which, although attached to the historical event, also has wider implications."[15] The *sabab* report thus helps narrow the scope of a Qur'anic verse's meaning and application by indicating in what situations it was deemed applicable by the Prophet or his Companions.[16] However, any implication that a verse's application is somehow limited only to the specific situation or persons identified in the *sabab* is generally regarded by the exegetes as dangerous and unacceptable.[17] This position reflects a "fear that doing so might suggest that the revelations were determined by historical circumstances, that is, that the *asbab al-nuzul* might be misconstrued as 'occasions *for* (not *of*)' revelation."[18] That is, the *sabab* may narrow a verse's application to a particular type of situation, but not so far as to limit its application exclusively to the instance referred to by the Qur'an. This reluctance toward the over-specification of a verse's application is compounded by the fact that "*asbab* information is frequently far too varied and flexible to allow decisions to be based primarily upon it"; instead, exegetes tend to use other tools of interpretation to understand the scope and application of a verse and then "[support] it ex post facto with the appropriate *sabab*."[19] In fact, the *sabab* may ultimately be used in the opposite manner: an exegete may utilize it to broaden a verse's meaning rather than limiting it. For example, in the view of al-Suyuti, a verse "may appear in its 'plain meaning' to be specific or limited in its application but, in fact, when the *sabab* is taken into account, the true intent of the verse is revealed; thus the *sabab* acts to 'reject the illusion of limitation.'"[20] That is, the specification of the verse's context allows the exegete to infer its overall intent, which then may be applied to numerous parallel contexts other than the original. A final point of clarification involves the assessment of who may be a reliable transmitter for *asbab al-nuzul*; according to some scholars of *'ulum al-Qur'an*, acceptable *asbab al-nuzul* may be transmitted only by Companions of the Prophet who were present at the event during which the given verse was revealed; in other words, in the estimate of some *'ulum al-Qur'an* scholars, one cannot accept just anyone's speculation on when a verse may have been revealed.[21]

The concept of broadening and reapplying a verse's meaning based on its intent is the basic premise underlying much of Fazlur Rahman's proposed model for interpreting the Qur'an—a model from which scholars of feminist tafsir repeatedly draw when using the historical contextualization method to reread the Qur'an. Rahman's approach is perhaps best understood through his position on the relationship between the Qur'an and history: "The Qur'an and the genesis of the Islamic community occurred in the light of history and against a social-historical background. The Qur'an is a response to that situation, and for the most part it consists of moral, religious, and social pronouncements that respond to specific problems confronted in concrete historical situations."[22] As such, it is most often the case that the Qur'an's statements correspond to particular historical situations that must be taken into consideration in order to understand the meaning of those statements. For Rahman, then, "one must understand the import or meaning of a given statement by studying the historical situation or problem to which it was the answer."[23] The study of a Qur'anic statement's specific socio-historical context constitutes the first step of Rahman's "twofold movement" model for distilling the intent and universal principles of the Qur'an. According to the model: "First one must move from the concrete case treatments of the Qur'an—taking the necessary and relevant social conditions of that time into account—to the general principles upon which the entire teaching converges."[24] Second, that general meaning is then applied to one's present socio-historical context of understanding.[25] This "double movement" of interpretation involves reading the Qur'an in light of its specific historical context in order to carefully understand its intent; then this intent is applied to the specific historical circumstances of the current context in order to understand its meaning in the present.

From Rahman, Wadud borrows the notion of deducing universal principles of the Qur'an from statements particular to the circumstances of the first audience of the Qur'an. Based on his work, Wadud calls for the development of an interpretive model for getting at the "spirit" of the Qur'an, the meanings of which are universally relevant and applicable in all times and places.[26] In *Inside the Gender Jihad: Women's Reform in Islam*, Wadud adds further nuance to Rahman's understanding of general verses; she clarifies that even though some *'amm* verses provide *general* meanings, they do not necessarily provide *universal* meanings.[27] Wadud argues that because "the idea of 'global pluralism' did not exist, general was limited to the immediate space and time of the revelation."[28] As a result, "universal, at the time of revelation, was not globally comprehensive."[29] Therefore, not only *khass* verses, but also *'amm* verses must be understood as statements *relative to* their historical contexts.[30] Wadud reasons that since "'general' can be relative to the general context of its revelation, there is space to re-examine those verses considered *'amm* against general contexts outside seventh-century Arabia."[31] In fact, if *'amm* verses are not treated with the same scrutiny of historical context as *khass* verses are, exegetes run the risk that erroneously derived general meanings could "misread" and "violate" the Qur'an, or conversely, that the Qur'an's "universal meanings could be lost by their modes of articulation."[32]

This interpretive approach—distinguishing between particular and general meanings of the Qur'an, and understanding them within their historical context—is especially useful with regard to Qur'anic passages that address women and gender, since, as Wadud points out, "some of the greatest restrictions on women, causing them much harm, have resulted from interpreting Qur'anic solutions for particular problems as if they were universal principles."[33] The universalizing of the particular in the Qur'an has led to the related problem of confusing the Qur'an's descriptive statements with its prescriptive statements. Wadud argues that though the immediate context of the Qur'an's revelation was a patriarchal and sexist society, the Qur'an does not impose the characteristics of such a society upon future readers. The Qur'an may refer to situations that are degrading to women, but that does not mean it is *prescribing* those circumstances for its readers. Barlas echoes this observation, noting that "the Qur'an recognizes men as the locus of power and authority in actually existing patriarchies. However, recognizing the existence of a patriarchy, or addressing one, is not the same as advocating it."[34] Wadud goes on to point out the limitations of failing to make this important distinction: "The Qur'an's accommodation of various social contexts has been viewed as implying support for the particular social order that existed in seventh-century Arabia . . . To restrict future communities to the social shortcomings of any single community—even the original community of Islam—would be a severe limitation of that guidance."[35] From such assertions, it is clear that scholars of feminist tafsir are keen to deflect criticisms that they limit or degrade the Qur'an's meaning by reading it historically. They draw on the exegetical tradition's own categorization of *khass* and *'amm* verses and its use of *asbab al-nuzul* literature to call for precise readings that uphold the universality of the Qur'an. By distinguishing particular statements from universal statements, and descriptive statements from prescriptive statements, they offer feminist rereadings of numerous Qur'anic statements about women.

Feminist Rereadings Using Historical Contextualization
Qur'anic Verses

Scholars of feminist tafsir apply the method of historical contextualization to a number of crucial passages. In her discussion of verse 4:34, Wadud makes the case for the historical contextualization of several terms.[36] The first portion of the verse reads: "*al-rijalu qawwamuna 'ala al-nisa'i bi-ma faddala Allahu ba'dahum 'ala ba'din wa-bi-ma anfaqu min amwalihim.*" These lines have most often been translated to the effect: "Men are in charge of women because God has preferred them and because they provide for them from their means." Most understandings of this verse imply the notion of men's absolute superiority and dominance over women. However, by delimiting this verse to a particular, rather than universal, situation, Wadud produces an alternative reading in *Qur'an and Woman*. According to Wadud, the verse is describing a specific socio-economic situation in which a husband is the *financial* provider (*qawwam*) for his wife and child, but only under specific conditions: first, he is one of those men whom God has preferred (*faddala*) in the matter of financial inheritance, and second, he financially supports his wife and child from his earnings.

As for the first condition, the man must be the beneficiary of a specific kind of preference (*tafdil*) by God. Wadud connects this preference to what she observes as the only Qur'anic instance in which "Allah has determined for men a portion greater than for women: inheritance. The share for a male is twice that for the female . . . within a single family."[37] That is, the first condition for a man's *qiwamah* (role as *qawwam*) is that he has benefited from this double inheritance. The second condition for a man's *qiwamah* is that he is the financial provider for his family. If either of these conditions is not fulfilled, then he is not the financial *qawwam* of his family. Wadud posits a further argument against the verse being read as an absolute or unconditional statement about all men and all women. She points out that the verse "does not read 'they (masculine plural) are preferred over them (feminine plural).' It reads '*ba'd* (some) of them over *ba'd* (others).'"[38] This nuance of the verse is another indication of the verse's particularity and specificity.

In her identification of the specific family circumstances to which the verse refers, Wadud also examines the question of whether male responsibility is restricted to the husband-wife relationship, or if it is applicable to societies more broadly in their responsibility to support childbearing women. She asks:

> What is the responsibility of the male in [his] family and society at large? . . . The Qur'an establishes his responsibility as *qiwamah*: seeing to it that the woman is not burdened with additional responsibilities [in the context of childbearing] . . . This ideal scenario establishes an equitable and mutually dependent relationship. However, it does not allow for many of today's realities . . . Therefore, the Qur'an must eternally be reviewed with regard to human exchange and mutual responsibility between males and females.[39]

For Wadud, the intent of the verse is an assurance of mutual and evenly distributed responsibility in the family, but as the historical context of family relationships changes, such as in the not uncommon case of single motherhood today, this intent must be reapplied to fit new situations. In the case of single motherhood, perhaps *qiwamah* would be reinterpreted and broadened as a communal responsibility. Thus, by contextualizing this verse, Wadud argues against any reading that would imply men's categorical dominance and superiority over women, and she also calls for a reading that is relevant to evolving socio-historical situations.

Azizah al-Hibri, author of numerous articles and essays in which she discusses verse 4:34, offers a parallel, though slightly different, reinterpretation of the verse by pointing to its particularities. For al-Hibri, *qiwamah* is an advisory role; under specific conditions, a man is entitled to offer advice to his wife (regardless of whether she chooses to follow it). Al-Hibri's reading of the first condition for *qiwamah* does not concern inheritance, as it does in Wadud's reading. In addition to the second condition that the male is the financial provider, the first condition is that "the male must also possess qualities (such as financial acumen, real estate expertise, etc.) that the advised woman needs to reach a particular decision but lacks (at that point)."[40] If the man does not possess this God-given "preference" (*tafdil*) in expertise or knowledge, then he is not the *qawwam* of his family. Because of the conditional nature of this verse, men "are not *qawwamun* over financially independent women, nor are ignorant men *qawwamun* over educated women."[41]

While al-Hibri's reading of the verse as a highly conditional one is similar to Wadud's, what is especially interesting is her understanding of the historical context that necessitated the revelation of this verse: "Because the Qur'an was revealed in a world that was and continues to be highly patriarchal, it engaged in affirmative action to protect women. The revelation about maintenance provided women against poverty."[42] Thus, al-Hibri claims that in this verse the Qur'an acknowledges and directly addresses its immediate historical context, in which women were financially disadvantaged and vulnerable to poverty in a male-dominated society; the Qur'an thus ensures that women living under these conditions are compensated and financially secure. In addition, al-Hibri points out that this verse is "describing (and not recommending)" a situation in which "some women were financially dependent [on some men]. In those circumstances . . . God gave the man supporting her the responsibility (*taklif*, not privilege) of offering the woman guidance and advice in those areas in which he happens to be more qualified or experienced."[43] For al-Hibri, the Qur'an is thus responding to the needs of this contextual situation but not endorsing the contextual situation itself. She also points out that while the verse is offering this protection to women, it is also placing important restrictions on men's presumed entitlement to *qiwamah* at the time of revelation and is "thus a limitation on then current practices."[44] As Wadud has also suggested, by speaking to its own historical context, the Qur'an is itself placing "a limitation upon the apparently general statement" of men's *qiwamah* "by specifying the reasons or circumstances ... that would entitle a male to be *qawwam*."⁴⁵ If the reader ignores this historical context, the understanding of the verse would likely be erroneously broad, thus misreading its intent.

Another verse that male exegetes have used in support of the notion of categorical male superiority over women is verse 2:228.⁴⁶ In referring to divorced women, a key portion of the verse reads: "*wa-la-hunna mithlu alladhi 'alayhinna bi-l-ma'rufi wa-li-l-rijali 'alayhinna darajatun*"; it is often translated to the effect: "Women have rights similar to the rights that are claimed of them, but men possess a degree more than them." Wadud points out that this statement is drastically restricted by the obvious context which the verse spells out for itself: divorce. The key term in this passage is *darajah* (translated here as degree), which is the focus of Wadud's rereading. Wadud posits that *darajah* refers only to the advantage men have over women in terms of unilateral repudiation in divorce.⁴⁷ The verse is not a statement of an absolute advantage given to all men over all women; rather, it is an advantage given to certain men under specific circumstances. The specific advantage that the verse refers to is the custom of men "being individually able to pronounce divorce against their wives without arbitration or assistance."⁴⁸ Moreover, this custom is itself limited by context. Wadud points out that the term *ma'ruf* (well known) indicates that the equitable balance of men's and women's rights and responsibilities in divorce is determined by each society according to its conventions; thus, she argues, the verse "places a limitation rather than a universal perspective on this issue because convention is relative to time and place."⁴⁹ Wadud argues that the Qur'an does not give men the unilateral right to repudiation; it speaks to a context in which men commonly had that right. She points out that the Qur'an "does not make a rule that men *should* have uncontrolled power of repudiation. Men *did* have this power."⁵⁰ Lastly, the Qur'an does not preclude the possibility of women obtaining the right to repudiation for themselves; it simply does not address this possibility since it was not the case during the time of revelation.⁵¹ Thus, Wadud reads this verse as situational rather than universal and descriptive rather than prescriptive, in order to produce an understanding of the verse that rejects its application as an absolute statement about men's natural or inherent superiority over women.

Wadud also uses historical contextualization to take on the controversial sanctioning of polygyny in verse 4:3.⁵² The verse reads: "If you fear that you cannot act justly toward orphans, then marry the women who seem good to you—two, three, or four; but if you fear you cannot be equitable, then one, or what your right hands possess. That is more appropriate so that you do not act unjustly."[53] This verse is often used by men to justify the taking of multiple wives to satiate their sexual desire for more than one partner. However, Wadud argues that this verse cannot possibly sanction multiple marriages for this purpose; its historical context makes it clear that the verse is concerned with just treatment of orphans under a particular set of conditions.

First, Wadud points out that the verse is speaking to an immediate seventh-century audience with a particular understanding of marriage: "marriage of subjugation at the time of revelation was premised on the need for females to be materially provided for by some male."[54] Second, the verse is specifically addressing a historical situation in which warfare had resulted in the orphaning of many children in the Muslim community. The immediately preceding verse provides the context: "Some male guardians, responsible for managing the wealth of orphaned female children, were unable to refrain from unjust management of that wealth."[55] In response, verse 4:3 allows these male guardians to marry up to four female orphans for the express purpose of protecting the orphans' wealth within the legal structure of marriage. According to this reading, the historical context of the verse makes it clear that the limited allowance for polygyny (limiting the number of wives to four) is concerned with the equitable treatment of orphans.[56] Furthermore, the allowance is a conditional one, as the verse stipulates that if a man is incapable of treating the orphans justly, then this allowance is nullified.[57] According to Wadud, this condition itself signals that the Qu'ran is speaking to "the archaic idea of marriages of subjugation" in which the measure of equitable treatment was solely financial; many would argue that this understanding of marriage has subsequently been superseded by a form of marriage that understands the just treatment of a wife to cover a territory broader than financial treatment alone.[58] Wadud argues that the verse is clearly speaking to a dated context since it is addressing a situation in which women are financial burdens to their families; it does not address modern situations in which women have the capacity to be financial providers.[59] Thus, the verse does not supply a rationale for taking multiple wives in a situation where women can, indeed, provide for themselves. Once again, Wadud demonstrates that an understanding of the historical context of revelation drastically limits the allowance of polygyny to specific conditions and situations.[60] She implies that since many of these particularities do not exist in the present, these verses must be reevaluated for their meaning under circumstances when these conditions do not exist.[61]

A similar set of historical conditions are considered by Wadud in her reading of verse 2:282, which addresses the issue of legal witnesses.[62] A portion of this verse indicates that in a legal situation requiring two male witnesses, if only one male witness is available to attend, then two female witnesses may take the place of the one missing male witness. It reads, "And call upon two witnesses from among your men, but if there are not two men, then a man and two women from among whom you approve as witnesses, so that if one of the two women errs the other reminds her." Responding to common interpretations of the verse, Wadud asks, "Is one male witness equal to two female witnesses and, therefore, one male equivalent to, or as good as, two females absolutely?"[63] Wadud's answer is a resounding no, pointing out that the verse is speaking to a particular historical context in which "women could be coerced" into producing inaccurate or false testimony, to the extent that "if one witness was female, she would be easy prey for some male who wanted to force her to disclaim her testimony."[64] Thus, the verse is not a general or universal statement about men and women's relative worth; it is specifically addressing a particular problem in the immediate context of revelation and providing a pointed solution for it.[65] She argues that the historical context belies any reading that would allow for the common assumption based on this Qur'anic verse that a woman's moral or human worth is half that of a man's. Furthermore, she notes that the context of the verse—women's inexperience and prohibitive vulnerability to men in legal matters—is now obsolete.[66] Therefore, even if one were to apply this verse to legal situations only, the present context would not match the verse's historical context, and the substitution of one male witness by two female witnesses would be highly questionable.

Wadud uses similar means to reread another portion of verse 4:34 that instructs men on proper conduct with their wives in the event of a quarrel.[67] A portion of the verse reads, "*fa-in ata'nakum fa-la tabghu 'alayhinna sabilan*"; it is often understood to the effect of, "if your wives obey you, then do not seek means against them." In reading the conditional phrase "if they obey you," Wadud points out that the Qur'an is not commanding women to obey their husbands, as other exegetes have assumed.[68] In order to combat such reading, Wadud places the verse in the context of marriages in seventh-century Arabia: the martial norm was one of "marriages of subjugation," where "wives did obey their husbands."[69] She argues that the verse is *describing* and addressing a specific type of marriage in a particular time period and culture, but it is *not prescribing* that model of marriage upon all readers of the Qur'an. (The issue of female obedience resurfaces in chapter 6).

Historical contextualization also serves Wadud in her reading of Qur'anic passages concerning the pleasures waiting believers in Paradise. Wadud's particular concern is the occasional references to *hur al-'ayn* in the Qur'an, often understood to mean fair, dark-eyed women whose companionship will be believing men's heavenly reward.[70] This interpretation has been troubling to many scholars because of the implication that women are objects used for rewarding men, the reference to a specific ideal of beauty for women, and the lack of concern for women's heavenly reward. According to Wadud, the specific physical characterization of heavenly mates indicated by the phrase *hur al-'ayn* would have appealed to the seventh-century Arab male audience of the Qur'an, who held a particular ideal of beauty: the "specific description here of the companions of Paradise demonstrates the Qur'an's familiarity with the dreams and desires of those Arabs."[71] Although in its immediate context the Qur'an often catered to those particular desires, Wadud argues that this description of the heavenly companion should be understood metaphorically, as a literal reading—implying that only men will be rewarded with companions and that they will be rewarded with companions who are beautiful by a single standard—is untenable. The general meaning that should be gleaned from these Qur'anic statements is the promise of desirable mates for all believers, both male and female, who enter Paradise.[72]

Many interpreters of the Qur'an examined in this book turn their attention, at some point, to the issue of women's veiling and seclusion. For the purposes of this chapter, I will limit my examination of the issue's treatment to the exegetes' use of the historical contextualization method in interpreting verse 33:59.[73] The verse reads: "O Prophet, tell your wives and daughters and believing women that they should draw over themselves their outer garments (*jalabib*). That is more suitable, that they should be recognized and not harmed. God is forgiving and merciful." Barlas argues that the instruction to all Muslim women to cover their bodies using their *jalabib* (sing. *jilbab*), or "outer garments" (which is itself an ambiguous directive since it does not clarify exactly which parts of the body should be covered), is specific to the social norms prevalent during the time of revelation. Barlas reads this passage in light of the historical context in which the verse was revealed: "the social structure of a slave-owning society in which sexual abuse, especially of slaves, was rampant . . . at a time when women had no legal recourse against such abuse."[74]

According to Barlas, in the context of a slave-owning society governed by pre-Islamic sexual norms, the Qur'an's directive constructs *jilbab* as a marker of Muslim women's sexual unavailability to men, as distinct from non-Muslim slave women who were considered sexually available to men according to *Jahili* (pre-Islamic) custom. In this sexually charged environment, the *jilbab* of verse 33:59 is meant to "render [Muslim women] *visible*" to and "recognizable" by "*Jahili* men, as a way to protect the women."[75] However, Barlas suggests, only in a slave-owning, sexually corrupt society would the *jilbab* protect and signal the sexual unavailability of women.[76] Barlas's implication is that outside these specific social conditions, the instructions of verse 33:59 would no longer serve the purpose of protecting women.[77] Thus, the meaning of the passage is specific and relevant only to its context and can be applied only under similar social conditions.

Finally, Wadud takes up the broader issue of why the Qur'an, as in many of the verses discussed thus far and subsequently, frequently addresses only male believers directly (addressing them in the second person while referring to women in the third person, if at all). In these instances, the Qur'an appears to address men to the exclusion of women, perhaps thus giving preferential treatment to men or implying that women are not equal or worthy recipients of Qur'anic guidance. On this matter, Wadud claims that the Qur'an, aware of the socio-historical context of its revelation, "made special address to those in whose hands were the power and privilege to establish social justice."[78] Since men possessed greater privilege and power over women in seventh-century Arabian society, they possessed greater ability and responsibility to counter the oppression of women and other disadvantaged groups. The Qur'an thus recognized within its revelatory context that justice was "the dispensation of the strong granted toward the weak."[79] Therefore, men may have been the focal point of Qur'anic guidance in that particular context, but only because the Qur'an recognized that in its specific revelatory context, men possessed greater capacity and responsibility for social reform. Thus, male address in the Qur'an is a reflection of the Qur'an's historical context rather than an indicator of preferential treatment of men.

Qur'anic Exegesis

As the preceding discussion of specific verses indicates, a major premise of feminist tafsir is that the historical context of seventh-century Arabia indelibly shaped the pronouncements of the Qur'an. A corresponding premise guides critiques of the exegetical tradition; that is, just as the historical context of the Qur'an shapes its content, the historical environments of exegetes shape interpretations of the Qur'an. Thus, scholars of feminist tafsir criticize common exegetical treatments of the Qur'an by uncovering the assumptions exegetes hold about gender as a result of their socio-historical, cultural environments.

In defending this critical approach toward traditional exegesis, Wadud argues that the "prior text" of any reader—that is, the "cultural context in which the text is read"—significantly influences how one reads the Qur'an.[80] Wadud counts social understandings of gender among the prior texts influencing the reader. She understands gender as a fluid social construction: "Femininity and masculinity are not created characteristics imprinted into the very primordial nature of female and male persons . . . They are defined characteristics applied to female and male persons respectively on the basis of culturally determined factors of how each gender should function."[81] Because the social construction of gender is among the prior texts influencing a reader, he or she is inevitably guided by his or her own historically and culturally determined views of gender when attempting to understand the Qur'an. Put another way, an exegete's historical and cultural contexts determine his or her perception of the roles of men and women in society (what Wadud refers to as the "functional distinctions" of men and women), which in turn powerfully impacts his or her interpretation of the Qur'an.[82] Wadud and Barlas hold that exegetes routinely insert historically determined views of gender into their interpretations of the Qur'an without acknowledging that these views belong to them rather than to the Qur'an. The problem of male exegetes failing to acknowledge the historicity of the gender norms guiding their exegeses is further compounded by the subsequent accumulative authority of their readings. In ascribing unparalleled knowledge of the first Muslims to early Muslim scholars and viewing their understanding of the Qur'an as more accurate and authoritative than Qur'anic interpretations by succeeding generations, the Islamic tradition effectively canonized readings of the Qur'an "generated over a thousand years ago in the name of sacred history and historical precedent," paradoxically generating a "historical defense of the sacred/universal" character of early interpretations while "refus[ing] to accept . . . a historicizing understanding" of them.[83] The overall effect of such reasoning has been to lock readings of the Qur'an into particular historical contexts without acknowledging their historicity; this in turn has impeded the process of distilling historical biases from exegetical meanings and developing interpretations of the Qur'an in line with new historical contexts.

Key to Wadud's argument is her observation that, in contrast to the various historical environments that produce gender norms and accordingly influence exegesis of the Qur'an, the Qur'an itself does not prescribe gender norms. Wadud asserts that although the Qur'an acknowledges the existence of "culturally-determined, functional distinctions" between men and women in society, it "does not propose or support a singular role or single definition of a set of roles, exclusively, for each gender across every culture."[84] (She notes that to do so would amount to "an imposition that would reduce the Qur'an from a universal text to a culturally specific text."[85]) The implication is that when an exegete proposes a single definition of gender roles based on the Qur'an, the proposal originates with the exegete, not with the Qur'an. An exegete's proposal of gender norms based on the Qur'an is informed by his or her historical context rather than the text of the Qur'an itself.

According to Barlas, demeaning and patriarchal interpretations of the Qur'an reflect the "misogyny" of the era in which the most definitive works of exegesis were authored.[86] Guided by the social norms of their times, exegetes would "project into Scripture their own desires."[87] Sa'diyya Shaikh's study "Exegetical Violence: *Nushuz* in Qur'anic Gender Ideology" demonstrates how medieval exegesis is colored by "the normative gender ideology and gender roles prevalent in these exegetes' socio-political and cultural realities."[88] Shaikh finds that their interpretations endorse a "notion of a qualitatively superior male constitution;" men are linked to "rationality, intellect, and spirituality," while women are characterized as "emotional, irrational, carnal, and sexual."[89] She concludes that the exegetes' "hermeneutical lenses are evidently created by a patriarchal worldview and thus their interpretations are the ideological products of male-centred society."[90]

On the whole, Muslim feminist works provide far fewer illustrations of the application of the historical contextualization method to exegetical texts than to the Qur'anic text. While revealing the historical constructedness of exegetical pronouncements on gender is significant to the Muslim feminist project, it is much less the focus of the exegetes' attention than the work of historically contextualizing the words of the Qur'an itself. This unevenness in focus suggests that it may seem more urgent or beneficial to scholars of feminist tafsir to elucidate the historical context of the Qur'an itself (in a sense, to "rescue" the Qur'an from the patriarchal context of its revelation) than to expose the historical context of traditional exegesis (and thereby draw attention to their disagreements with authoritative scholars). However, even as exegesis is given less attention than the text of the Qur'an, it seems that even less priority is reserved for approaching Hadith in relationship to the Qur'an.

Hadith

Generally speaking, scholars of feminist tafsir approach the Hadith with a marked ambivalence, and therefore their use of the Hadith in applying the historical contextualization method to the Qur'an exhibits some methodological inconsistencies. In some cases, the exegetes are inclined to cite certain Hadith reports positively without scrutinizing their historical authenticity when they support the just treatment of women, and they use them to buttress their interpretations of the Qur'an. In other cases, they argue for the inauthenticity of Hadith reports that demean women, rejecting those reports and maintaining that the Qur'an must be prioritized over them. Furthermore, in many of their interpretations of the Qur'an, they do not consult the Hadith tradition at all. Thus the application of the historical contextualization method in the field of feminist tafsir as a whole reveals an inconsistent usage of the Hadith and Sunna and a selective scrutiny of the sources of historical information.

Here it may be helpful to briefly revisit the role of the Hadith in the tafsir tradition (previously discussed in chapter 1). Throughout the tradition, "Muhammad is considered to be the first exegete of the scripture . . . The prophet, by his words and his deeds . . . elucidated many passages of the revealed text."[91] Like all Hadith reports attributed to him, the Prophet's elucidations of the Qur'an were passed on to Muslims through the transmissions of his family members and Companions, who, because they knew the Prophet firsthand and were among the first Muslims, are regarded with "extraordinary authority."[92] These oral traditions were likely not committed to writing until more than a century after the Prophet's lifetime, and it was not until the early ninth and tenth centuries C.E. that Muslim scholars developed an elaborate science for distinguishing between what they deemed as authentic Hadith reports and fabricated ones. This science concentrated on a report's *isnad*, its chain of oral transmitters. The validity of an *isnad* (and hence, the authenticity of a Hadith report) was accessed by scrutinizing the transmitters' moral reputation and mental acuity, the continuity and chronological soundness of the *isnad* chain, and the number of concurrent transmitters for each link in the chain.[93] The six canonical collections produced through this process of scrutiny excluded hundreds of thousands of reports.[94]

However, many contemporary scholars have questioned the authenticity of a Hadith canon that was not formalized until the ninth and tenth centuries C.E. Islamic historian R. Stephen Humphreys examines the tremendous challenges posed by the oral and written traditions of early Islam; as he puts it, a major concern of scholars of Islamic historiography is "how far, and in what ways, the concepts of historical process, the religio-political concerns, and the literary structures of the extent texts have diverged from accounts originally composed . . . during the [seventh century C.E.]."[95] Humphreys points out the problem of orally transmitted material prior to the development of the sciences of Hadith authentication (emerging around the early ninth century C.E.); he notes that those sciences' standards of scrutiny "could hardly be applied to the texts produced in earlier generations when these techniques were either unknown or at best far less regular. In brief, the way in which the ancient historical tradition was recorded and transmitted left room for manifold sins of omission and commission."[96] Furthermore, given the absence of any other whole, surviving historical sources from the first century of Islam, in Fazlur Rahman's words, the "disentanglement of the [Hadith's] historical Prophetic elements is perhaps incapable of complete achievement for want of early enough sources."[97] Even though there is plenty of such evidence that the Hadith canon is not built only on "strict historicity," it has withstood criticisms by modern scholars and resisted any serious or systematic revision by Muslims to date; thus the six canonical collections remain intact and largely authoritative for most Muslims.[98]

As mentioned previously, a number of modernist Muslim scholars and their contemporary successors are known for their skepticism of the criteria by which the Hadith were transmitted and canonized and have called for the reevaluation of the sources and content of suspect Hadith reports.[99] Though the authority of *al-tafsir bi-l-ma'thur* (tafsir by tradition) is derived from the statements of the Prophet's Companions and their Successors, these scholars question the assumption that their reports were "handed down from one generation to the other without the intervention of reason, discernment, selection, or rejection of the transmitters."[100] For example, Fazlur Rahman argues that "historical criticism was not the only principle of selectivity used by canonical collectors."[101] He suggests that in addition to the disqualification of reports that appeared to contradict the Qur'an, there were also murkier standards of selectivity applied by scholars who were engaged in doctrinal and political debates, and who were thus motivated by factors other than the historical method when favoring the canonization of some reports over others.[102] For Rahman, it appears that at times they were motivated by their own sense of what did or did not conform to the spirit of the practices of the Prophet and his early followers; thus, the "intuitive principle of selectivity" they employed "was not primarily historical, but doctrinal."[103] Often, as a result, "palpably post-Prophetic developments . . . were verbally attributed to the Prophet."[104]

The history of the Hadith's development, then, creates a serious dilemma for modernist scholars and their successors. On the one hand, for them the Hadith canon's veracity is suspect on several serious accounts and, therefore, arguments based on Hadith are also suspect. On the other hand, as Fazlur Rahman has argued, "if the Hadith *as a whole* is cast away, the basis for the historicity of the Qur'an is removed," since this would result in the loss of any documentation of how the first Muslims understood the teachings of the Qur'an.[105] For Rahman it is true that "the Hadith in part does not represent the verbal and pure Prophetic teaching."[106] However, despite its murky historical underpinnings, the Hadith is indispensable for understanding the historical context of the Qur'an and the practices of the first Muslims.[107]

Thus, scholars of feminist tafsir are left to confront an enormous literature of questionable historical authenticity. Barlas discusses at length the ways in which the Hadith reflects the historical contexts of its emergence and canonization, particularly its political functions and manipulations.[108] She argues that a number of "ideas, discourses, and practices, including some that were in tension with and even contradicted the Qur'an's teachings" became incorporated into the Islamic tradition via the Hadith.[109] Barlas also points out that the Companions of the Prophet were granted an unassailable authority in the Islamic tradition because of their proximity to the Prophet, contributing to the treatment of "the first Muslim community and its practices as . . . non-historical and eternal."[110] She also posits that much of the recorded Sunna "is not a reflection of the Prophet's praxis" but reflects the early Muslim community's understanding of it.[111] Furthermore, both she and Riffat Hassan deplore how the Hadith has been employed in the tafsir tradition. Hassan argues that the use of questionable Hadith reports to understand the Qur'an became commonplace and seamlessly interwoven into works of Qur'anic exegesis to the extent that "authoritative works both of Qur'anic exegesis and Islamic history have become colored by the *Hadith* literature. In course of time, many *ahadith* became 'invisible,' the later commentators referring not to them but to the authority of earlier commentators who had cited them, to support their views."[112] Barlas critically points out that some scholars went so far as to equate the authority of the transmitted Sunna with the Qur'an or even elevated it above the Qur'an in authority.[113] In some cases, then, scholars used "the *Sunnah* to read the Qur'an" and thereby "undercut the doctrine of revelation's self-sufficiency."[114] Hassan concurs, noting that the Hadith has often been the "lens through which the words of the Qur'an have been seen and interpreted."[115]

Hassan has implied in her work that many Hadith reports that demean women entered the Islamic tradition because Hadith scholars gave more weight to *isnad* criticism than *matn* (content). She argues for the rejection of any report that contradicts the Qur'an, repeatedly asserting that the Qur'an is unrivaled in its divine authority and that its meanings must always take precedence over anything conflictual in the Hadith. Hassan plainly states: "All Muslims agree that whenever a Hadith attributed to the Prophet conflicts with the Qur'an it must be rejected."[116] Wadud submits a similar position, noting that she prioritizes the Qur'an over the Hadith due to the "inerrancy of Qur'anic preservation versus historical contradictions within the *hadith* literature."[117]

In practice, this skepticism toward the Hadith has resulted in feminist tafsir's use of the Hadith in contradictory ways to both supply and rule out historical contexts for Qur'anic verses. Granted, some of this paradoxical use of the Hadith for opposite ends results naturally from the diversity that marks the Hadith canon. (The medieval collection of the Hadith was based upon the acknowledgement that some Hadith reports are more reliable than others; even those deemed reliable are divided into categories based on various levels of certainty about their reliability.[118]) The logical result is that some Hadith reports may be used with greater confidence to supply or confirm historical contexts for situations in the Qur'an, whereas other Hadith reports may be doubted in identifying historical contexts. This variant use of the Hadith reflects the diversity within the Hadith canon and does not necessarily pose a methodological problem in and of itself.

However, a methodological problem for the project of feminist tafsir as a whole arises when scholars of feminist tafsir variously use Hadith reports to produce or rule out historical contexts without subjecting all the reports to the same standards of scrutiny. When the reports are favorable, the exegetes do not discuss their reliability. However, when the reports are problematic, they devote considerable attention to criticizing their authenticity.[119] After studying the *isnad* and *matn* of Hadith reports about the creation of man and woman, Riffat Hassan rejects reports that claim that woman originates from the rib of man.[120] She questions the soundness of their transmission by studying their *isnad*, and she argues that they contain "generalizations about [woman's] ontology, biology, and psychology contrary to the letter and spirit of the Qur'an."[121] Hassan similarly rejects reports that appear to instruct women to bow before their husbands and obey them as a duty to God, as well as reports on the evil of women and their inferiority in intelligence and religiosity.[122]

In contrast, Wadud and al-Hibri use the Hadith positively to support their interpretations of verse 4:34. The reports on which they concentrate are concerned with the Prophet's stances on husbands beating their wives; they cite these reports in response to male scholars' use of verse 4:34 to claim that men's authority includes the directive for a husband to beat his wife (discussed in further detail in subsequent chapters). Wadud cites a report in which the Prophet once told a woman that she had grounds for retribution against her husband because he had beaten her; subsequently, when verse 4:34 was revealed to him, the Prophet stated in response, "'I wanted one thing and Allah wanted something else.'"[123] The Prophet's words, according to this report, are often interpreted to mean that although he himself wished to grant the woman recourse against her violent husband, his wish was superseded by God's Qur'anic allowance for beating. However, Wadud regards this report positively and uses it to encourage the emulation of the Prophet's nonviolent attitude and behavior. She argues, "He *never* implemented this text [portion of verse 4:34] in his life. He never struck a woman or beat a slave."[124] Wadud asserts that since the Prophet is the best practitioner of Qur'anic guidance, his practice of nonviolence toward his wives supports that 4:34 does not command beating one's wives.[125] Azizah al-Hibri makes a similar argument about the Prophet never beating women,[126] and uses the same incident in the Hadith to argue that the Prophet allowed women retribution for being beaten by their husbands.[127] She also cites reports of the Prophet chastising men who beat their wives[128] and advising men to treat women with kindness.[129] Al-Hibri uses all these reports to argue against interpretations of 4:34 that sanction domestic violence.[130]

The uneven use and scrutiny of the Hadith demonstrates a methodological inconsistency across the collective body of feminist tafsir works.

This inconsistency presents major challenges to the success of historical readings of the Qur'an because the information necessary to supply the historical context of the verses reread by the exegetes largely derives directly or indirectly from the Hadith, even when the exegetes do not trace the historical contexts they identify back to particular reports. The successful use of the feminist method of historical contextualization will require that scholars of feminist tafsir more carefully clarify their positions on the Hadith tradition as a whole, in part by treating the Hadith more systematically in all their readings of the Qur'an rather than referencing the Hadith in select cases when it is convenient to support or defend their interpretations.

However, these challenges are also accompanied by some exceptional work and call for further research on the Hadith and Sunna.[131] Sa'diyya Shaikh's "Knowledge, Women, and Gender in the Hadith: A Feminist Interpretation" is a promising start in this vein; in this work she analyzes the varying constructions of gender in Hadith reports on women's knowledge and sexuality.[132] Asma Barlas has called for the differentiation of "the *Sunnah* from its textualization in the *Ahadith*"; although she admits that such work will be difficult, she says it is "necessary for greater interpretive freedom and also for reading the Qur'an by the Qur'an" more fruitfully.[133] In *Inside the Gender Jihad*, Wadud notes the scarcity of feminist work on the reinterpretation of Hadith and encourages further research on the matter.[134] Thus, the field of feminist tafsir awaits the development of more consistent standards for utilizing the Hadith and a thorough examination of source difficulties to strengthen the use of the historical contextualization method in feminist readings of the Qur'an.

5

Intratextual Method

> *The innumerable Muslim commentaries on the Holy Book often take the text verse by verse and explain it. Quite apart from the fact that most of these project tendentious points of view, at great length, by the very nature of their procedure they cannot yield insight into the cohesive outlook on the universe and life which the Qur'an undoubtedly possesses.*
> —FAZLUR RAHMAN, Major Themes of the Qur'an[1]

FAZLUR RAHMAN'S INFLUENTIAL call to study the Qur'an's "cohesive outlook" is echoed in the keystone feminist exegetical strategy of reading the Qur'an holistically. This approach involves reading the Qur'an intratextually—comparing related Qur'anic verses and terms to one another instead of reading them in isolation, as well as reading verses in light of what the exegetes have identified as the Qur'an's overall movement toward advocating justice and equality for all human beings.[2] As in the use of the historical contextualization method, the intratextual interpretive strategy also finds a precedent in premodern and modernist exegesis of the Qur'an. Numerous scholars have observed an internal coherence within the Qur'an,[3] often referring to this quality of the text as the Qur'an's *nazm*.[4] In addition, among the most significant interpretive methods elaborated upon by classical exegetes is *tafsir al-Qur'an bi-l-Qur'an*, the method of "interpreting the Qur'an using the Qur'an itself." This method is based on the early exegetical premise that the Qur'an is "its own primary commentator and is the first source for understanding its meaning."[5] One part of the Qur'an may be used to understand another part; thus the Qur'an must be understood as a whole, unified text.[6] The celebrated Ibn Taymiyah (d. 1328 C.E.) comments on the authoritativeness of this method in his *Muqaddimah fi usul al-tafsir*. Ibn Taymiyah states: "The best way [method of tafsir] is to explain the Qur'an through the Qur'an. For, what the Qur'an alludes to at one place is explained at the other, and what it says in brief on one occasion is elaborated upon at the other."[7]

Modernist scholars and their successors note, despite the tafsir tradition's support of this method, that the execution of *tafsir al-Qur'an bi-l-Qur'an* and any substantive development of the concept of the Qur'an's *nazm* are largely missing from much of Qur'anic exegesis. Fazlur Rahman argues that far from treating the Qur'an as a unity, premodern Qur'anic interpreters generally exhibited an "atomistic approach" toward the text.[8] According to Mustansir Mir, a contemporary scholar of the Qur'an, despite the understanding of *nazm* in traditional tafsir works, "the basic unit of Qur'an study is one or a few verses taken in isolation from the preceding and following verses."[9] Rahman is among the most vocal critics of this characteristic of tafsir works; he observes in traditional Qur'anic scholarship "a general failure to understand the underlying unity of the Qur'an, coupled with a practical insistence upon fixing on the words of various verses in isolation."[10]

Building on Rahman's criticisms, Amina Wadud and Asma Barlas observe that by treating the Qur'an in a piecemeal manner, exegetes have contradicted their own consensus on how to interpret the Qur'an and have violated one of the "hermeneutic principles suggested by the Quran for its own interpretation," that is, the Qur'an's own stated directives for how it should be interpreted.[11] Among these Qur'anic instructions, Barlas cites the Qur'an's "praise for those who say 'We believe In the Book; the whole of it Is from our Lord'" as well as "its warning that 'Those who break the Qur'an into parts. Them, by thy Lord, We shall question, every one, Of what they used to do.'"[12] Wadud concludes that the tafsir tradition has proved inadequate in this regard by its own standards: "Starting from the position that we [Muslims] believe in the whole of the book, the atomistic approach that characterizes traditional exegesis does not sufficiently explain or exemplify the extent and impact of total Qur'anic coherence and perhaps never tried to nor made claim to such."[13] Wadud notes that as part of this deficiency in tafsir, the tradition of Qur'anic exegesis lacks a systematic manner for tracing and comparing parallel uses of language and themes throughout the Qur'an:

> Despite consensus [among exegetes] that the interpretation of the Qur'an by the Qur'an itself (*tafsir al-Qur'an bi-l-Qur'an*) is the number one tool [for Qur'anic interpretation], traditional Qur'anic

exegesis is atomistic, applying meaning to one lexical item or passage at a time. Occasional references to other specific verses are inconsistent, unsystematic, and haphazard.[14]

A brief mention of one verse's relation to another verse may be rendered but these are [sic] haphazard with no underlying hermeneutical principle applied. A methodology for linking similar Qur'anic ideas, syntactical structures, principles, or themes together is almost non-existent.[15]

From this viewpoint, traditional exegeses have generally neglected the coherence and holism of the Qur'anic text, failing to view verses comparatively using a consistent or systematic manner.

In response to this shortcoming of the tafsir tradition, modern and contemporary Muslim scholars have exhibited growing interest in studying the *nazm* of the Qur'an.[16] Mir observes: "In modern times . . . a number of Muslim scholars from various parts of the Muslim world have, with varying degrees of cogency, argued that the Qur'an possesses a high degree of thematic and structural unity, and this view seems to represent a modern consensus in the making."[17] Thus these scholars began to call for reading the Qur'an as a cohesive whole.[18] For Fazlur Rahman, "the Qur'an must be so studied that its concrete unity will emerge in its fullness."[19] He notes that "due regard must be paid to the tenor of the teaching of the Qur'an as a whole so that each given meaning understood, each law enunciated, and each objective formulated will cohere with the rest. The Qur'an as a whole does inculcate a definite attitude toward life and does have a concrete weltanschauung."[20]

Azizah al-Hibri echoes Rahman, aiming to read the Qur'an in a manner that "asserts the thorough internal consistency of the Qur'an."[21] Asma Barlas sets out to "treat the text as a unity," reading it "holistically, hence intratextually."[22] Calling for Muslims to reestablish the exegetical premise of the Qur'an as a unified whole, Wadud proposes a holistic method of tafsir based on the principle of tawhid, or unity, in the Qur'an: "I propose a hermeneutics of *tawhid* to emphasize how the unity of the Qur'an permeates all its parts. Rather than simply applying meanings to one verse at a time, with occasional references to various verses elsewhere, a framework may be developed that includes a systematic rationale for making correlations and sufficiently exemplifies the full impact of Qur'anic coherence."[23] Thus, Wadud calls for the development of an organized exegetical system for comparing different parts of the Qur'an with each other: studying recurring terms, linguistic structures, and themes in tandem to derive a broader and more unified picture of Qur'anic meaning and intent.[24]

On the whole, scholars of feminist tafsir argue that atomistic treatments of the Qur'an have resulted in misleading, distorted understandings of the text, especially in relation to verses about women. Their arguments echo Fazlur Rahman's assertion that "to select certain verses from the Qur'an to project a partial and subjective point of view . . . necessarily does violence to the Qur'an itself and results in extremely dangerous abstractions."[25] Barlas observes, for instance, that "patriarchal or oppressive" readings of the Qur'an often "result from reading the text in a piecemeal and decontextualized way, for instance, by privileging one word, or phrase, or line, or Ayah, over its teachings as a whole."[26] For these scholars, holistic readings of the Qur'an are essential to developing feminist interpretations of the Qur'an. As Wadud observes of the exegetical tradition, thus far "there has been no substantial consideration of the particular issue of woman *in the light of the entire Qur'an* and its major principles."[27] For Barlas, "recognizing the Qur'an's textual and thematic holism, and thus the hermeneutic connections between seemingly disparate themes, is absolutely integral to recovering its antipatriarchal epistemology."[28] This position is consistently at the center of several feminist readings of key Qur'anic verses, as discussed below, and is used to discount narrow interpretations of the Qur'an that discriminate against women.

Reading Equality in Creation

A central component of intratextual feminist readings is a shared understanding of the creation story in the Qur'an as evidence for its overarching, guiding message of human equality regardless of sex. This understanding of human creation serves as a central reference point when performing holistic readings of the Qur'an; the exegetes hold that if the Qur'an is read as a unified whole, all its verses relevant to male-female relations must then be read in comparison to, and in light of, its creation story. Riffat Hassan's work on human creation in the Qur'an is the most extensive and referenced of Muslim feminist works on the subject. Hassan's signature thesis is that according to the Qur'an, woman and man are created in egalitarian terms, from a single *nafs*, or soul, at the same time. The first woman is neither created from nor for man; nor does she cause man's "fall" from grace.[29] Collectively reading portions of the story of Adam and Eve (known as Adam and Hawwa in the Islamic tradition) found in various chapters of the Qur'an, Hassan finds that both Adam and Eve commit the sin of eating from the tree of knowledge; both are tempted by Satan and equally responsible for committing this sin, and there is no reference to Eve causing Adam's temptation.[30] Hassan also argues that the Qur'an does not narrate any sort of fall of humankind; though God banishes them from the Garden, both Adam and Eve are forgiven by God, and the rest of humankind does not bear responsibility for any unforgivable sin.[31]

In thus clarifying the Qur'anic telling of the creation story, Hassan seeks to differentiate it from a number of Hadith accounts that echo the biblical story of Adam and Eve. As in the texts of Genesis 2 and 3 and *isra'iliyat* texts based on them, these Hadith accounts presume that the first woman was created with a morally inferior nature and from the rib of the first man.[32] Hassan estimates that "almost all Muslims believe that the first woman (Hawwa) was created from Adam's rib" due to the influence of these Hadith accounts.[33] According to Hassan, this understanding of creation has led to the widely held belief among most Muslims "that women—who are inferior in creation (having been made from a crooked rib) and in righteousness (having helped Shaitan in defeating God's plan for Adam)—have been created mainly to be of use to men who are superior to them."[34] From this perspective, woman figures as God's secondary creation, is derived from man for man's use, and is not just lesser in virtue but also a vessel of evil and temptation.[35] In response to Muslims who accordingly presume that woman is the inferior and subordinate member of the first human pair, Hassan points out that the Qur'an itself, which does not contain the rib narrative, presents an entirely different understanding of the creation of the sexes.[36]

After comprehensively comparing the Qur'an's verses on creation, Hassan concludes: "In none of the thirty or so passages that describe the creation of humanity . . . is there any statement that could be interpreted as asserting or suggesting that man was created prior to woman or that woman was created from man."[37] In particular, Hassan focuses on verse 4:1, a key portion of which reads: "O humankind, be conscious of your Lord, who created you from [*min*] a single soul [*nafsin wahidatin*], and created from it [*min-ha*] its mate [*zawjaha*], and disseminated numerous men and women from the two [*min-huma*]."[38] As both Hassan and Amina Wadud point out, the word *nafs* (translated as "soul") is conceptually neither male nor female, though grammatically it is feminine;[39] it is to this grammatically feminine noun antecedent that the feminine pronoun *ha* in *min-ha* and *zawjaha* refers.⁴⁰ They argue that in contrast to common understandings of the verse, there is no textual or linguistic justification whatsoever for attributing maleness to the *nafs* from which all humankind originates or, for that matter, for assuming that this original *nafs* is Adam.⁴¹ Likewise, they point out that the *zawj* (translated as "mate") partnered with the *nafs* is conceptually neither male nor female, though grammatically it is masculine, which belies the assumption that the *zawj* of *nafs* is female or Eve for that matter.⁴² In addition, Wadud argues that the word *min* (translated as "from") need not carry the sense of "extraction from" connoted by the English word "from," a meaning that has been used to characterize *zawj* as a derivative and thus a lesser creation than the *nafs*; instead *min* may be understood to mean "of the same nature as," thus clarifying the equality and sameness of the *nafs* and *zawj* from which men and women originate.⁴³ Using this verse, Hassan asserts that according to the Qur'an, "Allah's original creation was undifferentiated humanity and not either man or woman"; in addition, "both man and woman were made in the same manner, of the same substance, at the same time." ⁴⁴ They "share a single point of origin" and thus are equal partners within creation.⁴⁵

In conjunction with this evidence for the equality of the sexes in creation, the exegetes also emphasize the Qur'an's explicit statements concerning the equality of the sexes in their potential for independent moral virtue and righteous acts. Citing key verses, they assert that, in Barlas's words, "both women and men have the same capacity for moral agency, choice, and individuality."⁴⁶ The exegetes unanimously cite verse 33:35, which features ten mentions of male and female pairs, overtly indicating the partnership of both women and men in exhibiting several examples of righteous qualities and deeds.⁴⁷ Barlas argues that by leaving no doubt as to women's inclusion in this statement of human beings' capacity for moral virtue, this verse clearly indicates that "women and men are able equally to acquire *taqwa* (moral personality)."⁴⁸ In addition to this partnership in moral capacity, men and women also share in the partnership of mutually encouraging morality among themselves. The exegetes frequently point out that in verse 9:71 (discussed further later), the Qur'an designates men and women each other's mutual *awliya'*, or "protectors," indicating a "shared moral discourse and mutual care between the sexes."⁴⁹ They argue that by describing men and women as each other's moral guides, the Qur'an emphasizes their equality in moral potential.

Not only are both men and women equally charged to righteous action, they are also both entitled to equal recompense in the afterlife for the (im)morality of their actions. In Barlas's words, "The Qur'an holds both men and women to the same standards of behavior and applies the same standards for judging between them."[50] The exegetes make two important points here. First, one's sex has absolutely no bearing on God's judgment of one's deeds. On the basis of verses 45:21–22, 3:25, 3:161, 4:110–112, 10:30, 14:51, 16:111, and 3:195, Wadud argues that "recompense is *acquired* not through gender, but through actions performed by the individual before death"; the "individual is not distinguished on the basis of gender, but on the basis of faith and deeds."[51] (Hassan makes the same argument also using 3:195, as well as the related verses 4:124 and 16:97.[52]) As men and women face God's judgment for their actions, "their only distinction is on the basis of *taqwa* (God-conscious piety)."[53] Second, every person is judged for her/his actions as a single moral individual; neither men nor women bear any responsibility for the other's actions. Barlas calls this concept "the Qur'an's view of 'ethical individualism,'" or "moral personality": the notion that "every individual, whether woman or man, is responsible for him or herself" and no one else.[54] Citing verses 2:48, 82:19, and 6:164 (on the impossibility of taking on what someone else earns or interceding on another's behalf), Wadud asserts: "No one can diminish the merits earned by another; neither can anyone increase them. No one can share in the merits achieved by another, nor in the punishment which will be given."[55]

Altogether, by reading Qur'anic verses on human creation, moral capacity and care, and recompense in the hereafter, the exegetes establish a substantial body of evidence in support of their claim to the Qur'an's overall position on the equality of men and women. As Hassan puts it: "Not only does the Qur'an make it clear that man and woman stand absolutely equal in the sight of God, but also that they are 'members' and 'protectors' of each other. In other words, the Qur'an does not create a hierarchy in which men are placed above women . . . They are created as equal creatures of a universal, just, and merciful God."[56] The importance of this interpretive maneuver—of establishing the equality of the sexes as an overarching, guiding principle of the Qur'an as a whole—cannot be overstated in its value to the Muslim feminist project. It is this understanding of the Qur'an's egalitarian ethic that allows the exegetes to argue that in order to be valid according to the Qur'an's own principles, any interpretive statement about women in the Qur'an must cohere with its core principles concerning the equality of men and women; by the same token, any interpretive statement that does not cohere with these core principles is invalid. By using this reasoning, for example, Wadud is able to declare: "To attribute an unrestricted value to one gender over another contradicts the equity established throughout the Qur'an with regard to the individual: each *nafs* shall have in accordance to what it earns."[57] Relying on the Qur'an's treatment of the *nafs*, the exegetes hold that any readings of the Qur'an that devalue or denigrate women must be categorically deemed incorrect on the grounds that they contradict a foundational premise of the Qur'an and are, in Hassan's words, "contrary to the letter and spirit of the Qur'an."[58] If the Qur'an's own instructions for interpreting itself—that is, to treat its content as a unified and coherent whole—are to be followed, then, as Barlas argues, all its "legitimate readings will cohere with the overall moral objectives of the Qur'an's teachings."[59] The impact of such statements is far-reaching; they help the exegetes to establish that the equality of men and women is a core moral objective of the Qur'an with which all understandings of the Qur'an must contend. For them, once it has been firmly established that the Qur'an unambiguously states that "man and woman have been created equal by Allah," none of its verses may be interpreted thereafter to render women "unequal, essentially, at a subsequent time."[60]

Verses on Marital Harmony and Tranquility

Scholars of feminist exegesis argue that an additional core principle of the Qur'an is its advocacy of harmony and mutuality within marital relationships. Employing the intratextual strategy, they argue that verses of the Qur'an on male-female relations should be read "in relation to the greater Qur'anic principles and their ultimate intent of harmonious and equitable relationships in society."[61] The exegetes commonly cite three verses as evidence that the Qur'an establishes marital harmony and mutuality as one of its overarching goals: 30:21, 2:187, and 9:71[62]:

> 30:21 And among [God's] signs is that [God] created mates for you from among yourselves so that you might find rest in them. And [God] has put love and mercy between you . . .
>
> 2:187 . . . They [your wives] are garments for you, and you are garments for them . . .
>
> 9:71 The male and female believers are protectors of each other . . .

Based on 30:21 and 2:187, Wadud states: "Within marriage, there should be harmony . . . mutually built with love and mercy. The marriage tie is considered a protection for both the male and the female."[63] Similarly, al-Hibri refers to verse 30:21 as the Qur'an's "Harmony Principle" or "Equality Principle": "The thought contained in it is repeated in various forms in the Qur'an, an indication of its significance. For example . . . verse 2:187 . . . is a reference to the fact that spouses are each other's sanctuary insofar as each covers the other's shortcomings and preserves his or her privacy; hence the tranquility and harmony."[64] As mentioned previously, Barlas notes that the reference to men and women as each other's *awliya'* ("guardians" or "protectors") in verse 9:71 indicates the Qur'an's advocacy of "mutual care between the sexes."[65] In addition, al-Hibri argues, on the basis of the related verse 2:229,[66] that "the letter and spirit of the Qur'an . . . states that husbands should live with their wives in kindness or leave them charitably."[67] Reading these verses together, the exegetes establish a body of evidence to which they frequently turn in demanding intratextual, holistic readings of difficult Qur'anic verses. They allow al-Hibri, for instance, to "conclude that the Qur'an articulates a basic general principle about proper gender relations; namely that they are relations between mates . . . which are intended to provide these mates with tranquility, and are to be characterized by affection and mercy."[68] The same grounding allows Sa'diyya Shaikh to confidently articulate the Qur'anic ideal for male-female relationships: "The notions that believing men and women provide friendship and mutual protection for one another; that they equally undertake moral agency in the world; that human beings strive to live in a state of tranquility with their spouses; that marital relationships are to be approached as the embodiment of Divine love and mercy, collectively reflect the Islamic ideal of gender relations."[69] In handling the interpretation of contentious verses about women (discussed later), the exegetes call for holistic readings of the Qur'an that cohere with this ideal for male-female relations, and they oppose interpretations that contradict it.

Gradualism across the Qur'anic Text

As a supplement to intratextual readings that support the equality of men and women and mutuality and harmony in marital relationships, the exegetes also argue that taken as a whole, the Qur'an exhibits an overall progression toward advocating justice and equality for all human beings. According to Wadud: "The Qur'an establishes a radical momentum towards continual reforms in gender relations. Even where it appears to fall short of explicit articulations these might be inferred by following the directions of the textual linguistic and moral momentum."[70] Wadud gives examples of where the text "seems to have remained neutral: social patriarchy, marital patriarchy, economic hierarchy, the division of labour between males and females within a particular family."[71] She argues that in these areas, the Qur'an does not clarify or demand immediate, drastic reform; its laxity may be understood as resulting from a gradual approach toward social change. "Although in some instances the Qur'an proposed immediate abolition of certain ill practices, most of the time it advocated gradual reform. Few reforms were completely implemented before the final revelation."[72]

For example, as al-Hibri notes, the Qur'an explicitly commands immediate reform of polytheistic practices and female infanticide; however, for "lesser though quite important matters," it calls for reform in gradual stages.[73] "The Qur'anic philosophy of gradualism is predicated upon the fact that fundamental changes in human consciousness do not usually occur overnight. Instead, they require a period of individual or even social gestation. For this reason, the Qur'an uses a gradual approach to change entrenched customs, beliefs, and practices, except in fundamental matters."[74] The exegetes suggest that this gradual approach to change helps to ensure the effectiveness and longevity of reform, reasoning that gradual change meets with less resistance and is therefore more successful in the long run.

The exegetes often point out that in the gradual prohibition of wine, for instance, the Qur'anic prohibition occurs through a sequence of revelations that build up to forbidding it. However, in the cases of slavery and women's rights, the Qur'an is more subtle and less specific in suggesting gradual reform. In these cases, as Wadud points out, "the text establishes a trajectory of social, political, and moral possibilities, but does not articulate them definitely."[75] On the matter of slavery—which is never expressly prohibited by the Qur'an—Wadud writes: "For complex social, cultural, and historical phenomenon like slavery, for example, following only the explicit references in the Qur'an would never have led to the eradication of it as an institution. The Qur'anic ethos of equity, justice, and human dignity, however, might contribute to such a reform."[76]

The exegetes argue that by the same token, when the Qur'an's advocacy for gender reforms is not clearly stated, it is implied by its overall "worldview, vision, and ultimate intent."[77] That is, the exegetes locate the Qur'an's indications for gender reform in its general intent and its larger "progression with regard to the development of human interactions, morality, and ethics."[78] According to Wadud, Qur'anic instruction on this matter comes not necessarily from direct statements but from observing the "Qur'anic trajectory" of "justice towards humankind, human dignity, equal rights before the law and before Allah, mutual responsibility, and equitable relations between humans."[79] Likewise, Hassan argues that the Qur'an advocates justice for women as part of its general impetus toward justice for all human beings, since as a whole the Qur'an is "profoundly concerned with freeing human beings—woman as well as men—from the bondage of traditionalism, authoritarianism (religious, political, economic, or any other), tribalism, racism, sexism, slavery or anything else that prohibits or inhibits human beings from actualizing the Qur'anic vision of human destiny."[80] Wadud concurs, "The whole of the Qur'an as guidance points toward the directions of moral excellence and ethical propriety."[81] The Qur'anic context of revelation was "only the starting place from which to begin the movement toward fulfilling the eternal nature of guidance which the Qur'an points humanity toward."[82] On this basis, she argues that "the continued change which the Quran put into motion was not meant to stop when the revelation was completed."[83] Wadud calls for interpretations of the Qur'an that treat its overall trajectory toward greater social reform as a "precedent" for ongoing transformation toward greater social justice.[84]

As part of this discussion, it is worth noting the possible parallels between this interpretive approach and the Qur'anic exegetical concept of *naskh* (abrogation), according to which some parts of the Qur'an are thought to be superseded or replaced by other parts revealed at a later time—even though scholars of feminist exegesis have generally neither invoked this concept by name nor placed much emphasis on it.[85] Among the proof-texts cited by commentators in support of *naskh* are verses 2:106 ("For whatever verse We abrogate or cause to be forgotten We bring something better or similar . . . ") and 87:6–7 ("We will teach you to recite so you will not forget, except for what God wills . . ."). Premodern exegetes sometimes turned to the concept of *naskh* in order to respond to seeming discrepancies or conflicts between Qur'anic verses. The jurist al-Shafi'i (d. 820 C.E.) stressed the importance of carefully determining the chronological order of the verses in order to assess if an earlier verse may have been abrogated by a later one.[86] As mentioned, the Qur'an's gradual prohibition of wine, over the progression of verses 16:67, 2:219, 4:43, and 5:91–92, is commonly deemed a case of Qur'anic *naskh*.[87]

Premodern commentators speculated that the Qur'an exhibits *naskh* in cases in which a later verse may not be "suitable for the people at the earlier time."[88] A common position is that God sometimes changed certain laws in the text "for the benefit of humanity, as . . . God recognized would be necessary, given the changing conditions of the world."[89] They may reason that "human beings are not able to bear all the truth at once," citing verses such as 3:159 (on dealing gently with the believers) as evidence.[90] Another common position is that the Qur'an introduces reforms within the text gradually and incrementally as a mercy toward humanity.[91]

However, premodern commentators were frequently at pains to defend the concept of *naskh* against charges that its use undermined the authority of the whole Qur'an. Opponents feared that frequent resort to *naskh* in interpretation would lead to the belief that the Qur'an contained contradictions or mistakes or was an incomplete revelation; it might come to imply that God's will and knowledge were imperfect or variable. Proponents defended *naskh* by arguing that although "God's law does vary according to the time and place," such variation is merely "reflective of the nature of human existence, not of the divine essence."[92] In other words, "when abrogation occurs people may perceive a change, but this is only a change from the human perspective."[93] Unconvinced by these arguments, however, many premodern scholars came to disapprove of the application *naskh* to the verses of the Qur'an and limited its application to whole revelations (i.e., the Qur'an) in relation to previous revelations (i.e., the Bible).[94]

Even some modernist scholars were averse to the use of *naskh* in interpreting the Qur'an. Modernists such as Sayyid Ahmad Khan (1817–1898) and Isma'il Raji al-Faruqi (1921–1986) objected to the notion of any verse nullifying another because of the threat it might pose to sustaining the authority of the whole Qur'an.[95] As Andrew Rippin has argued, "Modern Muslim attention and devotion to the text of the Qur'an . . . have led to an emphasis on the integrity of the text of the scripture, taken to the point of limiting or even denying the phenomenon of abrogation."[96] In line with this trend, and perhaps as a way to deflect potential accusations of undermining the Qur'anic text, scholars of feminist exegesis have refrained from any overt references to *naskh* in their works.

Regardless of its possible (though unnamed) relation to the concept of *naskh*, it may be observed that the feminist strategy of invoking the Qur'an's overall trajectory toward human equality and justice serves four major functions in works of Muslim feminist exegesis. First, the trajectory argument lends support to the notion that the interpretation of each of the Qur'an's verses must cohere with the whole Qur'an's overall progression toward greater social justice for humanity. Second, it provides an explanation for the appearance in the Qur'an of certain verses that may negatively impact women or limit their agency, and the exegetes do not have to "discard" these verses in order for the Qur'an to be just to women. Third, the problematic meanings drawn from these verses are explained by the error of the reader who reads them in isolation instead of in view of the larger progression of the whole Qur'an. In other words, the fault for such meanings lies not with the verses themselves but rather with the reader's shortsightedness. Fourth, the trajectory argument serves as a justification for the exegetes to depart from literal readings of the text that are problematic for women. By arguing that the text as a whole suggests movement beyond its literal form, the exegetes locate support within the Qur'an itself for reading the Qur'an "beyond" the Qur'an (a strategy I will revisit later).[97]

Feminist Rereadings Using the Intratextual Method
Verses 2:228, 2:223, and 2:282: Male Advantage, Sexual Access, and Legal Witnesses

As discussed in chapter 4, verse 2:228 is often understood as: "Women have rights similar to the rights that are claimed of them, but men possess a degree more than them."[98] This verse has been used to claim that men are given a moral advantage over women by God. In addition to pointing out that the verse is referring only to a specific right granted to men but not women in the context of divorce, Wadud uses the intratextual strategy to point out that common interpretations of the verse clearly contradict the Qur'an's other statements about the equal moral capacity and judgment of all human beings. Wadud states: "To attribute an unrestricted value to one gender over another contradicts the equity established throughout the Qur'an with regard to the individual: each *nafs* shall have in accordance to what it earns."[99]

A critical portion of verse 2:223 is often understood as "Your wives are your tilth; so approach your tilth as you wish."[100] Premodern and modern interpretations have often read this verse as giving license to men to have sex with their wives whenever and however men want. Such interpretations often imply that women are the sexual property of men and may be used to authorize forceful or violent treatment of women. Using verse 9:71,[101] Barlas points out that such interpretations are "incongruent with the emphasis of the Qur'an on equality and mutuality and its reference to spouses as each other's 'raiment.'"[102] Barlas speculates that in 2:223 the Qur'an is referring to "the cultivation of love and mercy, since these themes are central to its teachings on marriage and female-male relationships."[103] (This verse will be discussed further in chapter 6.)

Finally, as discussed in chapter 4, verse 2:282 makes the allowance that in a legal situation requiring two male witnesses, two female witnesses may take the place of one male witness.[104] Premodern and modern exegetes have often used this verse in support of the claim that a woman has only half a man's value as a human being. In addition to Wadud's point that the verse refers only to a specific kind of legal scenario in the context of a specific historical situation, Barlas notices that the issue of legal testimony appears numerous times in the Qur'an without indicating any such allowance. Tracing the issue throughout the Qur'an, Barlas observes that "there are a total of five cases of evidence giving in the Qur'an, and in only one does it make the provision about two women."[105] Thus by reading 2:282 alongside other parts of the Qur'an, it is less plausible to make a statement about men's superiority over women using this verse.

Verse 4:3: Polygyny

Readings of 4:3 by al-Hibri, Wadud, and Barlas feature the recurrent use of the intratextual method to reinterpret the Qur'anic verse that has most often been used to sanction the practice of polygyny. Al-Hibri translates the verse as

> If you fear that you shall not be able deal justly with the orphans, marry women of your choice, two, three or four; But if you fear that you shall not be able to deal justly [with them], then only one, or that which your right hand possesses. That will be more suitable to prevent you from doing injustice.[106]

As discussed in chapter 4, scholars of feminist tafsir use the historical contextualization method to argue that the context of this verse's revelation and its conditional nature severely restrict the Qur'an's allowance for polygyny. In further support of the position that the Qur'an's polygyny allowance is limited, the exegetes make three additional intratextual arguments. First, they point out that an accurate understanding of the verse's meaning must take into account a related verse within the same sura. The relevant portion of this verse, 4:129, reads, "You will not be able to act equitably toward your wives, even if you desire."[107] As the exegetes point out, if the allowance for polygyny in 4:3 is conditional upon men's ability to deal justly with multiple wives, and 4:129 states that men are incapable of meeting this condition, then the Qur'an itself renders the allowance at least questionable, if not altogether void.[108] Thus by placing the verses together, they produce an alternative interpretation whereby the Qur'an itself presents "a case against generalized polygyny."[109] Furthermore, Barlas argues that if one ignores verse 4:129, then the Qur'an's "assertion that men cannot do justice between wives . . . would hold no meaning."[110] To do so would be to imply that not all of the Qur'an is meaningful, and as Barlas notes, "for believers the Qur'an's teachings cannot be meaningless."[111]

Second, the exegetes argue for a reading of 4:3 that takes into account the Qur'an's guiding principle of justice and accountability for unjust actions. As al-Hibri observes, "The Qur'an expressly states that polygamy results in injustice."[112] That is, the Qur'an states that polygyny violates one of its overall core aims—that of establishing justice among human beings and families in particular. Wadud points to the apparent contradiction between the consequences of polygyny and the Qur'an's advocacy for justice and mutuality: "Surely, it is impossible to attain the Qur'anic ideal with regard to mutuality ('They [feminine plural] are raiment for you [masculine plural] and you are raiment for them' (2:187)), and with regard to building between them 'love and mercy' (30:21), when the husband-father is split between more than one family."[113] Reading verse 4:3 in light of the whole Qur'an and maintaining the premise that no part of the Qur'an can contradict another, the exegetes insist that the Qur'an discourages (or even rules out) the practice of polygyny based on its demand for just action.

Third, the exegetes argue that in light of the Qur'an's overall progression toward increasing justice, verse 4:3 sets the eventual goal of abolishing the practice of polygyny altogether but does so in terms that will make such a reform more successful and sustainable in the long run. For example, al-Hibri refers to the Qur'an's gradualism in her reading of the verse:

The Qur'an was revealed to a culture steeped in polygamy. In *Jahiliyah,* men married more than a hundred women at a time. It was therefore unrealistic, given human nature, to prohibit polygamous behavior abruptly. The Islamic approach to this situation as in other matters was to limit the practice severely, designate avenues for ending it, and provide a prescription/description of the ideal state of affairs that excludes the practice.[114]

Thus, the Qur'an's treatment of polygyny is not only *not* an obstacle to Qur'anic interpretations in support of justice for women but also the ideal route to ensuring such interpretations in the long term.

Verse 4:34: Male Authority and Marital Violence

As examined in chapter 4, the first portion of verse 4:34 is understood by scholars of feminist exegesis to mean roughly, "Men are the *qawwamun* of women on the basis of what God has favored for some men over others, and on the basis of what men provide for women from their means."[115] The exegetes have tended to understand *qawwamun* as "advisors" or "providers." In addition to treating this statement about *some* men's advisory/maintenance roles vis-à-vis *some* women as a conditional, particular, and delimited one, they also use intratextual strategies in interpreting the verse.

For example, Wadud understands *qawwam* as a potential designation for a man that might give him the opportunity to contribute to the process of childrearing, given that he does not bear the bodily burdens of pregnancy, birth, or nursing that a woman does. Thus, his work as a *qawwam* enables him to contribute in some indirect way to the childbearing process, to support his female partner, and compensate her for physical responsibilities. For Wadud, this understanding of a male *qawwam* is in alignment with the Qur'an's overall concern for justice in human relationships. In her words, "For simple balance and justice in creation, and to avoid oppression, his responsibility must be equally significant to the continuation of the human race."[116] In addition, al-Hibri and Barlas point out that any understanding of the man's *qiwamah* role in 4:34 as one based in men's intellectual and moral superiority and authority over women would contradict verse 9:71, in which the Qur'an designates men and women each other's mutual *awliya'* (guardians). Thus, interpretations of verse 4:34 that understand "the husband as a ruler over his wife or, at the very least, as the head of the household" (and use it in support of the claim that men are categorically superior to women) are flawed because they do not treat the Qur'an as internally consistent; in Barlas's words, such an understanding "ignores that the Qur'an appoints women and men each other's ... mutual protectors, which it could not do if men were in fact superior to women and their managers."[117] Al-Hibri writes that even though 4:34 "appears to conflict with the Equality Principle" of 30:21, when reading the verses intratextually, one must prioritize the latter; to make this argument, she refers to some juridical principles: "A basic rule of Islamic jurisprudence is the following: where ayahs appear to conflict, they must be carefully studied in search of a meaning that makes them consistent with each other. Another basic rule states that one way to resolve apparent conflict between ayahs is to check the scope of each."[118] Here al-Hibri incorporates some elements of the historical contextualization method that emphasize the conditionality of verse 4:34 with her intratextual reading of the verse. She argues that while 4:34 places limitations on the authority of the man by "specifying the reasons (*'illahs*) or circumstances . . . that would entitle a male to be *qawwam*," verse 30:21 which "articulates the Equality Principle is clearly general. It has no qualifiers, provisos, or carve-outs. It is also repeated in similar forms several other times in the Qur'an."[119] When reading both verses intratextually, the apparent contradiction between the two verses should be resolved by deciding that verse 30:21 (similar to verse 4:1) outweighs the other in terms of scope, ruling out the possibility that men are the superiors of women.[120]

However, the next portion of verse 4:34 presents more difficulties for scholars of feminist tafsir. The subsequent lines of 4:34 read:[121]

> *fa-l-salihatu qanitatun hafizatun li-l-ghaybi bi-ma hafiza Allahu wa-llati takhafuna nushuzahunna fa-'izuhunna wa-hjuruhunna fi al-madaji'i wa-dribuhunna fa-in ata'nakum fa-la tabghu 'alayhinna sabilan.*

Most male commentators have understood these lines to the effect:

> Therefore the righteous women are obedient and guard in their husbands' absence what God would have them guard. As for those women whose disobedience you fear, admonish them, abandon their beds, and beat them; but if they obey you, then do not seek means against them.

The three most contentious terms here are *qanitat*, *nushuz*, and *wa-dribuhunna*. First, the exegetes take issue with the interpretation of *qanitat* as referring to women who are obedient to their husbands. Wadud, for instance, tracks the appearance of the term *qanit* (masculine plural: *qanitun*; female plural: *qanitat*) throughout the Qur'an: "In the context of the whole Qur'an, this word is used with regard to both males (2:238, 3:17, 33:35) and females (4:34, 33:34, 66:5, 66:12). It describes a characteristic or personality trait of believers towards Allah. They are inclined towards being co-operative with one another and subservient before Allah."[122]

By clarifying the Qur'an's use of the word *qanit* to refer to both men and women, Wadud rules out the use of the term in 4:34 to claim that righteous women should be obedient to their husbands. In addition to being a term applied to both sexes, it is a term that consistently refers throughout the Qur'an to human beings' obedience to God, which is "clearly distinguished from mere obedience between created beings."[123]

Second, the exegetes use the intratextual strategy to reexamine the meaning of *nushuz*, which most premodern and modern interpretations have assumed to refer to a situation in which women are disobedient to their husbands. Wadud notes that similar to *qanit*, "the word *nushuz* likewise is used with both males (4:128) and females (4:34)."[124] The relevant portion of verse 4:128 reads, "If a woman fears *nushuz* or desertion on the part of her husband, there is no fault in the two reconciling with one another."[125] By the same logic used to understand *qanit* as a term applicable to both sexes, Wadud argues that the term *nushuz* refers to a situation that may also be instigated by a man. Taking into account the term's repetition in 4:128, Wadud understands *nushuz* as a situation of marital disharmony resulting from the actions of either the man or the woman, rather than as a wife's disobedience to her husband.[126]

Finally, in approaching the term *idribuhunna* (beat them), the exegetes also employ intratextual strategies, though arguably with more contradictory results. For the sake of background, before examining these intratextual interventions, it is worth mentioning that the exegetes often address the term by opposing the translation of *daraba* (the root verb of the command form *idribuhunna*) as "to beat." Their approaches to opposing this translation involve limiting the verse's application to a set of particular conditions and context, and thus are best classified under the category of the historical contextualization method. I summarize them here to aid the reader in understanding the intratextual approaches to this verse. According to al-Hibri, *daraba* refers to a very mild or symbolic form of striking that must not be on the face or leave a mark; for example, a husband may use something like a soft twig (discussed later).[127] Hassan points out that *daraba* has several variant translations in Arabic and is best translated in verse 4:34 as "holding in confinement."[128] For Wadud, "*daraba* does not necessarily indicate force or violence," as it is "strongly contrasted" with another term, "*darraba*," to "strike repeatedly or intensely."[129] In addition, the exegetes argue that rather than prescribing violence, the verse was placing restrictions on violence. Wadud argues: "In the light of the excessive violence towards women indicated in the biographies of the Companions and by practices condemned in the Qur'an (like female infanticide), this verse should be taken as prohibiting unchecked violence against females."[130] For Wadud, then, the verse "is not permission, but a severe restriction of existing practices."[131] Al-Hibri posits that verse 4:34 severely restricts permission for a husband to "beat" his wife to extremely serious situations (i.e., adultery or lewd behavior), and, even in such a case, grants this permission only if his attempts to use both verbal communication and physical separation to resolve the marital conflict have failed (as discussed subsequently, she argues that the verse "imposed a graduated approach to anger management designed to dissipate anger before reaching the final stage").[132]

Now turning to intratextual approaches to verse 4:34, al-Hibri connects her reading of *daraba* to what she calls the Qur'an's "philosophy of gradualism."[133] For her, verse 4:34 sets into motion the Qur'an's plan for gradually alleviating problems of marital violence in Muslim society. In her words, the verse "develops a graduated approach to the problem of wife abuse, which is aimed at cabinning the aggressive instincts of the patriarchal male, and re-channeling his anger into more productive, or less destructive, outlets. In doing so, the Qur'an takes into account the very nature of human beings and the need for [a] 'gestation period' for them to achieve a higher stage of development and communication."[134] Thus the verse enacts a "transitory stage" in the Qur'anic process of restricting, mitigating, and eventually eradicating marital violence against women.[135] In other words, the Qur'an offers a realistic, gradual approach to the problem of wife abuse in a society where such violence was overwhelmingly prevalent and deeply entrenched. It introduces a three-step model for conflict resolution (verbal communication, then physical separation, then "beating") to limit the possibility of a man's resorting to the final step of violence.[136] In addition, al-Hibri also uses the intratextual strategy of pointing to the Qur'anic story of the prophet Job as evidence for the Qur'anic trajectory toward mitigating marital violence. She notes that, based on her reading of the Qur'an's instructions to the prophet Job to strike his wife with some grass in verse 38:44, Job fulfills the oath he had taken to hit his wife in punishment for her disbelief in God's message while avoiding causing her physical harm.[137] Thus, the Qur'an offers the example of Job's decision as an illustration of a mild, "symbolic" method for admonishing one's wife; "this symbolic act defines the minimal standard below which no Muslim may stoop."[138] Bringing all these pieces together, al-Hibri reaches the conclusion that while verse 4:34 is pragmatic in its approach to mitigating marital violence in the immediate context of its revelation, it implicitly calls for the eventual elimination of marital violence altogether.

For her, this elimination would be in line with the Qur'an's overall advocacy of marital harmony. Al-Hibri claims that domestic violence is intolerable when 4:34 is read consistently with the rest of the Qur'an:

> The Qur'an is internally consistent because it is a divine revelation. The Qur'an repeatedly describes the relationship between husband and wife as one of tranquility, affection, and mercy. Further, it enjoins husbands to live with their wives in kindness or leave them amicably. Domestic violence is diametrically opposed to each of these Qur'anic views and ideals expressed in the various verses. Because of its internal consistency, the Qur'an could not be exhorting one ideal and enjoining the related conduct in some passages, and its opposite in another one.[139]

In contrast to verses on marital harmony, the *daraba* portion of verse 4:34 "is both conditional and structurally complex, leaving room for erroneous, culturally skewed, or subjective interpretations."[140] From these statements, al-Hibri seems to rule out the apparent allowance for hitting in 4:34 by favoring verse 30:21,[141] whose straightforward meaning in her view outweighs meanings derived from a complex verse such as 4:34.[142] Similarly, Barlas asserts that it is the interpretation, rather than the text of the Qur'an itself, that produces the apparent intratextual contradiction between verse 4:34 and Qur'anic principles of marital tranquility. In Barlas's words, any "reading" of 4:34 that sanctions hitting "contradicts the Qur'an's view of sexual equality and its teaching that marriages should be based in love, forgiveness, harmony and *sukun* [tranquility]."[143]

However, the exegetes' rereadings of verse 4:34 generally neglect to account for the existence of the word *daraba* in the text of the verse at all. An exception is Wadud's later work, *Inside the Gender Jihad*, where she offers an intratextual reading of *daraba* that problematizes the existence of the term within the verse and takes a much stronger stance against its use to condone any form of marital violence at all, regardless of its form or degree. Wadud draws once again on the Qur'an's overarching principles of justice and mercy in marital relations, arguing that 4:34 must be read in line with those Qur'anic concepts. In the following pages, I will examine the shift in Wadud's treatment of *daraba* in *Inside the Gender Jihad*; there she outlines two maneuvers that both invoke and complicate intratextual strategies for reading the Qur'an.

In *Qur'an and Woman* (1999), Wadud wrote: "the problem of domestic violence among Muslims today is not rooted in this Qur'anic passage . . . The goal of such men [who strike their wives] is harm, not harmony . . . they cannot refer to verse 4:34 to justify their action."[144] In this earlier work Wadud, like the other exegetes, traces the problem of domestic violence among Muslims to their misreading of the verse and/or violation of the Qur'an's overarching ethos of marital harmony. It is several years later, in *Inside the Gender Jihad* (2006), that Wadud admits that the language of the verse itself may serve violent ends.[145] Wadud writes, "I simply do not and cannot condone permission for a man to 'scourge' or apply *any kind* of strike to a woman."[146] Having taken this stance, Wadud's first maneuver is to approach the linguistic intent signified in the verse. Referring to the term *daraba*, she notes: "Multiple meanings can be deduced from the various uses and definitions for the word."[147] However, since there is no getting around the fact that one of these possible meanings remains "to strike," Wadud turns her attention to the possible intent behind the word. Revisiting *Qur'an and Woman*, she reimagines her work as engaging the intent of *daraba*: "I concluded with an alternative interpretation that the Qur'an meant to restrict unbridled violence . . . Perhaps the Qur'an did *not* intend to emphasize the narrowest reading, since violence against the innocent and oppressed is strongly discouraged elsewhere in the text."[148] Thus, according to Wadud, this verse—even while it contains the term *daraba*—still intends, in conformity with the Qur'an's overall positions on equity and kindness, to restrict domestic violence. Wadud grounds her earlier focus on textual intent in the work of jurists from the first three centuries after the Qur'an's revelation. She notes that in interpreting 4:34 and deriving rulings on its basis, early jurists pronounced limitations and restrictions on the act of striking one's wife.[149] Wadud suggests that in so doing, the early jurists were "asserting an understanding of textual intent" as well as "interpreting the Qur'an on the basis of the Qur'an, with 'justice' the overarching concern for human interaction."[150]

However, when revisiting the verse several years later, Wadud's views on the textual intent of 4:34 produce different results. In her second maneuver, she asserts that although reading 4:34 with the verse's linguistic intent in mind may have helped restrict violence against women in earlier centuries, doing so in the twenty-first century no longer mitigates violence against women.[151] For Wadud, fulfilling the overall objectives of the Qur'an in relation to this verse now means not just restricting or limiting its violent interpretations but also eliminating them altogether. She writes, "Any kind of strike, or any intention to apply the verse in that manner, violates other principles of the text itself—most notably 'justice' and human dignity."[152] Thus, in order to read this verse in line with the rest of the Qur'an in today's context, she rejects the meaning of *daraba* as "to strike," justifying this maneuver by pointing to principles of the Qur'an derived from other portions of the text. Here Wadud's usage of the intratextual method takes her to an impasse with regard to the existence of *daraba* in the verse, since the very presence of the term in the text makes the meaning of "to strike" possible. The intratextual strategy, then, does not produce a fully satisfactory rereading for Wadud, as this meaning of *daraba* is unacceptable to her and yet remains unavoidable. This impasse will be addressed further in subsequent chapters.

For now, in reflecting on the exegetes' collective use of the intratextual strategy, it is interesting to note how this approach might benefit from a better understanding of the nuances and progressions of Qur'anic language. The study of these elements would assess, for example, the process of signification in the Qur'an's use of key terms and phrasing; how Qur'anic language works to signify multiple levels of meanings through linguistic structure, syntax, and word choice; and how the Qur'an uses the same word over the progression of the whole text to communicate subtleties of meaning. Along these lines, Wadud has proposed that future scholarship should "compare all Qur'anic passages with lexical items based on the same particular root forms" and study "the larger textual development of [each Qur'anic] term" and the "trajectory of meaning and application" within the text.[153] A systematic intertextual evaluation of the language in the Qur'an would, of course, require painstaking, methodical, and lengthy treatment of the entire Qur'an, which is perhaps generations in the making. Wadud imagines the kinds of fascinating questions that are waiting to be explored about the Qur'an in this regard:

> Are certain [language] constructs preferred in different textual circumstances of Quranic guidance? . . . How do various Qur'anic

passages on similar themes or topics correspond to each other with regard to the do and be function of language constructs and textual implication or application? Is there a hierarchy of meanings that we can decipher? What is more, when key rungs in the ladder of this proposed hierarchy are empty, vacant or silent, the unspoken dimensions of meaning are hidden this way. How much is left unsaid along a linguistic trajectory that can be constructed theoretically to expand not only textual meaning but also application of meaning in unprecedented circumstances?[154]

The pursuit of such study has the potential to strengthen the exegetes' ability to use intratextual interpretative strategies for advancing meanings of the Qur'an that promote the dignity of women.

6
The Tawhidic Paradigm

I think that speaking for God and speaking in God's name are different things. The Prophet, through revelation, and the Qur'an, through dictation, in a literal sense, speak for God. Everyone else claims to speak in God's name. Everyone else is functioning in the realm of the possible and probable . . . To claim full or perfect knowledge of God's Will is to challenge the singularity and uniqueness of the Divine perfection.

—KHALED ABOU EL FADL, Speaking in God's Name[1]

THE DISTINCTION BETWEEN speaking for God and speaking in God's name—as Abou El Fadl so cogently puts it—is central to feminist tafsir's use of the "*tawhidic* paradigm" as a key interpretive method.[2] This approach takes its name from the core Islamic concept of tawhid, the doctrine of God's unity and incomparability. The exegetes employ the tawhidic paradigm to assert that sexism is a form of idolatry since it attributes a God-like role to men over women. They also invoke this paradigm in order to argue than one can never pronounce a final interpretation of the Qur'an, since to do so would be to claim to have God's knowledge and to place oneself in the role of God. Likewise, clear distinctions must be made between the divine text of the Qur'an and its human interpretation.

According to the concept of tawhid, God is wholly singular, unique, and indivisible. This indivisibility extends to God's authority and power over all of God's creation. No other shares in God's authority; in Barlas' words, "God is absolute Sovereign," and "no one—other deities, or divine consorts and offspring, or humans—can partake in it."[3] All creation is united under the one omnipotent creator. Wadud writes, "Allah is uniform, and unites . . . [all] multiplicities . . . in both the corporeal and the metaphysical realm."[4] Thus, all creation testifies to the unity of God. In this sense, creation emerges as a form of God's revelation or a reminder to human beings of God's oneness and unity. In addition to God's self-disclosure through the signs (*ayat*) of nature, God also reveals Him-/Her-/Itself through the scriptures sent to prophets, which serve as "reminders of the origin and end of the universe and of humanity."[5] Thus, one of the main purposes of the Qur'an is to remind human beings of their origins in God's unity, "to recall to memory the presence of the Only One."[6] It is left up to human beings "to direct the intelligence toward the knowledge of [God]."[7] However, human beings can only *attempt* to understand the revelations of God using their finite knowledge and limited capacities for comprehension. They are restricted in their ability to fully grasp the divine because of their humanity and the limits of their experience in bounded times and places. It is God alone who is all-knowing; no human being can attain the level of God's knowledge and awareness.

Any action that denies or fails to recognize the unity of God, such as idolatry or the ascribing of equals or likenesses to God, is *shirk*. As Barlas puts it, *shirk* is "the symbolic extension of God's Sovereignty to others" and constitutes the gravest of all sins.[8] The Qur'an explicitly forbids *shirk* in numerous passages and identifies it as an unpardonable transgression against God, as in 4:48 ("God does not forgive the association of partners with [God], but [God] forgives other than that for whom [God] wills . . ."). Thus God calls upon human beings to recognize His/Her/Its singularity and to strive to know Him/Her/It conscientiously through various forms of revelation.

The use of the tawhidic paradigm marks a departure from the use of other textual strategies utilized by exegetes of feminist tafsir in that it is most often used generally in articulating an overall relationship between human beings and divine revelation and less frequently for any pointed, direct intervention in understanding particular Qur'anic terms and verses. In this chapter I argue that scholars of feminist exegesis utilize the tawhidic paradigm to establish that designating men as the superiors of women or attributing maleness to God constitute acts of *shirk*; men's exegesis of the Qur'an is not equivalent to the Qur'anic text; interpretation of the Qur'an must be a dynamic and evolving process; and because the Qur'an is God's revelation in human language, its text cannot perfectly express God and thus cannot be equated with God. Although these derived concepts are sometimes applied directly to specific Qur'anic verses, they are most often employed as general guiding principles for approaching the Qur'an. In establishing these principles, the exegetes employ a core doctrine of Islam to substantiate their claims to male–female equality and their revised interpretations of the Qur'an.

Shirk of Sexism and Male References to God

According to the principle of tawhid, all human beings are united under one creator, and no one may share in the creator's authority. As discussed in chapter 5, the exegetes of feminist tafsir have argued that the Qur'an supports "the fundamental metaphysical sameness of all humans as creatures of God," treating them as equally capable moral agents, all created from the same *nafs*.[9] According to the exegetes, differences between human beings are based solely on their achievement of *taqwa*, their devotion to God, and "moral consciousness."[10] Thus, the only distinction between human beings exists on the basis of one's piety, not on the basis of superficial characteristics such as race, sex, or class. Furthermore, the sole distinguishing characteristic of *taqwa* may be judged only by God; it is "not an external matter accessible for human-to-human judgment."[11] Thus, the right to evaluate differences between human beings belongs to God and God alone. Therefore, to construct hierarchies between human beings—to attempt to evaluate the superiority of one group or individual over another—is to assume a role that belongs exclusively to God. Such an act amounts to putting oneself in the position of God and assuming God's authority; thus it is an act of *shirk*. Wadud argues: "When a person seeks to place him or her self 'above' another, it either means the divine presence is removed or ignored, or that the person who imagines his or her self above others suffers from the egoism of *shirk*."[12]

Azizah al-Hibri recalls the story of Iblis (Satan), who, in his arrogance, refused God's command to bow to Adam, whom he deemed inferior to him. His arrogance "led Iblis to disobey God, an act that posited Iblis's will as superior to that of God. By doing so, Iblis fell into *shirk*."[13] Based upon this story, al-Hibri develops the notion of "Iblisi logic," which she defines as an arrogant attitude that "emphasizes and magnifies difference as adequate justification for inequality."[14] She extrapolates that "actions that reflect a commitment to a hierarchy of humans based on various worldly factors reflect the same kind of logic used by Iblis."[15] According to al-Hibri, Iblisi logic forms the basis for "authoritarian, racist, classist, or patriarchal society."[16] Thus, using the doctrine of tawhid, the exegetes define acts of discrimination, including sexist discrimination, as violations of God's supreme authority and uniqueness. Wadud notes that the arrogance of Iblis is a form of *istikbar*, "considering oneself better than another, rather than obeying the will of Allah and acknowledging the necessary interconnection between all humans."[17] Thus, *istikbar* is the root of all forms of social oppression. She writes:

> Since God is the highest conceptual aspect of all, then no person can be greater than another person, especially for mere reasons of gender, race, class, nationality, etc. The *tawhidic* paradigm then acts as a basic theoretical principle for removing gender asymmetry, which is a kind of satanic logic or *shirk*, positing priority or superiority to men. Instead, women and men must occupy a relationship of horizontal reciprocity, maintaining the highest place for God in His/Her/Its uniqueness.[18]

Thus, al-Hibri and Wadud oppose attitudes of male superiority on the basis of their contradiction to the tawhidic understanding of God.

The exegetes rely on this position to assert that interpretations of the Qur'an which substantiate notions of male superiority are also acts of *shirk*. Al-Hibri states: "I find patriarchal interpretations (*ijtihads*) unacceptable to the extent they are based on Satanic logic and conflict with *tawhid*."[19] The exegetes' criticism of common interpretations of verse 4:34 is particularly illustrative of this approach.[20] With regard to this verse, the exegetes use the tawhidic paradigm to argue that interpretations of the verse that claim that women must be obedient to their husbands (rather than solely to God) are erroneous on the grounds that they are based upon *shirk*. As previously discussed, premodern and modern interpreters have used the term *qanitat* to suggest that the righteousness of women entails obedience to their husbands. They have also defined the *nushuz* of women as disobedience to their husbands and understood the conditional phrase *fa-in ata'nakum* to mean "if they (your wives) obey you (men)." Al-Hibri notes that in any such reading, "disobedience to the husband is subsumed under obedience to God;" and by this measure such a reading "borders on shirk."[21] Barlas notes that notions of wifely obedience amount to an extension of God-like authority to men, which "violates the concept of Tawhid that places God above such correspondences and also establishes the principle of the indivisibility of God's Sovereignty."[22] As an alternative, Al-Hibri reads this portion of verse 4:34 as referring to the honoring of "marital covenants," making the verse about (dis)obedience to God, not to husbands.[23]

Sa'diyya Shaikh discusses at length how interpretations of 4:34 that call for women's obedience to their husbands violate the doctrine of tawhid. The core problem of such readings, according to Shaikh, is that a "marital hierarchy" that is already in violation of tawhid becomes further "prescribed at a religious level."[24] In effect, "sacralised male authority and marital hierarchy become foregrounded in the relationship between female-believer and God."[25] In other words, the submissive relationship of woman to God is replicated in the relationship between woman and husband; in this scheme, obedience to one's husband is not only parallel to one's obedience to God but also becomes a requirement of one's obedience to God. This notion rests on the "assumption, no matter how indirect, that God's Sovereignty and man's are coextensive."[26] Shaikh notes that such an understanding produces a "spiritual hierarchy" in which "God occupies the pinnacle, men the centre, as mediators, and women ... the bottom rung."[27] Barlas makes a similar observation: "Masculinizing God is the first step in positing a hierarchy in which males situate themselves beneath God and above women, implying that there is a symbolic (and sometimes literal) continuum between God's Rule over humans and male rule over women."[28] Shaikh further explains, "The God-believer relationship [for women] becomes secondary and only accessible via a 'correct' man-woman relationship."[29] Because the husband figures as the mediator between the female believer and God, men effectively become "divine intermediaries if not demi-gods."[30] This arrangement disallows a direct relationship between woman and God and gives men God-like authority.[31] Thus, Shaikh argues, interpretations of 4:34 based on this scheme subvert the notion of God's uniqueness and absolute sovereignty and are thus "idolatrous."[32]

In addition to verse 4:34, Wadud addresses Qur'anic verses regarding the hereafter, particularly those that have yielded interpretations suggesting that men play a part in the judgment and recompense of their wives. Wadud studies interpretations of verses 37:21–22 and 36:55–56; these verses refer to the rewards and punishments awaiting human beings and their *azwaj* (mates). Premodern and modern exegetes have interpreted these verses to mean that a woman will be rewarded or punished on the basis of the record of her husband's deeds, even though, as Wadud asserts, "the Qur'an is emphatic that recompense is based on the individual."[33] Each person is justly judged only for his or her own deeds, not those of any other person, and regardless of one's relationships to others. Interpretations suggesting otherwise "contradict the Qur'anic stand against individual intercession at the Judgment."[34] These interpretations imply that men share in the determination of women's divine judgment in the hereafter. However, Riffat Hassan observes:

> Islam rejects the idea of redemption, of any intermediary between a believer and the Creator. It is one of Islam's cardinal beliefs that each person—man and woman—is responsible and accountable for his or her individual actions. How, then, can the husband become the wife's gateway to heaven or hell? How, then, can he become the arbiter . . . of her ultimate destiny?[35]

Hassan's comments point out that such notions are based upon the assumption that men share in God's authority, or that they are intermediaries in the relationship between women and God. For Hassan, it is inconceivable that Muslims could purport such notions; she expresses her bewilderment at "the audacity and the arrogance to deny women direct access to God."[36] As the exegetes observe, interpretations based on such assumptions attribute authority to men that, according to the doctrine of tawhid, belongs to God alone.[37]

Finally, if ascribing God-like qualities to men constitutes an act of *shirk*, by the same line of reasoning, the reverse act of ascribing male characteristics to God is an act of *shirk* as well. Barlas observes that since God is "Incomparable," God is also "Unrepresentable, especially in anthropomorphic terms."[38] As the exegetes point out, in addition to asserting repeatedly that God has no human associates, the Qur'an states that God does not beget and is not begotten.[39] Barlas observes that "these doctrines preclude associating forebears, partners, or progeny with God, or misrepresenting God as father, son, husband, or male."[40] Thus, the Qur'an's statement of "Divine Transcendence and Incomparability" provides "compelling theological reasons to reject God's engenderment."[41] It follows from this that any interpretive act implying or stating, directly or indirectly, that God is male or male-like constitutes *shirk*. Such interpretations amount to a kind of idolatry, as they portray God in anthropomorphic terms. Idolatry need not only be fashioning physical images or statues of human beings as likenesses or representations of God; idolatry may be equally operative on the level of interpretive language and concepts. Thus, references to God using male terms and pronouns are particularly problematic in terms of the tawhid doctrine. Barlas notes: "As the Qur'an's teachings suggest, humans (hence our languages) cannot comprehend, much less define, God."[42] This limitation of human language, along with the Qur'an's statement that Muslims "should not use similitudes (representations) for God," means that "the use of the pronoun 'He'" in reference to God is "a bad linguistic convention" that should be avoided.[43] At the very least, masculinized references to God in human language must not be understood as an "epistemological claim about God's Being."[44]

The comprehensive benefit of these deductions for the exegetes is their usefulness in rejecting both "patriarchalized misrepresentations of God" and "theories of father-right or male privilege" over Muslim women.[45] Debunking masculinized understandings of God becomes a tool in fighting Qur'anic interpretations that tout male supremacy and seek to legitimate a hierarchy of male authority over women.[46] By employing the tawhidic paradigm to criticize the notion of God's maleness, they disassociate divine authority from male authority. The exegetes are able to argue that associating man's authority with God's is a violation of God's Sovereignty, and thus tantamount to *shirk*.[47] In their criticisms of traditional exegesis, they cast interpretations in support of male domination as *shirk* and thus unpardonable sin.

Distinguishing the Qur'an from Its Exegesis

Scholars of feminist tafsir also use the tawhidic paradigm to argue that human interpretations of the Qur'an are not equivalent to the Qur'anic text; thereby they demonstrate that interpretations of the Qur'an that are demeaning to women are prone to error and open to criticism because of their authorship by human beings. The exegetes criticize Muslim tendencies to invest supreme authority in the interpretations of classical exegetes. Asma Barlas argues that their interpretations became treated as "sacrosanct" due to the "belief that these scholars were able to replicate the Prophet's own methodology because of their proximity *in real time* to him and to the first Muslim community."[48] As a result, Muslims have come to "canonize" their interpretations; they uphold their replication by "protecting the canon and by avoiding innovation."[49] Regardless of their content, Muslims have come to treat these interpretations as immune to criticism.[50]

Khaled Abou El Fadl makes a number of relevant observations about the fallibility of human beings in their efforts to comprehend the divine message. Although Abou El Fadl is not often directly cited by the exegetes, his observations are useful in explicating many of the implicit rationales of the exegetes on the topic of human interpretation. Abou El Fadl notes the limitations of human attempts to understand the divine, referring to human interpreters as "agents" and core Islamic texts as "indicators." This agent may be able argue that the text of the Qur'an indicates something of "the Divine Will in this or that direction. But the agent is not capable of encompassing or embodying the Divine Will."[51] For Abou El Fadl, to claim otherwise is an act of authoritarianism, an abuse of scholarly authority. Referring to God as the "Principle," he argues:

> Authoritarianism . . . is the marginalization of the ontological reality of the Divine and the depositing of this Divine Will in the agent so that the agent effectively becomes self-referential. In this authoritarian dynamic, the distinction between the agent and the Principal becomes indistinct and blurred. The Will of the Principal and the speech of the agent become one and the same, as the agent superimposes his or her own determination upon the instructions of the Principal.[52]

In effect, "the reader is able to displace the Author and set himself as the sole voice of authority. In essence, the reader becomes God."[53] This assumption of the role of God directly contradicts the tawhidic principle that no one shares in the authority of God. Despite the fact that, as Barlas points out, "the Qur'an distinguishes between itself and its exegesis," these interpretive acts of authoritarianism fail to distinguish between the word of God and its readings by human beings.[54]

Using similar arguments, the exegetes are quick to point out that regarding the *tafsir* of early scholars as incontestable contradicts the tawhidic notion of human beings' fallibility in understanding the divine text. Wadud asserts: "*Tafsir* is (hu)man-made and, therefore, subject to human nuances, peculiarities, and limitations. This natural limitation is unlike the divine will, which cannot be contained, explained, or even maintained by any one such limited being or community."[55] Barlas concurs: "A reading of the Qur'an is just a reading of the Qur'an, no matter how good; it does not approximate the Qur'an itself."[56] She adds: "The Qur'an is inimitable, inviolate, inerrant, and incontrovertible; however, our understanding of it is not."[57] Thus Wadud and Barlas criticize the attribution of indisputable authority to any interpretation of the Qur'an, claiming that all interpretations are subject to the limitations of human error. This allows the exegetes to counter the belief that "only males, and conservative males at that, know what God *really* means."[58] The exegetes fortify these arguments by establishing that the treatment of classical interpretations of the Qur'an as if they were unassailable is a violation of tawhid, since this treatment amounts to "equating their . . . authority with that of revelation."[59] Assigning classical interpretations this level of authority effectively "collapses divine discourse with its human interpretations" and confuses human interpretation with divine will.[60] Such notions imply that classical interpreters share in the knowledge and sovereignty of God. In declaring such attitudes contradictory to tawhid, scholars of feminist tafsir are able to distinguish between the Qur'an and its exegeses and to approach previous exegeses as open to criticism and revision.

Dynamism of Qur'anic Interpretation

Related to the argument that in accordance with the doctrine of tawhid no one may pronounce a perfect interpretation of the Qur'an is the argument that no one may produce a final interpretation of the Qur'an.[61] This concept also informs the exegetes' position that classical Qur'anic interpretations are not immutable and should be continually revised. They argue that human beings can do no more than *attempt* to understand God's mandates and engage in a continual process of searching for understanding. Since complete understanding of the Qur'an belongs solely to God, human beings are never able to produce a final, perfect interpretation of the Quran; all they can do is engage in an ongoing process of trying to understand the text, however imperfectly. Thus, the Qur'an must always remain open to continual, dynamic interpretation.

Khaled Abou El Fadl's comments on interpretive authoritarianism are again relevant to this argument. He observes that presenting an interpretation of sacred texts as "inevitable, final, and conclusive" is an attempt at "'locking' or captivating the Will of the Divine" as if it is one's own.[62] Finality of interpretation is not a possibility within reach of human capacity; attributing such finality to a Qur'anic interpretation is an act of authoritarianism: "Closing the interpretive process is a despotic act. If the reader attempts to 'lock' the text into a specific meaning, this act risks violating the integrity of the author and text . . . This . . . assumes that the reader is empowered or authorized to end the role of the author and the text. In fact, the reader's determination replaces the role of the author and the text."[63] Thus, in pronouncing an interpretation as final, a reader of the Qur'an takes on an authority that belongs only to its divine author. "Closing the text" is equivalent to "claiming a knowledge that is identical to God's knowledge."[64] It is a failure to distinguish between the knowledge and will of God and that of human beings.

In order to legitimate the development of new interpretations of Qur'anic verses that have traditionally been read in ways demeaning to women, the exegetes call on Muslims to reflect on the limitations of human understanding, arguing that these limitations oblige all human beings to produce evolving readings of the Qur'an. With regard to interpretations of the Qur'an that have denied full human dignity to women, Wadud speculates: "Perhaps Muslims have not fully understood the principles of human dignity established in the Qur'an because they are finite beings attempting to embrace ultimate meaning."[65] In other words, because human beings' insights into the Qur'an are finite, they have been limited in their understanding of the dignity that the Qur'an has granted to women. The fault, then, lies not with the Qur'an, but with human beings' fallible understandings of the Qur'an, which must always be updated. Thus, Wadud argues, a "plurality of meanings" is essential to "the development of various states and stages of individual and collective moral and spiritual development."[66] Evolving interpretations of the Qur'an are therefore necessary to the ongoing moral development of human beings set forth in the Qur'an. Barlas emphasizes the necessity of evolving interpretation because of the nature of human understanding: "New methods and readings are not only desirable but also essential because our knowledge of the Qur'an is eternally evolving."[67] Wadud echoes the notion of the broader relevance of treating Qur'anic interpretation as a dynamic process: "When it can be clearly seen that Qur'anic interpretation is a process that is never complete, then continual interpretations will become legitimate and necessary, regardless of how variant they might be from interpretations concluded in the past."[68] The exegetes thus ground their claim to new interpretations of the Qur'an in the concept of tawhid, pointing to the limitations of human beings and their never-ending process of understanding divine guidance and developing as moral beings.

Beyond the Human Language of the Qur'an

Finally, Amina Wadud and (to some extent) Asma Barlas use the tawhidic paradigm to argue that, as a form of revelation structured by human language, the Qur'an cannot perfectly encompass all divine meaning. This concept helps account for feminist impasses in the Qur'anic text that cannot be resolved using other textual strategies employed by the exegetes, such as that confronted by Wadud in relation to the term *daraba* in verse 4:34 (discussed in chapter 5). In *Inside the Gender Jihad*, Wadud reflects on certain Qur'anic verses that contain an unavoidable presumption of male dominance over women. Wadud writes of these verses: "I have come to places where how the text says what it says is just plain inadequate or unacceptable, however much interpretation is enacted upon it."[69] Unable to "rescue" such verses from their sexist or androcentric meanings, she reaches an impasse in conducting feminist readings of the Qur'an.

Wadud accounts for these instances in the Qur'anic text by positing that the expression of the divine message as stated in the Qur'an is limited by the medium of flawed human language. In other words, the blame for harmful meanings lies not with *God* but rather with human language as an imperfect medium for understanding God. These arguments are justified squarely on the basis of the tawhidic paradigm: God is wholly unique and cannot be represented in human terms. Because of the limitations of human language and humans' inability to fully grasp divine meaning, the text of the Qur'an cannot be understood as the exact or total expression of God's will.

Because human beings are incapable of fully comprehending God, the "Unseen is a part of reality concealed or hidden from human perception."[70] Because language is a human construct, it cannot encompass the divine message. As a result of "the deficiencies of all statements in language," and since God transcends anything that can be expressed using human terminologies, the Qur'an employs human language "to discuss what cannot be uttered in language."[71] Thus, the linguistic text of the Qur'an is "insufficient to completely contain and expose divine meaning."[72] Wadud points out that because of the flaws of human language, the Qur'an "did not and, as it says directly, could not exhaust the knowledge of Allah through language alone."[73]

Among the many flaws of human language are its androcentric tendencies and its inability to express concepts that transcend gender. Wadud observes that to a certain extent, "it is difficult to disentangle meaning from the patriarchal hegemony imprinted on the language of construction."[74] That is, the language of human beings is not a clean slate with which to communicate about the divine; it is already framed by the gendered biases built into it. For example, the Arabic language of the Qur'an employs the grammatical gendering of nouns and the use of grammatically male pronouns to refer to God. As Barlas points out, particularly in regard to the Qur'an's descriptions of God, "the androcentric nature of language is . . . likely to create persistent problems in signification."[75] Though God transcends any human linguistic concepts of gender, it is difficult to "perceive of the transgendered" and understand "ungendered spheres of reality" when "transcendent ideas are discussed in gender-stratified language."[76] These deficiencies in language, then, lend themselves to the error of equating God with misleading signifiers for God. As Wadud points out, "reducing Allah to the patriarchal contextual articulation [of Allah]" is "a kind of *shirk* (violation of *tawhid*)," since it reduces Allah to a human construct.[77]

It follows from this understanding of human language that the divine message cannot be reduced to the Qur'an. The divine message is greater and more complex than can be rendered in any humanly accessible form. Wadud understands the Qur'an as a reflection of a much greater ethereal message of which the Qur'an is only a partial indication. The Qur'an is a "phenomenologically perceptive realization of Divine word, *'the 'trace' which was left on earth by the non-material speech of God.'* . . . Thus the Qur'an 'is only an expression (*'ibara*) of God's speech, its created phonetical form.'"[78] As such, the Qur'an is a symbolic indicator of God's guidance, although it does not totalize God's guidance. Similarly, Barlas observes that the Qur'an "clarifies that the real, or archetypal, Qur'an remains with God."[79] That is, the divine message and the Qur'an are not one and the same.

Wadud goes on to argue that by this logic, the Qur'an should not be equated with God.[80] In her words, "Allah is and always was and therefore cannot be contained or constrained by text."[81] Likewise, Barlas warns that without taking into account the limitations of human language, human beings are likely to mistake the Qur'an for divine reality: "God's recourse to human language is meant only to communicate with us in words we can understand, not to delimit God's Reality. However, instead of recognizing the limitations of language, Muslim theology confuses it *with* Divine Reality, ignoring how this confusion results in humanizing God."[82] Wadud notes that when this confusion occurs, "Allah's particular textual exposure is equated with Allah's totality in Its transcendent and unknowable reality."[83] In this equation, human beings violate the incomparability of Allah and thereby commit *shirk*.[84] Thus, "if one truly believes in the eternity of the divine, then one cannot accept that Allah begins or ends with the particulars of Qur'anic utterances."[85] It is interesting to note how such observations about Qur'anic language echo some of the positions of classical Mu'tazilite theologians on the Qur'an in *'ilm al-kalam* (disputational theology) debates, who held that the Qur'an was created in time by

God rather than being co-eternal with God. However, neither Wadud nor Barlas address this parallel at length.

In using the tawhidic paradigm to distinguish between God and the Qur'an, the exegetes do not question the divine origins of the Qur'an. They maintain the sanctity of the message of the Qur'an but dissociate the Qur'an's sanctity from its human medium. Wadud states: "Human language limits Allah's Self-disclosure. If revelation through text must be in human language . . . then revelation cannot be divine or Ultimate. This is distinguished from the idea that revelation is from a divine source: rather, it indicates how the source availed itself of the limitation of human language to point toward the ultimate direction for human moral development, otherwise known as guidance."[86] Thus, the exegetes begin to explain some of the linguistic contents of the Qur'an that remain troubling from a feminist perspective without undermining the sanctity of the divine message, which the Qur'an merely approximates through signification.[87] By using the tawhidic paradigm to establish that the Qur'an does not perfectly encompass all divine meaning, the exegetes are able to fault human language, rather than God's message or the Qur'an, for pronouncements in the text that resist feminist interpretation. The Qur'an remains sacred and inviolable, whereas human language is culpable for deficiencies and errors in communication. This distinction prompts the exegetes, in Wadud's words, to look "through" the Qur'an's "particular linguistic confirmations and limitations" as if the Qur'an were "a window toward the transcendent."[88] It is to the problems and possibilities of this stance that I turn in part III.

PART III
Critiques of Feminist Qur'anic Interpretation

7
Initial Conclusions

> *Women's and feminist scholarship on the Qur'an is an attempt to read behind the text to make visible the historical contexts in which it was revealed and interpreted as a way of explaining its patriarchal exegesis. At the same time, women's and feminist scholarship on the Qur'an is an attempt to read in front of the text in order to establish the continuing relevance of its teachings to the lives of believers today. In the process, these readings seek to rescue the Qur'an from the sexism and misogyny that have marred our understanding of it for so many centuries.*
> —ASMA BARLAS, "Women's Readings of the Qur'an"[1]

HAVING CLOSELY EXAMINED the content of feminist exegesis of the Qur'an in chapters 4, 5, and 6, here I review overall trends in the works and offer some initial critical observations about them. I have argued that feminist tafsir works constitute a coherent field based on the observation of their common interpretive techniques. To recapitulate, scholars of feminist exegesis commonly employ the methods of historical contextualization, intratextual reading, and the tawhidic paradigm. They have argued that the Qur'an should be understood as a text revealed in the terms of its immediate seventh-century Arabian audience but also as a universally meaningful text for all its audiences. They have prioritized the Qur'an's general principles over its particular statements, observing the conditional and restricted meanings connoted within its syntactical structures. They have also resisted sexist and violent meanings of the Qur'an by insisting that its verses must be read in line with the Qur'an's larger messages of justice, harmony, and equality, as well as the principle of God's unity and oneness.

What also holds these works of feminist tafsir together as a correlated body of scholarship is the common influence of modern trends in Qur'anic interpretation. Like modernist Qur'anic interpreters, the exegetes of feminist tafsir are concerned with "going back to the sources" and reevaluating the Qur'an independently, laying claim to the right of ijtihad and bypassing traditional authorities. Both modernist scholars and exegetes of feminist tafsir advocate the holistic treatment of the Qur'an and the multiplicity and dynamic open-endedness of interpretation, and they are concerned with the Qur'an's overall movement toward greater social justice for human beings. They both distinguish the Qur'an's universal moral principles from its particular and contingent statements, and they examine the historical context of the language and revelation of the Qur'an as central to its meanings. In departing from traditional interpretations, they prioritize the Qur'an over the Hadith, which they treat as historically contingent or suspect. Finally, they both stress the limits of human knowledge and interpretation, attributing difficulties in understanding the text to human limitations.

Another aspect of feminist tafsir works that enhances their cohesion (though to a lesser degree) is the shared influence of developments in Jewish and Christian feminist theologies on them. The works reveal the resonances of Jewish and Christian feminist scholars' understandings of patriarchy, religious anthropology, and textual androcentrism. The exegetes are inspired by Jewish and Christian feminist approaches to "God-Talk" and interpretive devices such as the hermeneutics of suspicion. They share with Jewish and Christian feminists the assertion of female experience as central to more complete understandings of sacred texts, and they have also recovered the stories of exemplary female figures. In contrast to Jewish and Christian feminists, however, scholars of feminist tafsir unequivocally approach the Qur'an as entirely divine.

Equality, Justice, and Gender

I begin my critical observations of the field of feminist tafsir by outlining views of equality in its works. In numerous references to the principle of human equality, the works employ the notion of "equal but different" as a central qualification to the notion of male–female equality in the Qur'an. The exegetes repeatedly observe that the Qur'an recognizes the differences between men and women while treating them equally; indeed, for them the recognition of difference is key to the Qur'an's equal treatment of men and women: Wadud writes, "Women and men are equal in Islam, so are they considered distinct from one another."[2] For Barlas, the Qur'an's acknowledgment of differences between men and women is "fundamental to its desire to secure women's rights, especially in situations where they may be vulnerable to abuse."[3] Riffat Hassan notes, for example, that in distinguishing between the duties of males and females within the family, the Qur'an "ensures justice between men and women in the context of childbearing" and incorporates "safeguards for protecting women's special sexual/biological functions."[4] In fact, in the words of al-Hibri, the Qur'an provides women with a kind of "affirmative action" by granting them financial support and "added security in a difficult patriarchal world."[5] Wadud points out that men and women have "the same rights and obligations on the ethico-religious level," and, although distinct, their "responsibilities on the social-functional level" are "equally significant," and both receive "equitable compensation" for them.[6] Thus, the exegetes imply that the Qur'an treats men and women equally by regarding them as the same in terms of their moral capacity and worth (on the level of essential being) and by recognizing them as different in social matters (on the level of function)—thus endorsing a complementary view of difference on the social level. In *Inside the Gender Jihad,* Wadud concedes that complementarity may sometimes involve "an unequal power dimension" in "evaluating each player on a separate and unequal standard."[7] However, a few chapters into the same work, Wadud subsequently asserts that "functional disparity is not a precondition for, exception to, or exclusion from essential equality."[8] Wadud and the other exegetes imply that essential equality on the moral-spiritual plane is the most important measure of male–female equality in the Qur'an—it is the absolute determinant of equality. Barlas emphasizes that "the Qur'an does not conceive of difference as inequality,"[9] and it "does not use sex to construct ontological or sociological hierarchies that discriminate against women."[10] Therefore, for her the Qur'an "recognizes sexual *differences,* but it does not adhere to a view of sexual *differentiation.*"[11]

Barlas also argues that "the Qur'an does not define women and men in terms of binary oppositions," and it does not premise differences between men and women upon lack.[12] Drawing on the work of Sachiko Murata, she posits that the Qur'an embraces a polar conception of sexual difference that points to an "interconnectedness of opposite principles" that "manifests *the whole.*"[13] Rather than promoting the notion of oppositional sexual difference, then, the Qur'an's conception of difference "serve[s] to establish the principle of the fundamental unity of the human race."[14] Barlas concludes that in the Qur'an, "'difference differentiates laterally'" rather than "hierarchically."[15] In similar arguments, Wadud argues that the existence of man and woman is mutually contingent,[16] and she understands male-female equality in the Qur'an as a kind of "horizontal reciprocity" in which "women and men share perhaps distinct yet horizontal spheres" that allow for a nonhierarchical relationship of mutual "dynamism."[17]

The difficulty of accounting for both male-female difference and male-female equality in the Qur'an (and likely also the desire to avoid associations with notions of "equality" linked to Western feminism) makes the works prone to the inconsistent use of a number of ambiguous terms as a substitute for "equality." For example, in a passage from *Inside the Gender Jihad*, Wadud attempts to explain their distinctions in her own way: "The term egalitarian flexes its adaptability over the use of the term equal. Where equal is applied to the essential characteristic of being human, equity is applied to functional disparity, incongruence, or inconsistency. Egalitarian is the means by which both the inherent equality of human beings and the equity of responsibility toward other members in the family are reconciled."[18] The differentiated appraisal of the terms "egalitarian," "equal," and "equity" (as well as the term "parity" in other portions of her and others' texts) reflects the persistent need to qualify the notion of male-female equality within feminist exegesis in order to make sense of the co-existence of difference and equality in the Qur'an's references to men and women. However, the works' views on equality raise a number of questions: How does the different treatment of men and women on the social-functional level relate to their same treatment on the moral-spiritual level? Can those levels be so neatly separated? *What exactly* does different but equal treatment of men and women mean substantively? When the Qur'an recognizes or even accommodates social-functional difference, how does it do so while also continuing to distribute power and authority equally to men and women?

The question of power invokes the crucial concept of gender and its social designations and allotments of difference. In turning to the concept of gender in feminist tafsir we encounter further difficulties. One issue is the lack of clarity in the use of the terms "gender jihad" and "gender justice" throughout the works, both of which were first adopted by Wadud.[19] Wadud first uses the term gender justice, although without defining it, in the preface to her 1999 American edition of *Qur'an and Woman*.[20] In *Inside the Gender Jihad* she defines gender jihad as "a struggle to establish gender justice in Muslim thought and practice."[21] Wadud goes on to define gender justice as "a harmonious process in which women and men work together to remove barriers to women's full mainstreaming in all aspects of society."[22] This, in turn, prompts the question of what is meant by "mainstreaming." Wadud defines "gender mainstreaming" as "the inclusion of women in all aspects of Muslim practice, performance, policy construction, and in both political and religious leadership."[23] Wadud's references to "mainstreaming" still leave some things unclear, however. Her early work seems especially prone to this, where she calls for the development of a "cooperative and egalitarian system" with "maximum participation" from both sexes, where everyone's contributions are valued and respected, and where everyone is given "full access to economic, intellectual, and political participation" and men also "participate fully" in the household life.[24] On the one hand, the reference to mainstreaming denotes women's inclusion and appears to be an attempt to elaborate on the meaning of equality, which as discussed earlier, is used by Muslim women exegetes with qualification and ambivalence. On the other hand, mainstreaming as an alternative term leaves unclarified what the inclusion of women in all spheres of life would substantively mean or entail. Would men and women perform exactly identical roles in all spheres? How would such a system accommodate the biological differences between men and women acknowledged by the Qur'an? How would the system of mainstreaming evaluate and compensate for roles performed by only one sex because of biology? Beyond acknowledging the value and "importance of women's contributions" and "removing gender stratification" from the "public and private, ritual and political" spheres, this definition of gender justice does not fully articulate what actually constitutes the "justice" for Muslim women that is sought in gender justice or the gender jihad.[25]

Another area of confusion lies in the "gender" of gender justice and gender jihad, given that "gender" is not clearly defined by Wadud or the other exegetes. (Wadud herself points out, "precious little has been proposed to create an Islamic gender theory—whether from without or within."[26]) The exegetes have generally ignored theoretical issues around gender essentialisms, binaries, and social construction. On the whole, they appear to use "gender" as a synonym for "women," neglecting to address the male gender or the "queering" of gender. In neglecting an examination of gender, they do not deconstruct the processes by which the male subject has been universalized in the first place and the kinds of masculinity and femininity (and their relational formation) that persistently inform the verses of the Qur'an they are responding to; rather, they seem to take them for granted. It also appears that the phrasing of gender justice may be employed as another way of avoiding the terminology of equality because it is so complicated, but "gender justice" only further obfuscates meaning since it is used repeatedly without clear definition, and it never entirely rids itself of the phantom of equality, which the term seems to invoke while attempting to avoid it.

Apart from this, it is also unclear what is fully meant by the distancing of Muslim "gender justice" from Western, liberal notions of equality and justice based on the primacy of the individual. Al-Hibri notes that "Muslim women are in the midst of a debate as to whether Islam provides them with 'gender equality' or 'gender equity.' The former concept is viewed by its detractors as coming dangerously close to the Western concept of mechanical equality, based on an individualistic view of society. The latter concept is viewed by its detractors as leaving the door wide open for misuse by patriarchal adversaries."[27] Al-Hibri then notes that her organization Karamah opts for the term equality because of their firm belief in the Qur'an's principle of equality, but she does not directly address the concerns with the term she notes.[28] Wadud also refers to a distinction between Western and Islamic notions without much elaboration. She sees her work as located "within an indigenous Islamic worldview rather than as a mere by-product of or reaction to Western and secular developments, practices, and experiences of justice since the Enlightenment."[29] She also states: "My motivation has always been pro-faith in perspective. Any comparative analysis with secular Western theories or strategies for mainstreaming women in all aspects of human development and governance is coincidental and secondary."[30] A subsequent assertion foregrounding her perspective as a believing Muslim appears related to this stance. Wadud notes that her work "differs from secular articulations of social justice" because it acknowledges that "the total well-being of the human creature is not limited to the physical or material. At the end of the day, it is the moral center of one's being, or one's consciousness, that determines the nature of one's social actions and relationships."[31] Here Wadud seems to suggest that a faith-based morality and religious consciousness that accounts for the whole person within and beyond the earthly realm sets her perspective apart from Western secular views; however, it remains unclear how exactly such a consciousness allows her to definitively depart from the notion of the individual in the Western, liberal tradition from which the language of inclusion and mainstreaming derives.[32]

Neither Wadud nor the other exegetes clearly define the concept of equality or correlates such as mainstreaming. This lack of clarity and the exegetes' frequent references to equality, as if its meaning and parameters were self-evident, suggest that feminist tafsir has adopted a vague version of the liberal notion of "equal opportunity." The exegetes appear to inadvertently inherit the unresolved debates on equality and difference in liberal approaches to feminism without assessing them critically. In reflecting on feminist tafsir, Qudsia Mirza has argued for being "clearer about the concept of equality that is deployed in Islamic feminism," since in Muslim feminist thought "the concept of equality is one that is assumed, with little or no theoretical discussion of the implications of basing it on the concept of sexual difference, or sameness, with men."[33]

Another major set of questions around "equality" concerns the problem of not interrogating the commensurability of concepts of equality in the contemporary context with conceptions of male-female relations in a text revealed in the seventh century. Here, I point to feminist tafsir's unquestioned imposition of contemporary conceptions of equality on a sacred text revealed in a premodern society where such a notion was hardly a concern to anyone in the way it is today. In other words, the exegetes usually demand equality as if it is an ahistorical, timeless idea.[34] In response to this issue, Kecia Ali asks, "Why does equality matter, besides the fact that some of us have been conditioned by modernity to want it?"[35] Scholars of feminist tafsir have not offered a substantial answer to this question to date. As Ziba Mir-Hosseini argues, the historical record clearly demonstrates that notions of sexual equality (in our contemporary sense) were simply not a concern for premodern scholars and jurists, "as it was not part of their social experience."[36] Based upon similar observations, Elizabeth Leo criticizes scholars who "mistakenly pose modern questions that are more applicable to the lives of modern Muslim women than to the women who lived in the seventh-century world of the Prophet Muhammad," arguing that "sexuality, gender, and patriarchy are not useful concepts if they are applied backwards onto the past instead of having their evolution into our present understanding of them explored."[37] Likewise, Ali cautions that "the necessity of equality as a component of justice must be defended, not merely asserted."[38] As Ali points out, rather than demanding equality as a self-evident, ahistorical measure of justice from one's readings of the Qur'an, readers must explore the possible differences between contemporary concepts of male-female equality and understandings of men and women in the Qur'an.[39] In looking for Qur'anic support for contemporary notions of equality, the field of feminist tafsir has yet to carefully explain exactly what kind of "equality" is sought and to justify that endeavor on the basis of careful theoretical and philosophical inquiry.

Absolving the Qur'an and Faulting Tafsir

An additional set of challenges arises from the shortcomings of applying the textual strategies discussed in chapters 4, 5, and 6 to Qur'anic verses on women and male-female relations. In relying on these techniques, scholars of feminist exegesis have remained unable to account for the existence of certain Qur'anic statements that appear to be neglectful or harmful to women despite the application of the historical contextualization, intratextual, and tawhidic paradigm approaches. For the most part, the exegetes have not acknowledged the limitations of attributing anti-women readings of the Qur'an exclusively to human language and interpretation and never to the Qur'an itself.

In general, the exegetes have been reluctant to "hold the Qur'an responsible for its misreading," that is, the derivation of sexist or harmful meanings.[40] They do not resort to rejecting any language of the Qur'an because of their commitment to the divine origins of the entire text, in line with "the universal view held by Muslims . . . that rejecting any part of the Qur'an is tantamount to rejecting Islam."[41] They have attributed problematic meanings of the text to the interpretive errors or linguistic difficulties of human beings rather than to the divine text itself. Indeed, it is in response to the Qur'an's inviolable and unalterable quality that they have developed interpretive strategies to produce egalitarian meanings of the Qur'an, while neither faulting the Qur'anic text itself nor questioning its divine immutability.

Like most other scholars of feminist tafsir, Riffat Hassan asserts that "the Qur'an has *absolute* authority" since it is entirely the "unadulterated" word of God.[42] Hassan traces sexist readings of the Qur'an to the influence of Hadith reports "inconsistent with the Qur'an" that should have been disregarded by the standards of Hadith criticism.[43] Instead, such Hadith reports became "the lens through which the words of the Qur'an have been seen and interpreted."[44] For Hassan this misuse of Hadith, not the unassailable Qur'an, is to blame for its verses being "misread or misinterpreted."[45] By this logic, Muslims may combat all anti-women meanings derived from the Qur'an by purifying the Qur'anic text from the influence of faulty Hadith reports. Thus, for Hassan, "post-patriarchal Islam is nothing other than Qur'anic Islam."[46]

Asma Barlas is perhaps even more passionate in her defense of the Qur'anic text, admitting her intention "to absolve the Qur'an 'itself' of culpability for what Muslims have, or have not, read into it" and maintaining her position "against holding it responsible for how it has or has not been read."[47] In response to questions about the text's culpability, she asserts: "I believe that the onus for reading the Qur'an correctly lies with the reader . . . I see nothing wrong in arguing that meaning lies in the Qur'an, but the responsibility for recovering it *properly* lies with its readers."[48] It is human errors, not the Qur'an, that have yielded sexist meanings from the text; these meanings have arisen when human beings have read the Qur'an "timelessly," ignored its "egalitarian aspects," have failed to understand that "the Qur'an makes stipulations 'for a gender inequality that exists, but should not,'" or have drawn unnecessary distinctions between "religious and social/legal equality."[49] She substantiates this argument about human error by arguing that the Qur'an "anticipates the possibilities of its own misreading," citing verses warning against the perversion of its meanings, distorting its allegorical verses, or reading some verses to the exclusion of others.[50]

It was not until the publications of Kecia Ali's *Sexual Ethics and Islam* and Amina Wadud's *Inside the Gender Jihad* in 2006 that any of the exegetes had openly and extensively addressed the case of certain verses for which the interpretive approaches studied here fall short in "rescuing" the Qur'anic text from sexist and male-centered meanings. For example, the limits of the historical contextualization method emerge in cases in which historical context can explain but not prevent its androcentric meanings. According to Kecia Ali, unlike most Qur'anic verses on marriage, divorce, and polygamy, which simply "reflect the social norm of patriarchy, by addressing those with greater power in it,"[51] certain verses about sexual relations between men and women are more complicated: "In a number of verses concerned with sex, women are spoken about and men are spoken to in a way that presumes male control and is unconnected with ameliorative measures intended to restrict men's scope of action or enlarge that assigned to women."[52] Ali refers specifically to verses 2:187 (part of which the exegetes have highlighted for its famous description of husbands and wives as each other's mutual garments) and 2:222–223:

> 2:187 "On the night of fasting, (sexually) approaching your wives is permissible for you; they are garments for you, and you are garments for them . . ."
>
> 2:222–223 " . . . Withdraw from women during menstruation, and do not approach them until they are clean, but when they have cleansed themselves then approach them as God has commanded you . . . Your wives are (like) a field for you, so approach your field as you wish . . ."[53]

Describing husbands and wives as each other's garments, verse 2:187 grants men permission to engage in sexual acts with their wives after nightfall on days of fasting but not during the daytime, nor when they offer their prayers in retreat at the mosque. Verses 2:222–223 instruct men not to initiate sexual activity with their female partners during the course of their menstruation; the verses advise men to initiate sex as they wish after their women's purification from this course. First, Ali notes that these verses concerning sexual activity are addressed exclusively *to* men *about* women. Ali recalls that both Asma Barlas and Amina Wadud (in *Qur'an and Woman*) have argued that the instances in which the Qur'an addresses men exclusively reflect where the text "respond[s] to the practical exigencies of an extant patriarchy";[54] thus, they have argued, "such verses merely reflect the social norm of patriarchy, by addressing those with greater power in it."[55] Ali agrees that this argument is helpful in addressing some Qur'anic verses, such as those regarding marriage and divorce, which characteristically "direct men to allow women particular freedoms" and thus "suggest a trajectory away from male familial domination and control."[56]

However, Ali finds the historical argument ineffective in the cases of 2:187 and 2:222–223. For her, both passages undeniably "presuppose male agency and female passivity with regard to the initiation of sex."[57] Here, Ali argues, "women are spoken about and men are spoken to in a way that presumes male control" over women's bodies, a presumption which no amount of historical contextualization changes short of fully disregarding the verse.[58] In particular, Ali points out that, in its reference to women as the "tilth" of men, verse 2:223 "objectifies women in the most literal sense, discussing them as matter to be acted-upon" rather than "agents in their own right."[59] Ali concedes that these passages do remind men that ultimately their "access to women's bodies is controlled by divine regulation," since God judges them based on all their actions.[60] However, neither this reminder nor the historical contextualization method can fully explain away the androcentrism of these verses. She concludes that while such "androcentrism is not equivalent to misogyny ... neither is it unproblematic for interpreters concerned with matters of gender and justice."[61] In other words, the presumption of male control over women is entrenched within these verses to such an extent that the recognition of the patriarchal historical context of revelation does not alleviate the impact of the text's content. The historical contextualization method helps explain the patriarchal language and framing of certain statements, but it does not change that the Qur'an is not only describing but also *prescribing* behavior based on a presumption of male control.

Kecia Ali's criticisms also articulate a serious challenge to the effectiveness of the intratextual strategy for scholars of feminist exegesis. As discussed in chapter 5, the exegetes attempt to reconcile 2:223 with the emphasis upon mutuality and reciprocity of mates in other Qur'anic verses such as 9:71 and 30:21 and even the "garments" reference of 2:187.[62] Ali argues that "mutuality and love, however, are disconnected from the specific guidelines that the Qur'an establishes for sexual conduct."[63] She argues that despite the "powerful and moving (and gender neutral!) description of the divine purpose for marriage" in verse 30:21, it cannot be ignored that "the Qur'an *also* includes hierarchal and androcentric provisions for marriage and sex."[64] The Qur'an's statements about marital tranquility do not change the fact that "Qur'anic discussions of sexual intimacy contain no appeal for female freedom to act."[65] These verses presume in the first place that men, not women, are in control of sexual relations since they have almost unlimited sexual access to their wives and are the only active participants in determining the parameters of sexual conduct with them.[66] According to Ali, in the case of such verses, "the Qur'anic privileging of male sexual agency suggests that in some crucial sense the Qur'an is a thoroughly andocentric" text.[67] Ali concludes that "the strategies of historical contextualization and principle-extraction . . . are not useful in interpreting the Qur'anic regulations on sexual matters."[68] Interpretations of the Qur'an that ignore certain verses in insisting on just and equal treatment of women are guilty of "selective presentation of egalitarian verses," in contradiction to the feminist assertion that the Qur'an must be read holistically.[69] She asserts that ensuing "arguments about male/female equality built on the systematic avoidance of inconvenient verses" are "fundamentally dishonest and ultimately futile."[70] As Ali demonstrates, when these inconvenient verses are also acknowledged, the application of the intratextual strategy to *all* parts of the Qur'an fails to yield meanings that treat men and women as equally self-determining agents.[71]

An even more serious problem arises in the case of verse 4:34,[72] whose feminist reevaluation is most prominently undertaken by Amina Wadud.[73] As discussed previously, verse 4:34 instructs men on what actions they should take in the event of their wives' *nushuz* (often understood as disobedience to their husbands), including the suggestion of *daraba* (often understood as "to beat"); the meanings of both terms and the structure of the verse are reinterpreted by feminist exegesis to oppose the allowance for wife beating. In placing the blame for sanctioning violence on human understandings of verse 4:34, scholars of feminist tafsir have often failed to address problems in the text that are not resolved through their techniques.

One limitation is apparent in arguments on the Quran's philosophy of gradual social change. It is perhaps Azizah al-Hibri who most often refers to the "gradualism" of the Qur'an: "The Qur'anic philosophy of gradualism is predicated upon the fact that fundamental changes in human consciousness do not usually occur overnight. Instead, they require a period of individual or even social gestation."[74] This position reflects an apologetic approach to the question of why the Qur'an, in addressing the patriarchal context of its immediate audience, appears to tolerate attitudes toward women regarding marriage and sex at the time of revelation. Al-Hibri attributes the verse's apparent allowance for husbands to discipline their wives (albeit in mitigated form and with limitations) to the Qur'an's "graduated approach to the problem of wife abuse" that "takes into account . . . the need for 'a gestation period' for [men] to achieve a higher stage of development and communication."[75] The Qur'an thereby "introduced a transitory stage for change, while preserving the Qur'anic view of ideal marital relations."[76] Nevertheless, al-Hibri does not explain why the Qur'an did not mandate the same kind of urgent, dramatic reform on this matter as it did in other ways, such as in its prohibition of female infanticide. She offers only an apologetic defense for the slow pace of social evolution, neglecting to offer any explanation for why the Qur'an is clearly inconsistent in reforming all practices of violence against women. Al-Hibri goes so far as to uphold slow evolutionary change as the most effective route to lasting social reform: "Although gradual change is frustrating, it is, nevertheless, more stable and less destructive of society than a radical coercive change. Coercive change, which reflects a patriarchal preference for the use of force, lasts for only as long as the source of the coercion continues to exist. It also leaves a great deal of violence and pain in its aftermath."[77]

This approach, however, still begs the question of why the Qur'an does not treat the problem of wife abuse as one in need of reform as urgently as others. We are left only with al-Hibri's assurance that "gradual change need not be agonizingly slow. If Muslim women (and men) join efforts to dismantle patriarchal society, the objective could be achieved within our lifetime."[78] Women who experience domestic violence justified by means of the Qur'an would likely disagree with the notion that the Qur'an's solution is not "agonizingly slow" or that gradual change is an adequate or effective strategy toward eliminating marital violence.

Hassan, al-Hibri, Wadud, and Barlas have all offered alternative translations of the term *daraba* or argued that 4:34 allows for only symbolic or severely restricted or mitigated striking. However, as discussed in chapter 5, feminist tafsir has been unable to respond satisfactorily to the existence of *daraba* in the verse at all. As Farid Esack has pointed out, all these interpretations tend to address 4:34 without ever "questioning the legitimacy of physical chastisement itself," however mitigated it may be in form.[79] Scholars of feminist exegesis have thus produced apologetic readings of the verse that fail to respond adequately to its persistent use in justifying domestic violence against women.

In response to such observations about feminist interpretations of 4:34, Amina Wadud declares in *Inside the Gender Jihad*: "I accept the critiques of moving beyond my apologetics."[80] As discussed previously, Wadud examines how the very text of verse 4:34 may be among those statements in the Qur'an that are "inadequate or unacceptable, however much interpretation is enacted" on them.[81] She openly confronts the possibility that the Qur'an *itself* may cause violent readings, describing the process of revisiting verse 4:34 as "grappling with *textual* inadequacies."[82] For her, the violent meaning of *daraba* cannot be explained away through reinterpretation, since reinterpretation cannot change the existence of this term in the verse. Expressing her frustration in trying to rescue the text from its literal meaning, Wadud confesses: "There is no getting around this one, even though I have tried through different methods for two decades."[83] Wadud asserts that although reading 4:34 with the verse's linguistic intent in mind may have helped restrict violence against women in earlier centuries, doing so in the twenty-first century no longer produces the result of mitigating current levels of violence against women.[84] She writes, "I argue against any notion that it is acceptable for a man to beat his wife."[85] In this case, the Qur'an *itself* must be held responsible for its sexist and harmful readings.

In addressing verse 4:34, Wadud confronts the untenable situation in which scholars of feminist exegesis find themselves when, on the one hand, their interpretive techniques do not produce meanings congruent with their commitments to dignity and justice for women, but, on the other hand, as "believers in the faith tradition of Islam, [they] cannot rewrite the Qur'an."[86] In the case of *daraba*, the text of the Qur'an itself proves problematic for feminist exegesis, since no alternative translation or interpretive device can alleviate the possibility of it being read abusively. The potential translation of *daraba* into "strike" or "beat" cannot be entirely ruled out as one (although among many) of the possible interpretations of the term. According to Muslims' belief in God's omniscience, "God knew and intended" the possibility of this interpretation.[87] As Laury Silvers has argued, if one believes in the divine origin of the Qur'an, "one must acknowledge that God intended every meaning that can be drawn from within the semantic boundaries of the Qur'an. Divine knowledge is absolutely comprehensive. There can be no possible reading that was not ultimately intended by God."[88] In other words, the mere existence of the term *daraba* contravenes any interpretive possibility for ruling out the meaning of "to strike"; there is no act of interpretation that may eradicate this possibility.

In the case of such impasses with the Qur'anic text itself, the exegetes are left to develop alternative techniques that squarely address such statements in an unapologetic manner while also maintaining the divinity of the Qur'an. If, as Ali notes, "it is not enough to simply posit that 'the Qur'an is egalitarian and antipatriarchal,' and to blame interpretations that deviate from that perspective entirely on 'misreadings,'" where else are the exegetes to turn?[89] What can the exegetes do without undermining the Qur'anic text?[90]

Wadud's Strategy of Saying No

Since altering the term *daraba* or denying its full range of potential meanings is not possible, in *Inside the Gender Jihad* Wadud makes the decision to "say 'no'" to verse 4:34 in its linguistic form: "I have finally come to say 'no' outright to the literal interpretation of this passage."[91] Wadud argues that the Qur'an itself allows for human beings to say "no" to its literal pronouncements in limited cases. She claims that Muslims "can promote the idea of saying 'no' to the text" while "still pointing to the text to support this . . . It is therefore neither un-Islamic nor heretical" to do so.[92] She observes that "the Qur'an has necessarily left clues" for "challenging the limitations of the reasoning" possessed by the initial seventh-century audience of revelation.[93] The Qur'an has used such "clues" to serve the needs of both "linguistic compliance" and "contextual clarity" in its immediate context of revelation, while at the same time providing "eternal" and "universal" guidance for future contexts and civilizations.[94] (This recalls Wadud's argument, discussed in chapter 6, that since human language cannot perfectly express God, the Qur'an cannot be the exact expression of God.) Wadud argues that the Qur'an guides human beings "to higher moral practices even if not fully articulating these" in literal form in the context of its seventh-century revelation.[95] Thus, the text "constantly hints at and opens up to new meanings."[96] (This position also recalls the exegetes' intratextual arguments for the Qur'an's overall movement toward social justice examined in chapter 5.)

Wadud uses this reasoning to criticize the textual content of verse 4:34 while still attesting to the full sanctity of the Qur'an. She claims to criticize the Qur'anic text on the basis of the Qur'an itself. By pointing out the limitations of the Qur'anic text without denying the authority of the Qur'an or its divine origins, she proposes a radical solution for the most troubling feminist impasse within the Qur'an. In effect, she attempts to criticize the Qur'anic text without undercutting its divinity or the authority of God.

Wadud justifies saying "no" to the verse not only on the basis of the Qu'ran's own textual clues but also in terms of the history of its exegesis. Her interpretation of 4:34 "simply exemplifies the process or trajectory" of "the history of textual interpretation and application."[97] As mentioned previously, Wadud recalls that within the first few centuries of Qur'anic exegesis and jurisprudence, some jurists had already begun to interpret the "intent" of the verse as an allowance for nothing more than symbolic, nonviolent disciplining. Such an understanding of the verse amounted to "*an intervention opposing literal application*" of the text.[98] Thus, she argues, her interpretive maneuver is simply a continuation of what other interpreters have always done throughout the history of exegesis. Wadud writes, "The collective community has always manipulated the text in concert with civilizational . . . development. We must now simply acknowledge that it has always been done and accept the responsibility of . . . doing so openly."[99] She notes that in doing so, Muslims are merely "continuing the process of intervention between text and meaning, as believers in Allah and in revelation."[100]

Wadud acknowledges that the understanding of justice that guides her interpretation is different from that of the Qur'an's first audience of revelation. She admits that "the text actually states something unmeaningful from the perspective of current human developments and understandings."[101] She openly declares, "We need to make the text mean more for women's full dignity" than it did for its seventh-century audience.[102] For her, the verse reflects "an ethical standard of human actions that are archaic and barbarian at this time in history. They are unjust in the ways that human beings have come to experience and understand justice, and hence unacceptable to universal notions of human dignity."[103] As a way to substantiate this call, she recalls that the Qur'an "never overtly advocated the eradication of the institution of slavery and concubinage" even though later generations of Muslims came to understand the practice as unjust by the standards of the time.[104] She points out that Muslims "were able to stop practicing the institution of slavery and never charged ourselves with violating the text."[105] Therefore, adjusting understandings of the Qur'an in line with contemporary standards of justice should also be possible without accusing exegetes of corrupting the Qur'anic text.

In part, Wadud draws on the work of Khaled Abou El Fadl in her arguments for saying "no" to the Qur'anic text. In his *Speaking in God's Name: Islamic Law, Authority and Women* (2001), Abou El Fadl discusses the last-resort option of "faith-based objection" in the event of a reader's crisis of conscience resulting from a moral impasse in the Qur'anic text.[106] He notes the possibility of a reader coming across in the Qur'an "a text that seems to go against everything that he or she believes about God."[107] In such a case, Abou El Fadl argues, the "appropriate response is to exercise, what I have called, a conscientious-pause."[108] A "responsible and reflective person ought to pause. . . . not to simply dismiss the text . . . but to reflect and investigate [it] further."[109] One must engage in earnest investigation, "suspending judgment until such study is complete."[110] If the conflict between the text and one's conscience remains unresolved after seeking "all the possible avenues," Abou El Fadl notes, "Islamic theology requires that a person abide by the dictates of his or her conscience."[111] In part by drawing on Abou El Fadl's notion of conscientious pause, Wadud confronts verse 4:34 as "unacceptable" in terms of "current levels of human competency and understanding."[112] For Wadud, 4:34 is a case in which "the standards of age and place, or the standards of human moral development" have caused an "unsettling or disturbing of the conscience" that forces her to make a faith-based objection to the text.[113]

As Kecia Ali points out, the notion that "God does not demand that Muslims act contrary to the dictates of conscience" brings with it the weighty "responsibility for the individual human being to make ethical judgments."[114] Therefore, the notion of *khilafah*, or human agency, is also crucial to defending the decision to say "no" to *daraba*. Wadud argues that her objection to the literal form of the text is part of her responsibility to respond to the Qur'an as God's *khalifah* (agent). In her words, the Qur'an calls on "human beings to act as Allah's agents, responsible for making the meaning of the Qur'an implemental as universal guidance."[115] Accepting her responsibility as a human agent reading the Qur'an, she writes, "I am not afraid of my efforts to understand the text, to act upon my understanding."[116]

Building on Wadud's claim to human responsibility in reading verse 4:34, Laury Silvers has argued that *daraba* appears in the text in order to provoke a crisis of conscience within the human agent that purposefully forces him or her to object to the verse's literal form. Silvers makes the argument that God intentionally placed *daraba* in the verse, anticipating that some human beings would interpret it literally: "If we affirm divine knowledge, then we must admit that God intended this word-choice knowing it would be used to permit abusive behavior."[117] She asks, "If God did not intend men to beat their wives, then why use a word with a primary meaning of 'beat them'?"[118] For her, the answer is that God deliberately places the term in the Qur'an to present an important ethical challenge to human readers, signaling that as human agents, "we must struggle with our conscience *even in response to God.*"[119] Drawing on the work of medieval Sufi philosopher Ibn al-'Arabi (d. 1240 C.E.), Silvers points to the theological claim that God intends all "meaning[s] . . . from the Qur'an within the semantic boundaries of the accepted recitations."[120] Therefore, Silvers argues, "no amount of interpretive finesse would be able to cover over a reading of God's prescription in v. 4:34 as obliging husbands to hit their wives."[121] Thus, she concludes, God intends for the verse to convey "all possible meanings including 'beat them.'"[122] However, while "God may intend all meanings" implied by the term *daraba*, "it does not follow that [God] *approves* of all meanings."[123] Rather, the verse exists in this form "to inspire the crisis of conscience that would lead us to prohibit beating."[124] Therefore, the Qur'anic text deliberately contains a *"limited"* number of cases in which "one can and should say 'no' to the Qur'an."[125] It does so, Silvers argues, "to prompt the ethical crises that make us human."[126]

Interpretive Choice

In line with these observations made by Wadud and Silvers, Kecia Ali is perhaps the most prominent Muslim feminist voice calling for exegetes to take responsibility for their own exegetical decisions in reinterpreting the Qur'an in line with the aims of feminist justice. Ali calls for scholars to "justify the project of egalitarian interpretation" and acknowledge that "esteeming equality as the most important interpersonal value is a peculiarity of some modern Muslims" rather than "something inherent in the text of the Qur'an."[127] Ali's assertion is similar to Ghazala Anwar's suggestion that the "decision" to prioritize Qur'anic messages of justice and equality when confronting conflicting verses "is a personal one."[128] In the end, Ali proposes that exegetes "accept responsibility for acts of interpretation" and "acknowledge that they *are* interpretive choices" rather than purely self-evident in the text.[129] In *Secular and Islamic Feminist Critiques in the Work of Fatima Mernissi* (2010), Raja Rhouni criticizes Muslim feminist scholarship's inclination to "claim its reading" of the Qur'an "as the most original and truest."[130] Likewise, Qudsia Mirza has noted Muslim feminists' tendency to claim "their own interpretation as the expression of authentic or 'true' Islam."[131]

A number of scholars have pointed to the theological transgressions that may result from not taking responsibility for one's interpretive interventions. Ebrahim Moosa points out that in forcing certain egalitarian interpretations *upon* the text, interpreters obfuscate their own intervention in reading the Qur'an, in effect "ignoring [the role of] the reader" and turning the Qur'an into a "passive, non-interactive text."[132] But, as Moosa suggests, without its readers, the Qur'an "ceases to be the Qur'an."[133] In other words, whatever the Qur'an "says," "it says to actual readers"; essentially, the text does not "say" anything without speaking to a reader.[134] Thus, the Qur'an's revelation of God's meaning can never be independent of its readers, and human beings must interact with the text in order to yield its meanings.

As Khaled Abou El Fadl has argued, to claim to know the singular truth of God's words is to attribute God's will to oneself. It is for this reason, he observes, that a jurist or exegete must always disclose the personal or social assumptions informing his or her determinations regarding the Qur'anic text.[135] It is on the basis of such disclosure that one distinguishes between one's understanding of the text and the "truth" of the text, so that readers may be fully informed when they give credence to that understanding of the text.[136] To fail to make this disclosure is to engage in an act of textual "authoritarianism."[137]

As discussed in chapter 6, exegetes of feminist tafsir have argued that failing to distinguish between the Qur'an and its readers' interventions falsely implies that the human reader of the Qur'an has access to "a single, objectively verifiable meaning" from the text attributable to God.[138] Given the exegetes' use of this critique with regard to sexist interpretations of the

Qur'an, it is ironic that their works have sometimes been inclined toward the same tendencies. Ali asserts that the exegetes must be careful not to duplicate the absolutism of anti-women interpretations.[139] She warns: "Feminist exegetes must take care not to be as blinded by the commitment to equality . . . as classical exegetes were by their assumptions about the naturalness of male superiority."[140] When exegetes of feminist tafsir claim that their interpretive results are what the Qur'an actually "says" or really "intends," they risk making pronouncements that are just as authoritarian as those that they seek to combat.[141]

Despite these steps toward a greater consciousness of the active interpretive engagement necessary to the process of feminist interpretations of the Qur'an, scholars of feminist tafsir generally maintain the unquestioned premise of the liberating content of God's word, which awaits rediscovery and reclaiming. Since the Qur'an is the word of God, the Qur'an itself is just to women, and, according to the exegetes, their task is to uncover the egalitarian ethos of the Qur'an itself through alternative interpretation. Margot Badran's reflections on "Islamic feminism" are helpful in pointing to the entrenchment of truth claims about the Qur'an in this stance. Badran writes, "The key concepts of Islamic feminism are the Qur'anic principles of gender equality and social justice . . . Islam, through its scripture—the Qur'an as the word of God—introduced a message of fundamental equality of women and men."[142] However, with the historical progression of Islam, "the inherent contradiction between the revealed Word and patriarchy was obscured and Islam's call for gender equality and social justice was thwarted."[143] What is needed is "a realignment of Islam with the Qur'anic message of human equality and social justice," and change demands "returning Islam to itself (through the Book)."[144]

Raja Rhouni offers an incisive critique of these premises of the feminist exegetical project. For Rhouni, "The major flaw of Islamic feminism is its central assumption of recovering gender equality as a norm established by the Qur'an"; she observes that this inclination leads to "the tendency to put forward the project as essentially one of *retrieval,* retrieving the egalitarian truth of Islam," which is unjustified and assumed a priori.[145] Rhouni criticizes feminist exegetical efforts that "[seek], by any means, to retrieve gender equality as a norm *established* by the Qur'an, to the point of becoming a blinding dogma that weakens analytical rigor and produces mystifying narratives."[146] In line with Kecia Ali's criticism of the treatment of the Qur'an as a "repositor[y] of regulations," Rhouni calls for "a way out of essentialism" in the use of the Qur'an as a "repositor[y] of truths, from which we can 'retrieve' an egalitarian Islam."[147] Taking feminist tafsir to task for forced and inconsistent readings of the Qur'an, Rhouni writes:

> I do not agree with the methodology that chooses to give a more progressive, or egalitarian, meaning to a verse and presenting it as the truth, when it has the means to do so, while resorting to the idea that such and such verse needs to be contextualized in order to discover its contingency, when it reaches a semantic dead-end. To put it clearly, I disagree with the approach that reinterprets verses to invest them with a more modern and more egalitarian meaning, on the one hand, and that resorts to a historical and contextual reading when no progressive meaning can possibly be invented, on the other hand.[148]

Here Rhouni observes the problem in feminist Qur'anic exegesis of emphasizing "convenient" verses of the Qur'an that substantiate the notion of the Qur'an's egalitarian ethos and explaining away verses that are inconsistent with that position by citing the historicity of the Qur'an. This tendency is both methodologically inconsistent and obscurantist, ultimately undercutting the effectiveness of feminist exegesis and calling its soundness into question. It also reveals a manipulation of meaning to which not only conservative but also feminist readings are prone. Nasr Abu Zayd has also argued: "It is no longer sufficient to re-contextualize a passage or some passages when it is only needed to fight against literalism and fundamentalism or when it is needed to wave away certain historical practice that seems unfit in our modern context . . . These insufficient approaches produce either polemic or apologetic hermeneutics."[149] Employing the method of historical contextualization selectively thus results in capricious readings, leaving the Qur'an open to the manipulation of meaning by both feminists and their opponents.

According to Abu Zayd this problem in feminist exegetical approaches to the Qur'an occurs because "the Qur'an is dealt with as a text only" rather than as an interactive discourse between the Word and the reader; for him, "this means that the Quran is at the mercy of the ideology of its interpreter."[150] That is, as long as exegetes fail to think in new ways about the nature of the Qur'an's revelation, their methods will continue to engage in apologia and textual manipulation. In line with Abu Zayd's assessment,

Rhouni identifies the root of the problem with feminist exegetical approaches: "Rarely have these scholars engaged in rethinking the concept of the 'Word of God' itself, which . . . can allow scholars to deal with the Qur'an's androcentric discourse without apologies, or without mystification."[151] Rhouni suggests that feminist Qur'anic exegesis must reassess the nature of the Qur'an as God's speech and its revelatory relationship to human beings.

At the same time, it is important to examine the very real pragmatic concerns that have perhaps prevented feminist Qur'anic exegesis from taking such steps forward.[152] Suspected of participating in a project guided by foreign and imperialist notions of feminism, and of advocating a revamping of gender roles that are antithetical to Islam, Muslim women have relied heavily for their credibility and legitimacy on the argument that their calls for gender reform align with the foundational principles of Islam as grounded in the Qur'an itself. Rather than engaging in more radical new ways of viewing the Qur'an, Ali observes that those engaged in feminist rereadings generally remain focused on pragmatically expedient approaches to the Qur'an: "Often, they are attempting to sway public opinion or legislators by sticking as close to orthodoxy as they can or trying to convince audiences that a particular woman-friendly perspective *is* orthodoxy, just obscured by patriarchal cultural accretions. By strategic appeal to specific verses of the Qur'an and basic principles of fairness upon which many people can agree, they campaign for better laws."[153] However, Ali points out that in the process of doing pragmatically expedient scholarship to promote real-life change for Muslim women, advocates are often guilty of "mak[ing] ahistorical and superficial appeals to Islamic principles such as justice and equality."[154] They tend to resort—and for understandable reasons—to such claims rather than doing the more complicated work of confronting the problem of the Qur'an not always neatly aligning with their notions of justice and equality for women. The remainder of this book will consider what it might mean to undertake this more complicated work.

8

A Critical Reassessment

> *The process of establishing gender justice in Muslim society is neither simple nor straightforward. There is not one strategy, one method or one process. What works today may be unsuccessful tomorrow.*
> —AMINA WADUD, "What's Interpretation Got to Do With It: The Relationship Between Theory and Practice in Islamic Gender Reform"[1]

IN THE LAST chapter, I presented some initial conclusions about some of the conceptual problems and interpretive limitations and dilemmas in feminist exegesis of the Qur'an and ended by summarizing the criticisms of Raja Rhouni and Kecia Ali about some of the apologetic and absolutist tendencies within feminist Qur'anic interpretations. In revisiting those conclusions, I have been especially troubled by Rhouni's incisive criticism of feminist Qur'anic interpretation's tendency to treat "gender equality as a norm *established* by the Qur'an, to the point of becoming a blinding dogma."[2] In this chapter, I respond to Rhouni's admonition by reassessing the tenets of feminist Qur'anic interpretation from my perspective. Since, over the course of the decade I spent studying these works, I had come to share most of the perspectives at the core of feminist exegesis, the critical observations of Ali and Rhouni have challenged not only the works of the exegetes studied here but have also unseated many of my own views based on those works. Because the critical impact of Ali's and Rhouni's observations has dramatically affected my views, I depart from the form of the preceding chapters by speaking about feminist exegesis not only in the third person but also in the first person in this chapter.

In responding to Rhouni's criticism, I begin by admitting that when pursing the question of gender equality in the text of the Qur'an it is crucial to accept that one possible outcome of our work—though it may not be the one we hope for—is finding out that the Qur'an does *not* support gender equality the way we understand it. If we are to engage in this inquiry with honesty, we must be open to the possibility of an answer other than the one we desire. Otherwise, we are no longer asking an honest question, but rather beginning with an a priori answer that requires a retrospective explanation already bounded by the limits of that answer. We must be willing to face all possible answers, even the most painful and feared ones. In other words, we must be willing to be wrong about the hypothesis that the Qur'an supports our notion of gender equality.

In the interest of honest inquiry, even as we earnestly and faithfully attempt to find evidence of gender egalitarianism in the Qur'an, we must face our worst fears: What would it mean if we, as feminist, believing Muslims, eventually found that the text of the Qur'an *does* sanction gender hierarchy and male authority over women? What would happen if we were forced to concede that this is the case—would feminist exegesis of the Qur'an come to an end? What would that do to our relationship to the Qur'an? What would that do to our relationship to God? Could we go on as Muslims? Could we continue to be feminists? I argue that it is not pessimistic, but rather absolutely vital, for us to ask these questions of ourselves as believing Muslim feminists. They need not be questions following from dejection and defeat; they may also open us to new forms of faith and hope.

I will return to these most daunting questions after attempting an assessment of feminist arguments for gender equality in the Qur'an. My purposes in this chapter are to discuss how a methodological rigidity often detected in feminist tafsir has perhaps prevented it from questioning some of its foundational premises and to engage in a critical reassessment of those premises. The latter is an undertaking that leads me to make a difficult admission about feminist exegesis of the Qur'an: feminist exegetical conceptions of gender equality are historically specific to us and thus perhaps not in the end fully reconcilable with the Qur'anic text.

Feminist Methodological Rigidity

In reassessing many of the tenets of feminist tafsir, I am conscious of the seriousness of many of the claims I am making as well as the likelihood of resistance to my hypotheses among some Muslim feminists. One of the structural features of feminist exegesis of the Qur'an that may account for some of the resistance to major changes is its prescriptiveness. That prescriptiveness has constrained its development, at times causing it to exhibit an implicit intolerance for disagreement in the process of striving for authoritativeness, and often leads it to a position of deadlock.

Perhaps the basic modernist task of "taking back the Qur'an" is where the problem begins. In this endeavor, one claims not only that interpreters of the past got it wrong but also that one's own reading goes directly back to the source of meaning to set the record straight about what that source *really* says. To review some points made in chapter 7, one is struck immediately by statements of the kind made by Riffat Hassan that "postpatriarchal Islam is nothing other than Qur'anic Islam."[3] Here Hassan of course points to Muslim feminist thought's prioritization of the Qur'an over other Islamic sources, but her statement also relies on the presumption that her antipatriarchal assessments of the Qur'an are true to the Qur'an itself. This sentiment is perhaps strongest in the works of Barlas, who argues that sexist interpreters have read their biases "into" the text, implying her reading simply infers from what is actually in the text.[4] Hassan and Barlas share the company of Azizah al-Hibri and Amina Wadud in the common position that their readings point to the Qur'an's true egalitarianism.[5]

At first, such statements take on the appearance of opening the Qur'an to new meanings, but at second glance, they also reveal an implicit intolerance for contrary claims about the Qur'an. It is in observing this intolerant inclination that Kecia Ali warns feminists, "We must not arrogate to our own readings the same absolutist conviction we criticize in others."[6] In *Inside the Gender Jihad*, Wadud admits there are problems when claiming what the Qur'an "says." She takes responsibility for previously reducing the cause of Muslim women's subordination to "errors of interpretation," acknowledging that she had "inadvertently implied [she] actually had the power to express and possess the 'true' Islam."[7] She observes that "interpretations of Islam's primary sources, or even the very claim that what one is espousing *is* 'Islam'" can operate as a tool "to silence oppositional voices."[8]

This brings us to the problem of feminist tafsir's prescriptiveness. In assessing feminist thought on the whole, feminist legal theorist Janet Halley has observed that since feminist thought operates prescriptively and aims at becoming "normative," it is often the case that its proponents "want [their] theory to be total."[9] In other words, when one is deeply invested in equality and believes that one's way of thinking is the only route toward it, it is often excruciatingly difficult to question anchoring ideas; one fears that changing the foundations of one's thought will transport women back to a world where male domination remains unconquerable. This is to be expected; when an idea appears the only route to liberation, one will hold onto that idea at any cost. There is perhaps a parallel problem for Muslim feminists: because feminist tafsir often attempts to make normative statements about the true egalitarian core of the Qur'an, it is as if the Qur'an can only be unfailingly egalitarian and can never oppress women in its pure, uncorrupted interpretation or else the struggle for gender equality within Islam is defeated. For this reason perhaps, feminist exegesis has often been stubbornly resistant to considering other legitimate possibilities for the meanings of the Qur'an's pronouncements on gender relations.

One result of this rigidity is feminist tafsir's tendency to "deflect the logic of [its] ideas" to the extent that it has not traced its own "trajectories" to their logical end as a way to test their complete plausibility.[10] I attempt, in this critical reassessment of Muslim feminist exegesis, to perform this test—to point out where feminist tafsir's rationales lead when they are fully applied and taken to their limits. I attempt this exercise in order to confront whatever dead ends they may lead to, with the ultimate aim of opening new avenues in their place. Rather than fearing changes that lead to the undoing of fundamental tenets, we might find in the discovery of certain limitations an exciting impetus to transform.

Taking Interpretive Responsibility

As part of my reassessment, I would like to do what Kecia Ali prompts us to do at the end of *Sexual Ethics and Islam*: to take responsibility for our interpretive choices as feminist readers of the Qur'an. It may be true, as exegetes of feminist tafsir have argued, that the Qur'an accords with our sense of justice—despite centuries of interpretation that suggests otherwise—because it anticipates and accommodates evolving conceptions of justice in all times and places by being a divine and universal message. But, I argue that if this is true in our search for equality in the Qur'an, the onus is on us as Muslim feminist interpreters to defend and support such a claim while taking responsibility for prioritizing our contemporary sensibilities in the course of our interpretations. We must take responsibility for reading the Qur'an the way that we do; it is not the Qur'an's responsibility to support our desires for the text. Therefore, it is we—rather than the text—who must account for moments when the Qur'an does not seem to align with our notions of justice, and we must do so by routes other than apologia and textual manipulation. Instead of putting so much pressure on the text to say things that we wish it to say, we must relocate the intensity of our demands elsewhere: to an honest interrogation of our interpretive aims and objectives. When we seek "gender justice" from the Qur'an, what exactly do we want from the Qur'an and why? And how are our demands perhaps fundamentally different than what has been asked of the Qur'an before?

I have begun to see the increasing urgency of such self-examination and interpretive responsibility after paying closer attention to the criticisms made by some of the fiercest opponents (male and female) of feminist Qur'anic interpretation. These critics have repeatedly asserted that we have abandoned the principles of Qur'anic tafsir, we interpret the Qur'an in a manner in which it should never be interpreted, we lack *adab* (proper manners) with regard to the revered tradition of Qur'anic tafsir, and our readings are solely based on personal opinion. In short, they claim that we have left the Islamic tradition and distorted the meanings of the Qur'an and that is why our feminist readings are categorically incorrect. Our answer to these accusations has often been an insistence that our readings *are* correct because our exegetical methods *are* authentic to the Qur'an and the exegetical tradition; our critics' interpretations differ because *they* draw on the principles of tafsir selectively and distort the Qur'an by being guided by sexist prejudices. This response has placed us in a position of deadlock in relation to our critics.

However, after studying feminist interpretations of the Qur'an as well as the arguments of our opponents, I have come to the conclusion that our critics' continued abrasiveness to feminist interpretations of the Qur'an may not always be due to their sexist prejudices. I am willing to entertain the possibility that our critics *may be correct* in their assessment that feminist interpretation of the Qur'an makes false assertions and inappropriate demands of the text. But, I argue that if their assessment is correct, the reasons are more nuanced than they might think. It is my position that feminist interpretations may very well be inappropriate to the Qur'an and subvert the exegetical tradition—not because feminism is necessarily or categorically mistaken, immoral, foreign, or sullied in some other way—but because in placing feminist demands on the Qur'an, we have projected a historically specific (and at the same time theoretically unclear) sense of "gender justice" onto the text without fully considering how our demands might, in fact, be anachronistic and incommensurate with Qur'anic statements (and the exegetical tradition, which I discuss in chapter 9). This possible incommensurability with the Qur'an has not been readily apparent to exegetes of feminist tafsir in the past, in part, because the exact definitions and assumptions of "gender justice" have not been clearly articulated. This vagueness has kept us from seeing that the Qur'an might approach difference and sameness between the sexes distinctly from what many feminist readings have assumed about sexual difference and equality.

When scholars of feminist tafsir have come across portions of the Qur'anic text that have not easily yielded meanings in line with contemporary notions of gender equality, we often forget that our notions of equality are guided by historical values of our own that we bring to the text; we have perhaps become blind to the historicity of our feminist viewpoints in encountering those instances when the Qur'an does not easily conform to our understandings of gender egalitarianism. As a consequence, we have developed interpretive techniques and complex interpretive maneuvers to try to prove that, in spite of what the text appears to mean, the Qur'an somehow coheres with our notion of gender egalitarianism. This strategy is inadequate and at times disingenuous, as it obfuscates the inclinations of the Qur'an that may be irreparably nonegalitarian from our contemporary perspective. To put it bluntly, on some level our critics are correct: we have sometimes tried to make the Qur'an mean what we want it to mean, manipulating the text in our desire to derive textual support for our notions of justice.

I propose that scholars of feminist tafsir openly admit that it is our particular contemporary ideas about equality and justice that prompt us to see a dissonance between evidence for male-female mutuality and evidence for male-female hierarchy in the Qur'an—to admit that readings of the Qur'an that do not observe a dissonance between them or are unconcerned by them altogether are not necessarily defective readings of the Qur'an (often the claim has been that not reading hierarchy verses in cohesion with mutuality verses is to read the Qur'an atomistically). Indeed, as Ayesha Chaudhry has shown, many premodern interpreters who derived meanings of sexual hierarchy did not read the Qur'an atomistically but simply had a different view of the holistic message of the Quran.[11] The "dissonance" that registers with us between Qur'anic statements on mutuality and hierarchy is produced through our contemporary point of view; it is we who perceive their coexistence as contradictory, and it is we as feminist readers who desire to resolve the contradiction we observe. It is important to consider the possibility that in the Qur'an's revelatory context, however, the coexistence of mutuality and hierarchy verses may not have necessarily produced a dissonance. Thus, it is not true that only sexist interpreters have read their desires and specific views of (in)justice into the text;[12] scholars of feminist tafsir have also at times been guilty of a similar imposition of their views. What feminist tafsir might treat as an "ecumenical" definition of justice and injustice often turns out to be a very particular view of justice informed by contemporary feminist sensibilities.[13] Therefore, it is high time to own up to the historical particularity of our claims to feminist justice—as well as to what this means for our relationship with the Qur'anic text.

In view of the historical particularity of our feminist values, my position is that while the Qur'an takes remarkable steps toward equality as defined by our contemporary standards, it is still problematic enough by those standards so that the Qur'an perhaps cannot in the end be fully reconciled with our understandings of sexual equality and justice. I argue in this chapter that while the Qur'an makes numerous pronouncements that are indeed compatible with our contemporary understandings of sexual mutuality, reciprocity, kindness, female inclusion, and reverence for women, the Qur'an also endorses notions of male domination that ultimately make parts of the text incommensurate with our contemporary understandings of sexual equality and justice. The point here is not, as it has frequently been argued, that verses connoting male-female reciprocity and verses connoting male-female hierarchy are in tension with one another (a notion that has led scholars of feminist tafsir to argue for privileging reciprocal verses over hierarchical verses to substantiate the claim of the Qur'an's sexual equality) but that they are perhaps *not* in tension with each other—if we consider that there may be other understandings of the relationship between hierarchy and mutuality that inform the text of the Qur'an (a possibility I will discuss later). I offer this observation in the service of the larger argument: one significant reason why the Qur'an may not yield meanings that fully accord with our understanding of justice is that we are demanding a standard of sexual equality from the Qur'an that is specific to us and perhaps not reflected in the Qur'an.[14]

Recent works contain some recognition of the historical specificity of our demands for sexual equality but do not fully address it with the seriousness it deserves. Even as she continues to argue for the Qur'an's inherent egalitarianism, Asma Barlas, for example, has stated that she does not "believe that the Qur'an offers a *theory* of sexual equality. Theories of sexual/gender equality are pretty new . . . and I do not attempt to read one into the Qur'an."[15] However, she still insists that the Qur'an's antipatriarchal character allows for Muslims to develop such a theory "from its teachings."[16] A number of contributors to the volume *Gender and Equality in Muslim Family Law* (2013), an edited collection that builds upon the feminist exegetical works studied in this book, acknowledge the gap between the vision of justice they seek for women and notions of justice in the premodern contexts. However, they tend to reduce the gap to one of competing premodern and contemporary *interpretations* (rather than observing a gap between their interpretive views and the Qur'anic text itself), or, when they do notice that premodern concepts of justice are central to the *text*, they tend to fault the text's historical context without pursuing further what this might mean about the text itself.[17]

Before proceeding, it is important to make one small clarification in light of an explanation recently offered for the Qur'an's hierarchical treatment of the sexes: the hypothesis that the importance of equality between the sexes is not an inherent priority of the Qur'an[18] and that sexual equality is not a necessary component of justice in the Qur'an.[19] My assessment is slightly different: we should not be too quick to conclude that equality between men and women is not a value of the Qur'an, since such an assessment would be based on our standards of sexual equality. It may very well be that according to the premodern valuations of the Qur'an's revelatory context, what appears to us now as a lack of concern for equality may in fact be something quite different by the Qur'an's standards. Plenty of anthropological studies suggest that systems of equality, hierarchy, agency, and justice in other contexts reveal vast differences from our conceptions of them from twenty-first-century Muslim feminist perspectives. Variant understandings of equality should perhaps be the subject of future research, but my present concern is something else: from a contemporary perspective in the here and now, the Qur'an perhaps endorses a notion of sexual hierarchy as we define it today that is incompatible with sexual equality as we define it today.

I argue in this chapter that given the marked differences between the treatment of male-female relations in parts of the Qur'an and our notions of justice, no amount of interpretation can make the text definitively cohere with our contemporary sense of justice; claims to the contrary most often rely on anachronisms and textual manipulations. No interpretive technique can rule out the possibility that parts of the Qur'an may be guided by a very different view of sexual relations. We must admit that the Qur'an may not fully align with our contemporary calls for equality and justice, rather than engaging in apologetic maneuvers that aim at explaining away certain textual elements or in interpretive gymnastics that end up distorting the text. We are responsible for accounting for the possible gap between the text's notions of male-female relations and our notion of justice; the Qur'anic text is not responsible for closing this gap. Instead of trying to manipulate the text to cohere with our feminist demands, we must closely examine the logics that undergird our sense of justice and acknowledge their historical specificity; we must also revisit some of our foundational arguments about the Qur'anic text.

The Premise of No Gender Roles

In revisiting the many arguments upon which feminist exegetical work on the Qur'an has been based, certain claims about gender roles have seemed to me most in need of revision. Here I attempt to lay out how Wadud and Barlas, in whose works we find most of the discussions of gender that occur in feminist tafsir, have approached the question of gender roles in the Qur'an. I then explain my disagreement with their implication that the Qur'an does not prescribe gender roles.

Based on a critical approach to gender that treats it as an unstable social construction, both Wadud and Barlas hold that the Qur'an recognizes sexual differences between men and women but does not advocate specific gender roles for them.[20] For Wadud, this means that the Qur'an "does not attribute explicit characteristics to either one or the other, exclusively."[21] According to her, "the Qur'an does not propose or support a singular role or single definition of a set of roles, exclusively, for each gender,"[22] and it contains no "explicit Qur'anic prescriptions for dividing labour" between the sexes.[23] Likewise, Barlas claims that the Qur'an recognizes "sexual specificity" but does not define women or men in terms of attributes that are unique to them.[24] According to her, the Qur'an does not assign "gender symbolism;" nor does it "locate gender dimorphisms in sex."[25] Barlas goes so far as to claim that "the Qur'an does not even associate sex with gender, or with a specific division of labor" or "invest biological sex with content or meaning."[26] She writes, "Not a single verse . . . define[s] their roles as a function of their biology."[27] For example, she extols the Qur'an for never attributing motherly roles other than childbearing itself to women, noting that the Qur'an locates motherhood strictly "in the *womb*" and not in social performance.[28]

I agree that the Qur'an demonstrates remarkable restraint in assigning specific social roles and characteristics to men and women. However, the claim that the Qur'an never assigns any particular social roles to the sexes is not entirely defensible. The Qur'an does, in fact, assign some gender roles in certain instances—demonstrated through evidence provided by Wadud and Barlas even as they argue to the contrary. Perhaps the clearest case of the Qur'an's assignment of gender roles is found in their discussions of men's *qiwamah* in verse 4:34 (arguments similar to those of Hassan and al-Hibri as well).[29]

Barlas argues that the verse's statement on *qiwamah* "charg[es] men with maintaining women from their economic resources," in which they have been "preferred" (given more of than women).[30] Thus the verse assigns men who meet the financial requirements "the duty of being the breadwinner" of the family.[31] She asserts, however, that the breadwinning role does not make the man "head of the household."[32] Wadud has even more to say about *qiwamah*. For her, the verse lays out men's *qiwamah* as "an ideal obligation . . . to create a balanced and shared society."[33] As part of her overall rationale for understanding the verse, she points out that "woman's primary distinction is on the basis of her childbearing ability."[34] Childbearing is the only function in the Qur'an "exclusive to one gender,"[35] but the Qur'an does not treat it as women's primary or necessary function.[36] Therefore, women are not reduced to this biological function. Wadud goes on to explain verse 4:34's approach to balancing men's and women's responsibilities:

> For obvious biological reasons, a primary responsibility for the woman is childbearing . . . For simple balance and justice in creation, and to avoid oppression, [the male's] responsibility must be equally significant to the continuation of the human race. The Qur'an establishes his responsibility as *qiwamah*: seeing to it that the woman is not burdened with additional responsibilities which jeopardize that primary demanding responsibility that only she can fulfill.[37]

Wadud asserts that a man's compensatory role in relation to a childbearing woman is an ideal: "Ideally, *everything* she needs to fulfill her primary responsibility comfortably should be supplied in society, by the male: this means physical protection as well as material sustenance," though it can also be other things, such as moral or intellectual support.[38] Here Wadud demonstrates that *qiwamah* is an ideal social role or "responsibility" attached to men, though she argues that it is "neither biological nor inherent."[39] For her, the point of the verse is "balance"[40] between "equally significant responsibilities on the social-functional level,"[41] whose fulfillment yields "equitable recompense"[42] and "equitable compensation."[43]

However, if—as Barlas and Wadud point out—the Qur'an compensates women for their biological function as child-bearers by advising men to play some supportive role for them, then it is *not* in fact true that the Qur'an *never* associates sex with a specific division of labor. While it is useful to point out that men's *qiwamah* is rooted in social obligations and not in any moral or ontological superiority, we are still left with the plain fact of the Qur'an assigning a social role to men in the context of women's biological function in childbearing. If *qiwamah* is an assigned (or ideal) role for men as a balance to women's childbearing, we must admit that this role follows directly from a *biological difference* the Qur'an recognizes between men and women (i.e., the ability or inability to bear children).[44] There is no escaping that here the Qur'an is deliberately linking the social role of *qiwamah* to men and clearly associating it with men more than with women, even if not necessarily confining it to one sex. Since only women can bear children, men should support the family structure in some other way, if they are able. Regardless of whether this role provides balance and equity in the relationship or tips the balance in favor of male leadership in the family—that is, whatever the specifics of the *qiwamah* role are—there is no getting around the fact that in the most basic sense, here the Qur'an does in fact assign a gender role to men. That the details of this role are unstated and that its performance is conditional upon on a preferential designation (*tafdil*) by God and certain financial means does not in the end change the fact of the *gendered-ness* of the role's assignment. Moreover, the exegetes' discussions do not take into account that sex can never be so easily separated from gender, whether in the Qur'an or not; as discussed in chapter 9, even the recognition and assignment of biological distinctions between men and women is not innocent of social assumptions that frame the criteria by which one defines and attaches particular importance to certain biological differences while imagining those differences as stable. Thus, the Qur'an does in fact invest biology with content and meaning.

The Unresolved Problem of Different but Equal

The existence of the gendered role of *qiwamah* poses a direct challenge to the common Muslim feminist claim that men's and women's roles in the

Qur'an are "different but equal." Even if feminists interpret *qiwamah* as a supportive rather than authoritative role in providing for the family, various Muslim societies are free to decide what social values they assign to this role—creating a loophole for sexual inequality. Even though it is true that the Qur'an does not specify the details of *qiwamah* and does not appear to confine women's roles to childbearing, once the Qur'an assigns the role of *qiwamah* to men, women become vulnerable to how a society will attach social values to that role (however it may be defined). Depending on what value is attached to men's *qiwamah* in a given society, the result may very well be a power imbalance. Even if the Qur'an is mercifully advising the functional balance of different responsibilities between the sexes in the context of childbirth, social equality is only one of many possibilities the Qur'an leaves open for how to treat male-female difference in this verse. The social values attached to the difference between men and women declared in this verse are up to interpreters to decide, since the Qur'an advises the role but does not clarify its social meanings. While other interpreters might agree with Wadud, for instance, that men and women "have equally significant responsibilities on the social-functional level" because God will reward them equitably, the Qur'an does not spell out how God's reward relates to social equality.[45] It is Muslim communities who decide the social significance of men and women's different responsibilities. Wadud points out that "various social systems" have attributed "different values" to men's and women's roles on the "social-functional level."[46] In assigning the gendered role of *qiwamah* to men, here the Qur'an's statement on male-female *difference* is not necessarily a statement on male-female *equality*.

Another peculiar characteristic of some feminist interpretations of *qiwamah* is the argument that it is a responsibility for men rather than a privilege. This is implied in the work of Wadud and al-Hibri as discussed in chapter 4; at one point, al-Hibri explicitly refers to the role of *qiwamah* as one of "*taklif* (an obligation)" rather than "*tashrif* (privilege)."[47] Here it is instructive to refer to the arguments of Shaykh Abdallah Adhami, an Arab-American scholar with considerable popularity among U.S. Muslims today. Adhami also makes the claim about a man's *qiwamah* being a responsibility or service to his wife and family, and a review of his arguments aids us in dissecting the logic of the argument of *taklif* employed by some scholars of feminist tafsir. Though his views could hardly be described as feminist, Adhami is often admired by his female followers for his relatively fair-minded views on gender relations, likely due to his explicit position on the moral and ontological equality of men and women in the Qur'an. In order to explicate women's feminine "nature" in a manner that makes it appear coherent with the moral-ontological equality of men and women, Adhami emphasizes that women are neither inferior to men nor their servants. He stresses the tremendous importance of women in society and men's responsibility to them. For Adhami, women are strong and indispensable contributors to the family and society: they keep men upright and are an "anchoring presence" for men and the whole family.[48] For this reason, men rely on women, and women are key to preserving society.[49] Thus, he argues, women should be respected and appreciated, and Muslims should recognize their strength and significance.

In explaining his views of the nature of men and women outlined in verse 4:34, Adhami argues that while women are "guardians of the unseen" (men's personal needs), men are "guardians of the family."[50] In his view, according to the cosmic order implied by this verse and others, men are the "maintainers" of the family.[51] Here Adhami is careful to point out that man is the "pillar," not the head, of the family since he is *serving* the family by "holding up" the family; he is created "innately" to serve his family and society.[52] Adhami reminds us that both men and women are servants of God only; woman is not the servant of man.[53] He goes so far to state that women should question men's authority when they become domineering,[54] since men might do so if they forget their surrender to God or become overprotective of women.[55]

The problem with Adhami's argument is his use of euphemisms to obfuscate where exactly the "importance" of women lies: in upholding male authority in the family and community. Women's indispensable contribution to society is to support men's decision-making power over the family. Rebecca Groothuis has observed parallel arguments made by some conservative Christians: "Traditional male privilege and authority [is] spoken of as man's 'responsibility' to 'serve' . . . This makes it sound as though men are saddled with an onerous obligation, of which women are fortunately free. What is meant, however, is that men and not women have the exclusive right to decide and determine the direction of things."[56] Such reasoning mirrors Adhami's rationale. Even by encouraging respect for women's strength, and in representing men's role in the family as humble service rather than as domination (which women should protest), in the end his prescribed gender assignments are perhaps, to borrow from Groothuis, "*not* 'different but equal' functions," if "the male role entails having control over one's own life, as well as the lives of others. The female role entails placing the control of one's own life into the hands of another."⁵⁷ Here the idea that men and women are different but equally valuable members in the family is undercut by the effect of women's role in supporting men's leadership. Whether or not the male is called the "head" of the family, and even if men are warned against dominating their wives, and women are the servants of God rather than men, it remains that women's domain of influence is sequestered to that of the "unseen," while men's role is the management of the overall affairs of the family and community. Respect for women is likely respect for women's importance in maintaining male authority over their lives.

I refer to Adhami's approach to gender roles in order to demonstrate that even when one defines *qiwamah* as some exegetes of feminist tafsir would like—as a man's responsibility rather than privilege—the verse still may lend itself to an interpretation that creates a power imbalance between men and women. Such an interpretation would not only be plausible according to the text of the verse, but also—given social conventions among many contemporary Muslim communities—the most likely one today. My point is that even if the Qur'an's acknowledgment of male-female difference does not necessarily mean inequality, neither does it necessarily mean equality.

Admittedly, the portion of the verse we have discussed thus far does not preclude the possibility of an egalitarian interpretation. I am willing to entertain—for now at least—the argument that social inequality would result from this verse because of bad human interpretations or applications of the verse—in which case it could be argued that the text is not directly to blame for what it does or does not say. I revisit this issue again in the next section, where I demonstrate reasons why other indicators in this and other verses in the Qur'an make it increasingly difficult to rule out the text's acceptance of inequality as a legitimate organization of difference.

The Assumption that Mutuality Rules Out Hierarchy

One of the most important feminist exegetical arguments that requires revisiting is the notion that Qur'anic statements about mutuality between the sexes rule out the possibility of the Qur'an's endorsement of hierarchical relations between men and women. Feminist tafsir's understandings of equality are averse to any suggestion of hierarchical difference between the sexes, deeming it *shirk* (a violation of the oneness of God). Any sexual hierarchy is idolatrous because it assigns God-like authority to one class of human beings over another. Men and women have been created by God from a single source as moral equals, and the only real measure of difference between human beings is their *taqwa*—their devotion to God, which men and women are endowed with equal potential for and which can be judged by God only. Thus, treating one's sex as superior or in authority over the other is to take on a role that belongs to God only.

Scholars of feminist tafsir have argued that the mutuality of the sexes ordained by the Qur'an must translate into the social equality of the sexes, since inequality on the social level contradicts the moral and ontological equality and mutuality of the sexes. However, building on Kecia Ali's interrogation of the relationship between mutuality and hierarchy,[58] I will argue in this section that in the Qur'an's framework of male-female relations, mutuality between the sexes does not *necessarily* preclude or contradict hierarchical division between them. I will argue in the following section that social inequality does not *necessarily* violate the incomparability and oneness of God (i.e., social inequality does not necessarily constitute *shirk*). There is no necessary contradiction between these things, since within the framework of the Qur'an, it is possible that mutuality could exist in harmony alongside vertical divisions between the sexes, and that hierarchical division of the sexes need not mimic or compete with God's authority over human beings.

I offer evidence for the position that mutuality between the sexes may not necessarily contradict hierarchical division between them by briefly revisiting some of the verses that have been addressed by scholars of feminist tafsir, grouping them into two sets: First, those that suggest (by our contemporary standards) female inclusion; reverence for women; and mutuality, reciprocity, and kindness between the sexes. Second, verses that indicate (by our contemporary standards) male control or privilege over women. To avoid redundancy with the extensive discussion of feminist readings of the Qur'an in previous chapters, I will not offer here a comprehensive discussion of such verses but rather some brief references to illustrate the two Qur'anic tendencies I have identified. I use the illustration of these tendencies to support my argument that mutuality might possibly exist in harmony alongside hierarchical divisions between the sexes in the Qur'an.

Among the first set of verses (let us call them verses of "mutuality" to use shorthand) is 4:1, where we find evidence that human beings originate from the same creative source (*min nafsin wahidatin*);[59] God creates men and women from the same substance in the same manner, and thus they are created equally in this sense. In verse 30:21, we find evidence of reciprocity and mutuality between marital partners; here again, God creates mates for human beings from among themselves (*min anfusikum*) with love and mercy between them (*baynakum mawaddatan wa-rahmatan*). Verse 9:71 indicates that men and women have the same capacity for moral and pious action; male believers (*al-mu'minun*) and female believers (*al-mu'minat*) are protectors (*awliya'*) of one another, and both of them are identified as enjoining goodness, forbidding evil, praying, practicing charity, and obeying God and the Prophet. In verses 4:124, 40:40, and 3:195, believers are held to the same moral standard of righteousness for recompense in the hereafter whether they are male or female (*min dhakarin aw untha*); in both 4:124 and 40:40 they are assured entry into Paradise for good deeds regardless of their sex. Verse 9:72 features a similar assurance for the entry of both believing men (*al-mu'minin*) and women (*al-mu'minat*) into Paradise. Verses 81:8 and 16:58–59 feature condemnations of female infanticide. Verse 33:35 goes to extraordinary lengths to clarify that both men and women will be granted forgiveness and reward by God for their faith, devoutness, sincerity, patience, humility, charity, fasting, chastity, and worship; the verse accomplishes this by repeating masculine and feminine participle pairs ten times.

In describing the second set of verses (let us call them verses of hierarchy), I attempt to point to the most basic and literal indicators of male advantage and control in these verses by reading them as plainly as I possibly can and by leaving the meanings of contentious terms open-ended (while admitting, of course, that any translation is always inherently an interpretation). My aim is to point out that even within a variety of interpretations, there are certain basic indicators of male advantage and control that persist in these verses. To start, verse 2:222 instructs men to approach women in the manner willed by God (*fa-'tuhunna min haythu amarakumu Allahu*) after women have purified themselves following menstruation; verse 2:223 declares that wives (*nisa'ukum*) are something that men cultivate (*harthun la-kum*) and directs men to approach what they cultivate (*fa-'tu harthakum*) as they will (*anna shi'tum*). However verses 2:222–223 might be interpreted, it is clear at the very least, as Kecia Ali points out, that these verses discuss women "as matter to be acted-upon," not as "agents in their own right," even as this acting upon occurs "within the scope of divine regulation."[60] Verse 2:187 points to a certain kind of mutuality between men and women in its reference to men and women being each other's mutual garments (*hunna libasun la-kum wa-antum libasun la-hunna*); however, the verse addresses only men on how to lawfully approach their wives (*al-rafathu ila nisa'ikum*) for sexual activity. However we might interpret this verse, it remains, as Ali says, that the verse "presumes male initiation of sexual activity" in the absence of any parallel mention of women's activity in sex.[61] Verse 2:228 stipulates that something unspecified (the verse does not literally spell out what this thing is) is owed to women (*wa-la-hunna*) in an amount/in a manner similar to (*mithlu*) what is owed by them (*alladhi 'alayhinna*), according to what is customarily appropriate (*bi-l-ma'rufi*); however, men have (*wa-li-l-rijali*) a degree (*darajatun*) of that unspecified something over women (*'alayhinna*). Regardless of what the unspecified thing possessed by women and men in this verse is, the proportionate fairness of the something granted to women in this verse is accompanied by the lesser amount of that something which women are granted in comparison to men.

In verse 4:34, men are described as inhabiting some role of supportiveness or responsibility not spelled out in exact terms (*al-rijalu qawwamuna*) in relation to women (*'ala al-nisa'i*) that is linked in some way (*bi-ma*) to two things: how God exhibits a preference (*faddala Allahu*) of something unspecified toward some men (*ba'dahum*) over some others (*'ala ba'din*), and how men spend their wealth (*anfaqu min amwalihim*). The verse then identifies righteous women (*al-salihatu*) as those who are deferential (*qanitatun*) to something/someone unspecified, and who guard an unspecified thing that is unseen (*hafizatun li-l-ghaybi*) according to God's will (*bi-ma hafiza Allahu*). In relation to the role inhabited by men in this verse, men are given directions on how to treat their wives in the event of an unspecified disturbance related to their wives (*nushuzahunna*): men should provide an unspecified warning to their wives (*fa-'izuhunna*), depart from their wives (*wa-hjuruhunna*) in their beds (*fi al-madaji'i*), and strike them (*wa-dribuhunna*) in an unspecified manner. Finally, the verse commands that if the women defer to their husbands (*fa-in ata'nakum*), then the men should not engage in unspecified action against them (*fa-la tabghu 'alayhinna sabilan*). However anyone might interpret any part of this dense verse, and whatever it is exactly that men and women are being instructed to do in it, there is no way to get around the fact that women in this verse are always cast in one or more of the following roles: as *recipients* of something, as actors *in deference to* men or God, potential performers of something to be *curtailed* by men, or as people *acted upon* by men. In all cases, their roles involve some form of passivity (even in instances when they act). In contrast, men's roles in relation to women in this verse are clearly active roles; with respect to women, they are the *performers* of actions, not the recipients or objects of action. The only time they are acted upon is in relation to God (i.e., when God prefers some of them in some way or commands them to act or not act in some way).

Lastly, there is the matter of the Qur'an's conditional instruction for polygyny with up to four women (verse 4:3) and the allowance for men's sexual access to female slaves to whom they are not married (the term for these women is *milk al-yamin*, referred to as *ma malakat aymanukum/ aymanuhum* in verses 4:3, 4:24, 23:6, and 70:30). No matter how many historical and conditional limitations may be attached to the allowances for male sexual access to women in the interpretation of these verses to mitigate their scope and impact, there is no getting around the fact that these allowances exist in some form (no matter how limited) that is stubbornly asymmetrical in comparison to the treatment of women's sexual allowances. Whatever the historical explanation may be for the disparate treatment of men and women's sexuality in these verses, and whatever interest or benefit it may actually provide for women, it is men who are singled out in these verses' explicit allowances of active roles. In these verses, the allowances are exclusively for men to act upon women, and there are no parallel verses referring to allowances for women in active roles of sexuality. Even those who would argue that the intent of these allowances is to ensure the care of vulnerable women and that they have nothing to do with sex would have to explain why the care of women implied in these verses should necessitate sexual access to them.

Having illustrated examples of Qur'anic verses of mutuality and those of hierarchy, I contend that a crucial weakness in the arguments of Muslim women exegetes has been their insistence upon a tension between them that must be reconciled in favor of the tendencies of the mutuality verses. To examine this insistence at work, it is helpful to turn to some of the statements made by Asma Barlas and Amina Wadud about patriarchy. Barlas defines patriarchy as "a politics of sexual differentiation that privileges males"[62] and states that it denies women "agency and dignity."[63] For Wadud, patriarchy often functions as "a hegemonic presumption of dominance and superiority" over women; in patriarchal frameworks, woman may be "treated as an object" and "recipient" of decisions in which she does not take part.[64] Here we observe that Wadud and Barlas identify patriarchy with characteristics that are common to hierarchy verses: male privilege and dominance, impingement upon women's agency, and the treatment of woman as an object and recipient. Though these are precisely the characteristics of the Qur'an's hierarchy verses, both Barlas and Wadud claim that patriarchy is at odds with the Qur'an. Barlas argues that patriarchy "[does] not originate" in the Qur'an and has "been read into the text."[65] Wadud regards patriarchy as *shirk* and thus antithetical to the overarching ideals of the Qur'an,[66] claiming that "egalitarian notions of family" are "more commensurate with the Qur'anic social and moral ideals."[67]

To maintain their insistence that Qur'anic ideals are antithetical to patriarchy Barlas and Wadud try to resolve—what appears to them as—the contradiction between those ideals and the apparent meaning of certain verses.[68] Barlas attempts to minimize the Qur'an's tendencies toward male control. For her, verse 2:223's instruction to men to "go into their wives" functions as a limitation on how men approach their wives sexually, rather than an as endorsement of unchecked sexual access.[69] She argues that verse 2:222 does not employ the word *harth* as a metaphor for women's bodies to mean property but rather to connote "the cultivation of love and mercy, since these themes are central to its teachings on marriage and male-female relationships."[70] (Note that neither explanation totally eliminates the verse's implication of woman as something to be acted upon.) She justifies these readings with the claim that interpretations suggesting male control and nonconsensual sex in marriage are "incongruent with the emphasis in the Qur'an on equality and mutuality."[71] Even though Barlas admits that "the idea of consensual sex in marriage" is only a recent value, she claims that disregarding a woman's will would not allow adherence to the Qur'an's values of marital kindness.[72]

In *Inside the Gender Jihad*, Wadud chooses a different route. She admits to the "imbalanced expression of human sexuality in terms most specific to masculine, heterosexual dominance" within verse 4:3 on polygyny; verse 2:223 on women as men's *harth*; and verses 52:20, 55:72, and 56:22 on the *hur al-'ayn* as a reward for men in the afterlife.[73] She admits that "no equivalent articulations exist in the Qur'an about women's sexual satisfaction."[74] She refers to the problems in these verses as "glitches" and argues that they exist in the Qur'an as a response to the specific context of social relations in the Prophet's society.[75] Wadud reconciles these verses by claiming that the "substance of the Qur'an cannot be constrained by its particular utterances," implying that they should no longer be read literally.[76] She also sees 4:34 as a "recognition" but not an "edict" of "unequal power dynamics of masculine and feminine sexuality" in which "women must yield sexually" to men.[77]

Barlas's and Wadud's approaches to the problem of *daraba* in 4:34 follow similar patterns. For Barlas, interpreting 4:34 as "license to batter wives, or to compel obedience upon them, is not acceptable," and it "contradicts the Qur'an's view of sexual equality and its teaching that marriages should be based in love, forgiveness, harmony, and *sukun*."[78] Barlas suggests that *daraba* could merely be a symbolic rather than punitive gesture.[79] (Note here that she does not address the issue of what this symbolism might imply about male control over women.) As for Wadud, who pronounces the famous "no" in response to 4:34, she holds that "any kind of strike . . . violates other principles of the text itself—most notably 'justice' and human dignity, as Allah has led humankind to understand today."[80] For her, the *daraba* portion of the verse cannot be interpreted prescriptively in line with the Qur'an's other principles.

In these discussions, Barlas and Wadud view mutuality as an overarching value of the Qur'an, and they use this value to justify mitigated or nonliteral readings of hierarchy verses, treating mutuality and hierarchy as contradictory.[81] They argue that literal readings of the hierarchy verses ignore the mutuality verses and thus treat the Qur'an nonholistically. Wadud therefore advocates using "liberative and egalitarian references" in the Qur'an "to free the text from the potential snares in some of its own particular utterances."[82] I disagree with this methodological approach; in contrast to Barlas and Wadud, I hold patriarchal characteristics to be central to many of the Qur'an's hierarchy verses, and I am not convinced that literal readings of hierarchy verses necessarily conflict with the Qur'an's mutuality pronouncements, considering that their meanings may not have been at odds with one another in the Qur'an's revelatory context. There is perhaps no tension to resolve between the two sets of verses, since I do not find any definitive reason to assume that male control over women in the Qur'an would conflict with its values of kindness and mutuality between men and women. In the premodern context of the Qur'an's revelation, equality may not have been understood as a premise of loving, caring relationships; relationships of male-female dominance may not have necessarily offended ideals of mercy and tranquility. Classical and premodern views of love and sexuality exhibited a range of attitudes on the relationship between mutuality and hierarchy, including ones that saw possession, passivity, and submission as natural to loving relationships.[83] We cannot assume that in the context in which the Qur'an was revealed, for instance, that authority over another person's body would have ruled out kindness. Perhaps according to the premodern social and sexual norms of the Qur'an's historical context (according to which, as Kecia Ali points out, sexual consent was not a precondition for sexual licitness), being the guardians of women's bodies would not necessarily be an affront to women's dignity or overall worth. Love and mutuality may not have necessarily contradicted notions of female passivity and lack of sexual consent. To the contrary, both men and women might have seen patriarchal norms as fitting and even comforting, nurturing, and supportive of what they agreed was women's more passive nature; they may have seen honor and protection in those norms. It could be that in the context of the Qur'an, "patriarchy is not bigotry, hatred, or oppression, but rather the natural social order."[84] As Barlas observes, not all people "view patriarchy itself as a manifest case of *Zulm*."[85] Indeed, Ayesha Chaudhry has rigorously demonstrated with regard to the premodern interpretive tradition that notions of protective patriarchy were often not at all averse to the physical disciplining of wives.[86]

Feminist readers in the twenty-first century may find this preposterous, but according to premodern sexual mores that the Qur'an might reflect (being framed in the terms of a seventh-century Arabian context, as the exegetes have emphasized repeatedly), there may not be a necessary contradiction between the mutuality of men and women and the notion that husbands are "guardians over their wives," as has been presumed by most scholars of feminist tafsir.[87] In contrast to our perspectives, perhaps there was no contradiction between the equality of men and women in their creation, moral capacity, and moral recompense, on the one hand, and male privilege, authority, and control and female disciplining, on the other. To assume a *necessary* contradiction is to project our values onto the Qur'an in a manner that is anachronistic and not fully justifiable. For this reason, I do not agree with statements to the effect that "the answer to patriarchy" is "reciprocity," as there is no clear reason to treat one as clearly separate from the other, as at odds with one another, or as a replacement for the other in the framework of the Qur'an.[88] I disagree with the argument that the Qur'an's "framework of mutual love and recognition . . . presupposes the absence of hierarchies and inequalities."[89]

Here it is of course worth noting that there is a colorful history of women in the Prophet's time, particularly Medinan women and the outspoken female companions of the Prophet, who demanded the Prophet's recognition of their needs and desires, including sexual ones; it has even been suggested by many exegetes that the Qur'an responded to their outspoken demands in some cases.[90] However, their very protest indicates the prevalence of a set of social values and sexual norms which granted men authority over women, and it seems that these are the conventions to which the Qur'an may be immediately responding. Coming across no definitive evidence to the contrary, we cannot assume that male control is antithetical to the Qur'an's ideals of male-female mutuality. Therefore, we cannot mitigate or explain away verses of hierarchy in the Qur'an; their meanings remain in place.

At this point, I would like to revisit the issue raised at the end of the last section on the problem of "different but equal" with regard to *qiwamah*. I do this by pointing to an interesting shift in one of Wadud's positions on verse 4:34. Here I point not to her well-known shift in interpreting *daraba* but her shift on the term *qiwamah*, which is found buried deep within her discussion of HIV/AIDS in *Inside the Gender Jihad*. As noted in the previous section, Wadud referred to 4:34's pronouncement on *qiwamah* (men's support for women) as a prescriptive or ideal statement in *Qur'an and Woman*. However, in *Inside the Gender Jihad*, she refers to 4:34's statement on *qiwamah* as "a recognition of the unequal power dynamics of masculine and feminine sexuality"; the word *qawwam* "is stated in the form of an active participle recognizing agency and being. A man may fulfill *qiwamah*. Therefore women must yield sexually to this *Qa'im* (responsible male)."[91] We might infer that Wadud sees this as another instance in which the Qur'an's language assumes the historical context of marriages of subjugation. Here we find that Wadud's new position on *qiwamah* now lines up consistently with her new position on *daraba*. In other words, her approach to the first half of verse 4:34 now becomes consistent with her approach to the second half of that verse. As a result, we find an implicit admission that *qiwamah* is perhaps best understood in line with the hierarchical elements of the second half of the same verse (where *daraba* is found) that assume male agency and control (rather than simply responsibility). The question at the end of our discussion of "different but equal" about the possibility of an egalitarian interpretation of *qiwamah* is now implicitly answered by Wadud's admission: interpretations of *qiwamah* guided by social values that attribute power and authority to men find support in the hierarchical tendencies of the verse itself.

The Loophole of God-Centered Hierarchy

Having argued that male-female mutuality in the Qur'an might reside congruently with male-female hierarchy in the Qur'an, I address another prominent feminist argument about men and women in the Qur'an:

horizontal reciprocity between the sexes based on tawhid, the unicity of Allah. Here I propose that social inequality does not *necessarily* violate the incomparability and oneness of God, since hierarchical division of the sexes *need not* mimic or compete with God's authority over human beings. The model of sexual equality that has most prominently guided Muslim feminist interpretations of the Qur'an thus far is one of sexual difference reconciled through horizontal reciprocity. Wadud has famously argued that the only possible relation of verticality within the relationship between God, men, and women is the one between God and humans. Wadud concludes that the relationship between men and women, both vertically positioned under God, can then only be horizontal. Barlas also insists that "in the Qur'an, 'difference differentiates laterally' not hierarchically."[92]

Before pointing out areas of potential weakness I find in this argument, it is perhaps best to quote Wadud to describe her understanding of horizontal reciprocity between the sexes. She argues that "each and every human-to-human relation can be represented as a triad formed with Allah as a supranatural component;" in it "each two persons are sustained on the horizontal axis because the highest moral point is always occupied metaphysically by Allah."[93] She reasons that both persons "are of equal significance and neither can be above the other because the divine function establishes their reciprocal relationship."[94] She adds that the "horizontal plane is mutually cooperative because the role of the one can be exchanged with the role of the other with no loss of integrity."[95] *Taqwa*, or God-consciousness, is key to this arrangement: "The continual awareness and active reflection of Allah's presence ... creates a means for understanding that there can only be parity on a horizontal basis between any two persons or any two collectives"; verticality "can appear only if Allah is absent from the formula."[96]

If my understanding of this triad model is correct, I argue that this model lacks a total explanation of how man and woman are fully horizontally equivalent under God at the same time that they each have a *distinct* vertical relation to God. After all, if God's relation to men and God's relation to women were identical to each other, then the model would not need in the first place to bifurcate the relation between God and human beings into two separate vertical relations. But the fact that the model is in fact a triad and not a dyad with a single vertical line suggests there is something irreducibly different about each vertical relation to God. In addition, the fact that both men and women are both positioned vertically lower than God does not guarantee that they both exist at exactly the same level below God. The concept of tawhid, of course, necessitates that God is greater than both men and women. However, this concept on its own does not necessarily indicate anything further about men and women in relationship to one another in the triad model. Difference need not mean inequality, but neither must two entities that are both positioned below God be therefore equal to one another. Wadud's tawhid argument may tell us where God's position in the triad is, and that men and women are both positioned at coordinates that are below God, but it does not definitively tell us man and woman's coordinates in relation to one another on the triad. I remain open to some other theological reasoning against male-female inequality (and I, in fact, discuss stronger theological arguments later in the chapter), but the triad model alone does not suffice. I would hypothesize that this "loophole" is perhaps one of many reasons why centuries of Qur'anic interpreters did not view male-female hierarchy as a violation of tawhid.[97]

In fact, as the work of both Ayesha Chaudhry and Karen Bauer (among others) has shown, premodern exegetes (with some exceptions) overwhelmingly operated under the common presumption of what Chaudhry calls "a God-centered social hierarchy" whereby God's authority over women is mediated through men's authority over women; the exegetes commonly presumed that God "privileged and 'preferred' husbands over wives."[98] The predominance of this idea is evidence that according to premodern conceptions, men's authority over women is often seen as ordained by God. Premodern exegetes do not appear to think that men's God-granted authority resembles God's authority over human beings. The historical record also shows that Muslim understandings of leadership often presumed that "authority and power are a trust from God and not a sign of human sovereignty."[99] That is, there is a distinction between men's authority and God's authority, and men who stand in authority over women do not necessarily view themselves as sharing in *God's* authority over women. The authority of God and the authority of men are two different kinds: divine and human respectively. It is possible that the Qur'anic text might reflect this sort of premodern understanding of a "God-centered hierarchy," in which male authority is distinct from God's authority. If this is true, then the Qur'an would appear to perhaps support sexual hierarchy—unless there are different arguments that can persuade us otherwise (I discuss this possibility further).

The Last Resort of Moral-Ontological Equality

Having posited the possible presence of male-female hierarchy concomitant with male-female mutuality in the Qur'an, it is helpful to state clearly the ramifications of this for the possibility of equality between men and women in the Qur'an. Since we cannot rule out male-female hierarchy in the Qur'an, we must concede that perhaps the Qur'an tolerates it or even endorses or prescribes it. However, since mutuality can coexist with hierarchy according to certain value systems, even with the possibility of male-female hierarchy in the Qur'an, we may still lay claim to male-female mutuality in the Qur'an. Even so, since male-female *equality* cannot logically coexist with male-female hierarchy (from our contemporary perspective), we can perhaps no longer lay claim to full equality between the sexes in the Qur'an.

At this point some may argue—as a last resort to preserve the claim of the Qur'an's sexual equality—that what we have discovered is only a possible *functional* inequality between the sexes in the Qur'an rather than an ontological inequality (an inequality of being), and that the latter is far more important than the former. It is certainly true that feminist work on the Qur'an has produced some powerful arguments for the moral-ontological equality of the sexes. I briefly review two of them here before explaining their flaws. First, there is the argument for the equality of men and women in creation, moral capacity, responsibility, and recompense. According to this argument, women and men are created by God from the same substance (*nafs*) at the same time, and neither man nor woman has any essential quality of *being human* that the other does not have. Both man and woman are created with the same *fitrah* (moral capacity) and will be judged by God according to the same moral standards; neither man nor woman is responsible for the other's moral or spiritual condition.

Second, there is the *taqwa* argument, which is a better argument for tawhid-based equality than the horizontal reciprocity argument discussed earlier. All people are the same in the sight of God in every way except with regard to their differing levels of *taqwa*. As Wadud states, we as humans "might attribute greater or less value to another on the basis of gender, wealth, nationality, religion or race, but from Allah's perspective those do not form a valuable basis for distinction between individuals (or groups)—and His is the true perspective."[100] Thus levels of *taqwa* constitute the only real difference between human beings, and that difference can be assessed by God only (as it is "not accessible for external human judgment"[101]), which means that the assessment of one person's superiority over another can be performed by none other than God. To attempt such an assessment, including to engage in *istikbar* ("thinking of oneself as better than another"[102]), is to take on a role that belongs to God and thus attribute a God-like authority to oneself, which constitutes *shirk* (a denial of God's oneness). In the end, notions of male superiority are tantamount to *shirk*.

Both of these arguments for the moral-ontological equality of men and women are quite effective. However, one stubborn challenge to the notion of the ontological equality of the sexes remains: the possibility that in some cases the functional inequality of men and women in the Qur'an perhaps cannot exist *except as an effect of ontological inequality*. Granted, there could certainly be instances in which functional inequality in the Qur'an is unrelated to the question of ontological equality. These would be cases in which functional inequality is neither permanent nor essential to one's being. For example, an unequal function or role that is "limited in scope or duration" (temporary) can exist alongside equality in being.[103] Functional inequality can also coexist with equality in being when the given function or role has no relationship to one's inherent being or essence. However, in cases where the function is of "permanent duration" or based on a permanent feature of one's being, functional inequality is necessarily linked to inequality in being.[104] This is because in such a case, the function is not just a role, since it becomes tied to the person's being.[105] The role "designates not merely what [one] does (or doesn't do) but what one is."[106] Thus, when function is related to being, functional inequality will be necessarily rooted in ontological inequality. When we look closely at the Qur'an, we find some instances in which a man or woman's role is directly related to his or her being. As previously discussed, *qiwamah* and roles of sexual control are attached exclusively to men; in these cases male control appears to be a function related to being a man. The receipt of *qiwamah* and sexual passivity are attached exclusively to women; female passivity appears to be a function related to being a woman. When functional inequalities are assigned based on being a man or woman, they are rooted in a permanent difference of being. If, according to our contemporary standards of justice, the Qur'an may sometimes outline functional inequalities related to being, then we must concede that ontological inequalities might also come with them. This relationship of functional inequality to ontological inequality poses a formidable challenge to arguments for the ontological equality of men and women.

"Beyond" the Qur'anic Text

It is important to clarify that in calling for us to be honest about the Qur'anic text, I do not "surrender" the Qur'an to patriarchy and sexism. I do not seek to replace a view of the egalitarian "core" of the Qu'ran with a view of the gender-hierarchical "core" of the Qur'an. Rather, I present what I feel to be a more forthright view of the possible existence of *both* kinds of impulses within the Qur'an—whose coexistence is not to be explained away through our forcible readings of the Qur'an. Admitting that the Qur'anic text supplies *some* meanings that are perhaps irreconcilably sexist from our perspective is *not* the same as saying that the text is *entirely* sexist from our point of view. The reciprocal resonances of the text, even when they are complicated for us by its hierarchical resonances, still remain. They do not disappear into thin air because of those hierarchical meanings. This would be the case only if we were so arrogant and intolerant as to attach universality to our views of justice (in which hierarchy and mutuality are contradictory) and that anything different is wholly without meaning. There are still plenty of good arguments to be made about the Qur'an's indications of dignity, respect, and care for women—but we can no longer make those arguments as definitively as we once did. We can certainly point to the Qur'an's tremendous advancements for women relative to its time (as many have before us), but we must do so *without* drawing the anachronistic conclusion that those advancements can ground contemporary feminist advocacy and fully support our particular understandings of equality and justice.

In this chapter I have attempted an honest inquiry into the question of what undergirds our commitments to justice, pursuing answers other than the simplistic assertion that Muslim feminists stand on the enlightened side of justice. I have pursued this inquiry in part because of my fear that we have been so tied to our attachments to feminist justice that we have been unable to see the historicity and particularity of our positions and have thus produced anachronistic readings of the Qur'an. In pursuing the questions posed in this chapter, I have posited that what we seek as proponents of a particular conception of equality and justice is perhaps not reconcilable with the text of the Qur'an. Once we have historicized our feminist values and admitted to the possible lack of full commensurability between our notions of equality and pronouncements about men and women in the Qur'an, we must confront the full implications of this admission: it necessitates that feminist positions can no longer be based conclusively on the Qur'anic text itself. We recognize that the Qur'an's pronouncements are not wholly oppressive, but that they are problematic enough so that we cannot claim with certainty that its framework of justice is fully the same as our own. We must face the fact that we have reached the end of this strand of feminist interpretation of the Qur'an.

We can be thankful for the boon of Qur'anic verses connoting male-female reciprocity and female dignity. However, their existence in the Qur'an cannot erase the hierarchical resonances of the text for us. Though feminist tafsir has often claimed with certainty that statements on male-female hierarchy in the Qur'an do not reflect the values of the text, I argue that the only thing we can be fully certain of is that *we* prioritize the Qur'an's statements on male-female mutuality; we cannot be certain that the text prioritizes them. We can be sure only of what we do and what our values are as feminist interpreters. It is *we* as feminist interpreters who have upheld our readings. As Wadud puts is, in the project of feminist tafsir *"we are the makers of textual meaning."*[107] To continue its work, we must take full ownership of our interpretive intervention, and we will require new ways of relating to the Qur'an that reflect our authority to privilege certain values but also allow us to maintain the divinity of the text.

I call for us to demand a standard of justice that is limited neither by complete reliance on the Qur'anic text to "say" things for us nor by a relationship to it that grants its words unassailable authority in any straightforward sense. We will need to pursue a vision of the Qur'an as a divine text that allows us to imagine justice outside the text's limited pronouncements. I propose this not as an act of irreverence but rather as an act of faith that upholds the divine guidance of the Qur'an while acknowledging the Qur'an's framing within the time of its revelation. It is a position that is by no means new, following from the well-tread path of early theological debates about the createdness of the Qur'an among some of the most reputed scholars of Islamic tradition.

In the introduction, I argued that much of feminist tafsir has been propelled by the urgency of enacting real change in the lives of Muslim women. The field's prescriptive tendencies and pragmatic pressures have caused exegetes of feminist tafsir to subscribe to the notion of the primacy of the Qur'anic text in an attempt to ground their calls for justice in an authentically Islamic framework. In the process, it has had to wield tremendous—indeed, as we see in some cases, unbearable—pressure on the Qur'an to yield feminist meanings. In doing so, feminist tafsir has often distorted the text, claiming that the Qur'an says something that it perhaps does not actually say in any definitive sense and also frequently claiming that the Qur'an does not say what it possibly does. Chapter 7 pointed out that such inclinations make the readings prone to apologia and intolerance for other points of view. (It is also worth noting the added drawback that these tendencies make feminist tafsir even less credible to those who do not share its values; opponents of feminist tafsir have often criticized it exactly for these tendencies.) But here I would like to emphasize the most counterproductive outcome of these tendencies: the reinforcement of a form of Qur'anic authority that ultimately renders us passive readers of the text. As Raja Rhounu has argued, in laying claim to the "true" meanings of the Qur'an, feminist readings are "reinforcing the authenticity discourse by espousing its very logic," that is, partaking in the discourse through which one clamors for the authority of one's position by claiming that it echoes the Qur'an's own unquestionable position.[108] As Kecia Ali notes, these readings "inadvertently shore up the authority of certain texts or discourses."[109] The reinforcement of this kind of authority is detrimental not only because the Qur'an cannot fully support our claims to justice, and not only because it places us in deadlock with sexist readers who make the same claim to the "truth" of the Qur'an, but also because it diminishes *our* authority as readers to call for forms of justice beyond the pronouncements of the Qur'an.

As Ghazala Anwar has keenly observed, feminist tafsir has already incorporated notions of justice beyond the Qur'an's pronouncements even if its exegetes have not admitted to doing so. She notes that the exegetes have often sought "a vision of justice nourished by some verses of the Qur'an" and used it "to judge other verses which seem to shatter this vision of justice."[110] In noticing this, Anwar asserts that such an interpretive device is actually "*extra-Qur'anic* to the extent that it takes some verses as the standard to which the interpretation of other verses must adhere."[111] That is, one takes cues from outside the Qur'an in order to read the Qur'an in this manner.

Some readers of this book are likely to claim that I am reducing the Qur'an to its historically contingent elements and ignoring the Qur'an's universal principles, disregarding its overall trajectory toward forms of justice meant to be realized beyond the seventh-century context of the Qur'an's revelation. However, if the problem were simply one of historically contingent elements, it would not be nearly as serious as what I observe. There is no universal conception of equality indisputably reconcilable with ours to be distilled from the Qur'an, even after "clearing away" the historical specificities that are part of the text. The historical specificities are precisely what encode the Qur'an's principles of mutuality. As Kecia Ali has pointed out, these historical elements cannot be treated purely as description.[112] On some level they also may function as prescriptions if they embed into the text certain principles and assumptions about male-female relations that prefigure and thus structure whatever principles of mutuality we can draw out of the text. Those assumptions cannot be removed without denying the content of the text altogether.

Here it is important to address the "trajectory" argument commonly offered by scholars of feminist tafsir (discussed in chapter 5), which holds that the Qur'an signals a trajectory of social justice to it readers, "pointing us to higher moral practices even if not fully articulating these because of the context."[113] The trajectory argument functions similarly to two other arguments discussed as part of the feminist historical contextualization method studied in chapter 4. One is to argue that the Qur'an describes models of male control found in seventh-century marriages of subjugation, but that it does not prescribe them as models to be emulated.[114] The other is that the Qur'an's particular (*khass*) verses and even some of its general (*'amm*) verses are not meant for universal application.[115] All three arguments attempt to explain hierarchical pronouncements in the Qur'an by chalking them up to the Qur'an's need to communicate in the terms of its immediate historical context. One problem with such a justification is that at some point in history, one's conception of justice may be so far removed from the context addressed by the Qur'an that, in Wadud's words, it will begin to "[state] something unmeaningful" for us in the present.[116] Enough of the Qur'an's pronouncements connote male-female hierarchy that, if we were to follow the logic of the trajectory argument to claim that we have to move beyond the Qur'an in order to follow the Qur'an's trajectory, we will end up having to move "beyond" numerous portions of the text. As Ali notes, "one cannot argue for moving 'beyond' [the text] without being caught in a major contradiction."[117] Once this happens, we can no longer readily base our claims to equality directly on the Qur'anic text, as they are rooted in a conception of justice that does not derive direct support from the Qur'an.

Here I want to emphasize that in moving beyond the historical elements of the Qur'anic text, one is not just leaving behind something but also moving toward something else. In making the trajectory argument, one is making a claim based either upon faith or upon something other than the Qur'an. In any case, the justice of the "beyond" does not derive directly from the Quranic text. In order for the project of feminist tafsir to continue productively, we must openly admit that we are guided by conceptions of justice not definitively traceable to the Qur'anic text.[118] The demand for feminist justice is ours.

Instead of being defeated by these admissions, I argue that they can help us forge new beginnings and develop better feminist approaches to the Qur'an. New possibilities emerge when we depart from straightforward notions of the unassailable authority of the text and hold up the authority of our visions of justice. Like Raja Rouni, I posit that there are ways to pursue this route while also maintaining the belief in the divine revelation of the Qur'an if we are able to rethink the nature of God's speech in the Qur'an. Thinking in new ways about the nature of the Qur'an's revelation and our relationship to it can provide a viable route for reading the Qur'an as both feminists and Muslims who believe in the Qur'an's divinity. In proceeding in this manner, we are honest about the Qur'an without giving up on our feminist commitments or our faith, and we become free to think in new ways about the text.

Some of Amina Wadud's later work has taken initial steps toward a new treatment of the concept of the Qur'an's revelation. As discussed in chapter 6, Wadud articulates the position that because of the limitations of human language, the message of the Qur'an cannot be understood as the exact or total expression of God's will. The linguistic content of the Qur'an is imprinted with the norms of the historical context in which it was revealed, and human language is incapable of capturing the fullness of divine meaning.[119] Therefore, God cannot be equated with the Qur'an.[120] One drawback in Wadud's use of this approach, however, is her treatment of Qur'anic utterances as pointing to a trajectory beyond the speech of the Qur'an, without acknowledging that this trajectory must remove us from the Quran in certain ways. Raja Rhouni has also critiqued Wadud's saying "no" to 4:34 for the way she continues to attach normativity to the rest of the Qur'anic text instead of treating all the other parts of the Qur'an she examines as also delivered in a historically contingent manner.[121] However, Wadud's distinction between Qur'anic speech and God's revelation is still an important start toward rethinking the Qur'an in ways that offer new opportunities for feminist tafsir.

Nasr Abu Zayd's approach to the Qur'an as a "discourse" instead of a text offers another helpful avenue. Abu Zayd has famously argued that the Qur'an should be understood as a dialogue between itself and its addressees; as the living discourse of God's word, the Qur'an has a central human dimension. According to Abu Zayd, the Qur'an is a revelation that interacts with human comprehension to yield human understanding, and thus, its audience contributes to the text's meaning. The Qur'an is not delivered upon humanity but rather to humanity, in conjunction with its needs and understandings. He writes, "the Qur'an we read and interpret is by no means identical with the eternal word of God."[122] Therefore, "if we elevate historical aspects of the Qur'an to divine status, we violate the word of God."[123] For Abu Zayd, to do so is to "lock God's Word in time and space. We limit the meaning of the Qur'an to a specific time in history."[124] Abu Zayd's approach to the Qur'an as discourse, then, offers feminist tafsir a way to rethink the nature of divine meaning.[125] The leads provided by Wadud and Abu Zayd allow feminist tafsir to pursue a new future in which we approach the Qur'an both honestly and faithfully.

9
Confronting Feminist Edges

As to those to whom to work hard, to begin again and again, to attempt and be mistaken, to go back and rework everything from top to bottom, and still find reason to hesitate from one step to the next—as to those, in short, for whom to work in the midst of uncertainty and apprehension is tantamount to failure, all I can say is that clearly we are not from the same planet.
—MICHEL FOUCAULT, The History of Sexuality[1]

The wall of impossibility is an invitation to enter, not a prohibition against critical thought. Its impasses become passages, its aporias become porous.
—CATHERINE KELLER, "The Apophasis of Gender"[2]

THE ADMISSION IN chapter 8 that feminist conceptions of justice and equality may not be fully reconcilable with the text of the Qur'an takes us to the "edge" of the Qur'an: we have reached and exceeded the limits of clear-cut Qur'anic support for our ideals. Arriving at this edge means that we have come to an impasse in current strands of feminist approaches to the Qur'an, requiring us to search out new ways of relating to the Qur'an as believing Muslim feminists. In this chapter I explore another edge: the borders of the exegetical tradition. Alongside the issues I raised in chapter 8 about our authority as interpreters in relation to the Qur'an, here I raise questions about our authority in relation to the exegetical tradition. I examine how the androcentrism of exegetical authority with respect to the Qur'an might make it constitutionally averse to feminist inclusion. I then propose the revision of concepts of sexual difference in feminist tafsir related to the challenges of reconciling difference and equality discussed in chapter 8. I end by reflecting on what it means to question many of the foundations of feminist tafsir, and I embrace a position of "radical uncertainty" in relation to that questioning.

The Challenge of Androcentric Exegetical Authority

Besides the problem of male-female hierarchy in the text of the Qur'an, we must revisit the issue of androcentrism in the exegetical tradition and its ramifications for the acceptance of feminist authority to interpret the Qur'an. As I make these observations, I am aware that neither Islamic authority nor Islamic tradition is monolithic. As alluded to in the introduction, Richard Bulliet has argued that over the course of Islamic history, Muslim leaders have consolidated their authority by laying claim to a "real" Islam, invoking the past to construct an orthodox center of Islam that excludes heterodox religious developments. The authoritative center of Islam is continually challenged by these developments at its edge, in response to which elite authorities have "frequently expressed horror of innovation (*bid'ah*) in matters of faith and practice."[3] However, as Bulliet argues, because of serious challenges to the consolidation of authority absent a clerical structure in Islam and given modern transformations in structures of authority, the edges of tradition do not remain clearly or permanently defined.[4] Similarly, Muhammad Qasim Zaman, drawing partly on Talal Asad, has argued that definitions of tradition are based on competing claims to an "authentic" past that is imagined, manipulated, and constructed in different ways in the present.[5] Despite the dynamic character of Islamic authority and tradition, I maintain that both present formidable obstacles to the inclusion of feminist perspectives. I point out two major roadblocks to the acceptance of feminist exegetical authority: (1) the fact that feminist-interpretive results radically subvert traditional exegetical assumptions about male-female relations; and (2) the vulnerability of the argument that the Qur'anic text cannot be equated with its human interpretations.

First, it is important to observe that in a certain sense, interpretive authority works "backward." Interpretations obtain their legitimacy by repeating not only the *methods* of traditional exegesis but also by repeating the *results* of traditional exegesis. That is, legitimacy derives not only from the starting point of interpretation but also from its ending point. Ayesha Chaudhry argues that "the authority of the tradition is not generally considered to be its methodology but rather its substantive [conclusions]."[6] As Juliane Hammer has pointed out, often the conclusions of an interpretation are used to determine whether that interpretation falls in line with tradition, and consequently whether the interpretation has any real authority.[7] In such cases, it is unlikely for an interpretation to claim *both* authority and a radically new conclusion at the same time; often it is possible to claim only one. Since the authoritative premodern exegetical tradition (and many of its iterations in the contemporary era) largely reflects hierarchical views of male-female relations, one could argue that the authority of subsequent exegetical efforts depends on them also endorsing the same view of the sexes (or at least a congruent one)—which poses a serious obstacle to the authority of feminist interpretations. This means that grounding feminist interpretive methods in traditional exegetical methods is perhaps nowhere near enough to lend them authority.

Here one might submit the case of Umm Salamah (the Prophet's wife) often narrated in the exegetical tradition as evidence that the Qur'an recognizes women's authority to question the text.[8] Commentators cite a number of Hadith reports in which Umm Salamah boldly questions the Prophet about why the Qur'an appears to exclude women in its pronouncements. This incident has been variously linked to verse 33:35 (attributed to Umm Salamah questioning why women are not being mentioned by the Qur'an), verse 3:195 (attributed to Umm Salamah questioning why women are not recognized for their sacrifices as emigrants to Medina), and verse 4:32 (attributed to Umm Salamah questioning why women cannot fight in battle to receive the same amount of inheritance as men). It is remarkable that commentators treat reports about Umm Salamah as plausible *asbab al-nuzul* for the Qur'anic verses; we may certainly point to this treatment as evidence that the exegetical tradition recognizes women's request for inclusion in the Qur'an's address as a legitimate and intelligible inquiry. While the *asbab al-nuzul* related to Umm Salamah are certainly significant in demonstrating a tolerance for women's interpretive engagement with the Qur'an, they do not, however, indicate a tolerance for women's questioning of fundamental ideas about the nature of men and women and the balance of power between them. A request for inclusion does not, after all, necessarily call into question the firmly held beliefs about human nature that have produced women's exclusion in the first place. I will return to conceptual fallacies about women's inclusion at the end of this section.

In pointing to the exegetical tradition's intolerance for radically new ideas about sex equality, I am not rehearsing the common Orientalist claim that the Islamic exegetical tradition is stagnant. It has often been argued that the Prophet's condemnation of *bid'ah* (innovation) "was not a categorical prohibition of innovative ideas or practices"; rather it meant that "new ideas and practices had to be consistent with established precedents and recognized principles."⁹ In addition, Karen Bauer has noted that in premodern exegesis about verses related to women, earlier interpretations do not dictate later ones, as exegetical works demonstrate at times surprisingly variant readings.¹⁰ I do, however, point to self-confirmation as a possibly constitutive feature of exegetical authority in the sense that it perhaps does not allow upending basic ideas about human nature challenged by feminist criticism of the Qur'an.

The second roadblock I observe to the acceptance of feminist exegetical authority is the vulnerability of the position that the Qur'anic text cannot be equated with its human interpretations. This position is a not a necessary conclusion when we take into account the radical difference between our contemporary understanding of time and history and that of premodern exegetes. As Peter Wright has persuasively argued, beginning in the twentieth century, some Muslim thinkers (Muslim literary scholars influenced by European Romanticism, particularly in Egypt) began to understand time and temporality in a manner drastically different from the way their predecessors understood time; they became aware of a gap between the "natural" progression of time and their own view—or memory—of time.¹¹ As a result, they, along with their Muslim modernist successors, came to view history as an *account* of time authored by human beings. In contrast to premodern Muslim thinkers, they began to emphasize the role of human agency in the making of history, positing that time cannot be experienced except through a human-authored account of it. Thus, modernists developed the view that time and its events can be experienced only through (a human-authored) *history*.

This new understanding of time and history had a dramatic impact on the way that modernist Muslim thinkers viewed texts, since the authorship of texts was among the events in time which could be experienced only through history. In other words, modernist thinkers who inherited this view came to see the authorship of texts as no different from any other event in history: like anything else, it occurs *in* history. Therefore, all texts bear the mark of the historical environment of their authorship; all texts are "encoded" by their historical context. Modernist thinkers also applied this view of texts to their understanding of the Qur'an as a text. (Here, it is important to note that the application of this view to the Qur'an goes beyond the Muʿtazilite view of the createdness of the Qur'an, which posited the creation of the Qur'an in time. For modernists, the Qur'an was not only created in time but also in *history*.) This led to the view commonly held among modernist thinkers that the Qur'an is best read historically—understood according to the meanings it had for its first audience. They came to see that the *asbab al-nuzul* are more than just occasions of the revelation of the *text*, as premodern interpreters had thought of them; they are also the occasions of the *meanings* communicated by the Qur'an.

This new understanding of time and history was inherited by Muslim feminist scholarship later in the twentieth century but with some important additions. Scholars of feminist tafsir share the modernist view that the Qur'anic text was created in history and that history directly affected its meanings. They agree that the premodern *mufassirun* had often misunderstood the meanings of the Qur'an because they had failed to read the Qur'an in its historical context. But for Muslim feminist scholarship, there is a more crucial thing amiss in the readings of premodern interpreters: premodern interpreters had failed to understand not just that that text of the Qur'an was created in a historical context but also that their own *interpretations* of the Qur'an were produced by their *own* historical context.

To clarify, modernists had paid attention to the fact that the text of the Qur'an was created in history, but not as much to the fact that *interpretations* of the text were created in history. Granted, modernists such as Fazlur Rahman did, of course, advocate for the application of the Qur'an's meanings according to one's contemporary historical context—with which scholars of feminist tafsir agree. But feminist approaches to the Qur'an go a step further. Feminist approaches point out not only that the Qur'an *should* be interpreted according to contemporary history but also that it *always already* is, since one cannot help but read a text through the lenses and limitations of one's own historical moment. Modernists argued that the Qur'an should be continually revisited and interpreted dynamically, which is an argument echoed by scholars of feminist tafsir. But stated more precisely, the feminist interpretive position is that the Qur'an is *always* "revisited" every time it is read. The former position, held by modernists (and shared by feminist readers), is a prescription for ensuring the most accurate understanding of the Qur'an's intent. The latter position, emphasized by feminists, is the observation of an inherent condition (or limitation) of reading the Qur'an at all.

Perhaps the most important issue at stake here is that for premodern readers (and their contemporary traditionalist counterparts), the meaning of the Qur'an is based purely on authorial intent. As Adis Duderija has pointed out, to them, understanding the Qur'an is nothing more than the retrieval of an objectively accessible meaning from the text that reflects the author's intent.[12] For feminist readers, however, understanding is not a passive process but rather the product of a dialogue between the text and reader, who always reads the text from within a particular history. The reader does not retrieve an objectively accessible meaning from the text but rather participates in the mediated production of the text's meaning.[13] Thus the role of the reader (not just the author) becomes central to reading the Qur'an, and the reader can never objectively know the intent of the author/God. This feminist view is held in sharp contrast to the traditional exegetical view that objectively identifiable meanings can be gleaned from the Qur'an.

It is on the basis of the view of texts and textual interpretation being encoded by history that scholars of feminist tafsir have criticized premodern and contemporary exegetes who adopt the premodern assumption that Qur'anic meaning is objectively accessible. Barlas, for instance, criticizes the defense of the "objective" quality of their exegesis through "the denial of [its] historicity."[14] Barlas and others have argued on the basis of the tawhid paradigm that when male interpreters fail to distinguish between the Qur'anic text and their necessarily subjective interpretation of it, they are attributing God's knowledge to themselves and thereby committing a form of *shirk*. Barlas laments the repetition of this tendency in the tradition due to the fact that authority has principally derived from a "scholarly lineage" rather than the merits of one's interpretation.[15] This has resulted in the "tendency to accumulate meanings rather than to (re)create them, and the growth of a self-referential and self-reproducing methodological paradigm."[16]

It is crucial to note, however, that in accordance with many premodern interpreters' views of time and texts (often inherited by traditionalist contemporary interpreters), it *is entirely possible* to access objective meaning from the Qur'an, and this *is* in fact *how* meaning is derived from any text, including the Qur'an. According to this way of thinking, it is not *shirk* to assume that one's interpretation is objective. It is *not* an equation of God's knowledge with one's own knowledge to assume that one's reading is objective; it is simply the logical result of how texts are read by human beings. Interpretive objectivity does not necessarily have anything to do with God's authority. By the same logic, one may also decide that once a meaning has been objectively obtained, its fundamentals do not require revisiting. Subsequently derived Qur'anic meanings may reflect a certain degree of diversity and disagreement with previous ones (differences that might result from the acknowledgment of different customs and circumstances, as we see in the juristic record for instance, but not because of an awareness of *historicity*). However, any meanings that fundamentally and radically contradict the established meaning—such as those relying on a radically different understanding of human nature—cannot be correct. Thus, according to this logic, there is nothing at all amiss in relying on a tradition of accumulative knowledge in the manner that Qur'anic exegetes have. This is a view that is produced not only through the prioritization of tradition over reason, as has been commonly suggested, but is also crucially affected by the exegetes' view of time.[17]

As this discussion demonstrates, the feminist claim that equating one's interpretation of the Qur'an with what "God says" is the result of holding the particular—and relatively new—view of time and history that radically departs from premodern and neotraditional exegetes' views of time. It is only through a particular logic of time and history that the equation of text with interpretation, or the accumulative approach to Qur'anic exegesis that invests premodern male interpretations with unassailable authority, appears to us as tantamount to *shirk*. (In this sense, critics of feminist interpretations are perhaps correct in their assessment that feminist tafsir approaches the Qur'an in a manner that is historically and methodologically anomalous.) By other logics, the accusation of *shirk* does not hold up and thus does not disrupt the cumulative authority of the exegetical tradition or the fixity of its positions on male-female hierarchy.

I now return to the larger problem of women's inclusion in interpretive authority. In order to examine the full ramifications of feminist criticism's intervention in Qur'anic interpretation, we should perhaps consider how views of male-female hierarchy premised by the premodern exegetical tradition might structure exegetical authority. It is important to interrogate the possible structural role of androcentrism in Qur'anic interpretation and ask what Qur'anic interpretation can actually *be* without it. To put it another way, we must question how the authority of Qur'anic exegesis might fundamentally rely on—be constitutionally dependent on—androcentrism as its premise. We must ask how Qur'anic interpretation is "forever"—that is, constitutionally—changed by the challenges posed by feminist exegesis.

Here, I propose that we cannot simply "add and stir" feminist perspectives into Qur'anic tafsir, since in the process of applying feminist criticism, we perhaps remove something constitutive of the tafsir tradition and thus alter it fundamentally. The question becomes: When we undercut the androcentrism that has perhaps been constitutive of Qur'anic interpretation, what is left of Qur'anic interpretation? Is it still the same endeavor? If not, then what is it now? When we ask these questions, we must be willing to consider the possibility that feminist interpretation is not a solution to the problem of sexist interpretation of the Qur'an but perhaps the symptom of another, much deeper problem—that the tradition of Qur'anic tafsir relies on a notion of interpretive authority that is *constitutionally* averse to feminist inclusion. Perhaps our deep attachment to finding affirmations of male-female equality in the Qur'an has obscured this deeper problem from our view. That is, our approach to feminist interpretation of the Qur'an has perhaps concealed the problem we have been struggling with all along: it is possible that according to the exegetical tradition the authority to interpret the Qur'an is essentially androcentric.

We may certainly argue (citing historical examples of numerous women interpreters) that interpretive authority is open to the *inclusion* of women. However, this does not mean that interpretive authority is necessarily open to feminist interpretations that challenge the basis of androcentric authority. In other words, the mere inclusion of women does not necessarily pose a threat to it. Women's inclusion would not be the problem so much as the radical questioning of fundamental tenets about gender undergirding exegetical authority.[18] In fact, it could be that opening exegetical authority to women who do not undertake this radical questioning simply *reproduces* androcentric authority "under the sign of its erasure"; that is, the inclusion of women may simply perpetuate the masking of exegetical authority's androcentrism and thereby reinforce it.[19] Rather, it is feminist criticism that makes visible the structural bases of male power in the exegetical tradition and questions why women have been excluded in the first place. It is for this reason that I offer the hypothesis that feminist exegetical authority cannot be claimed through a call for greater inclusion of women in Qur'anic interpretation that simply leaves intact the structure of male power over women. We must also consider the possibility that once feminist criticism does enter the picture to undercut the androcentric basis of exegetical tradition, what is left of exegesis is no longer authoritative. This is because feminist criticism would fundamentally destabilize what is perhaps constitutive of exegetical authority, transforming the latter into something else. Whatever that something else is, it is may no longer be authoritative, as it radically overturns some of the standard premises of traditional authority concerning gender. It is this possible irreconcilability that has perhaps prompted our critics' claim that our approaches to the Qur'an lay outside the boundaries of tradition and are based on personal positions, despite feminist claims to the contrary.

Sex, Difference, and Equality

My proposals in this book for reassessing operative positions in feminist tafsir are also driven by the belief that we require revised understandings of sex, gender, difference, and power. Here I revisit concepts of sexual difference in feminist Qur'anic exegesis, not as way to revoke our demands for justice for women but rather to consider other notions of subjecthood that may help us approach the conundrums of difference/equality and mutuality/hierarchy, discussed in chapter 8, in new ways.

While exegetes of feminist tafsir have understood gender as a dynamic social performance (i.e., roles, behavior) of sexual difference, they have inadvertently—often contrary to their stated intentions—remained attached to essentialized conceptions of sex and sexual difference. While they have usually approached gender construction and performance critically, they have not, however, approached sex in an adequately critical manner. Here we find that in the process of insisting that the Qur'an does not specify gender roles and simply protects women on account of their unique biological function, the works of Barlas and Wadud for example, maintain an essential view of sex that treats it as a fixed state of biology. Barlas even attributes many instances of inequality to the collapsing of (permanent) sex with (the culturally determined roles of) gender.[20]

However, works of feminist theory since the 1990s have demonstrated that not only gender but also sex is an unstable social and cultural construction. Judith Butler noted in her groundbreaking work *Gender Trouble* that gender is the "apparatus of production whereby the sexes themselves are established"; gender is the "cultural means by which 'sexed nature' or 'a natural sex' is produced."[21] Sex then takes on the appearance of being "prior to culture."[22] In the words of Joan Scott, sexual difference "acquired its natural status only retrospectively, as a rationale for the assignment of gender roles. In other words, nature (the difference of the sexes in this instance) was produced by culture as culture's justification—it was not an independent variable, nor an ontological ground, nor the invariant base on which edifices of gender were constructed."[23] Thus, neither sex nor gender is "objective or independent of human belief systems"; in short, neither are "natural."[24]

With a view to these insights, I propose that feminist tafsir begin to treat not only gender but also sex as a fluid and historically contingent concept and sexual difference as a shifting relation of interdependence.[25] To the credit of Wadud and Barlas, both attempt to advocate models of dynamic interdependence between the sexes. Barlas insists that the Qur'an "does not endow humans with a fixed nature," and it "does not define women and men in terms of binary oppositions."[26] Both Wadud and Barlas call for a polar view of sexual difference whereby both men and women possess both masculine and feminine oppositional attributes. Wadud refers to one sex as "contingent upon the other."[27] Barlas argues that each one is an "internally differentiated unity."[28] Unfortunately, these fluid conceptions of sexual difference often do not cohere with the way both scholars treat sexual difference in their arguments about specific verses of the Qur'an.

I argue that the difference between the relation of God to men and the relation of God to women cannot be fully explained as equal through the negative assessment that difference does not necessarily mean inequality. In part, this explanation is insufficient because the implicit model of sexual difference it depends on, and thus sustains, is an essentialized notion of difference between the sexes that ultimately undermines sexual equality. A model of sexual difference that is predicated on fixed binary opposition "conceal[s] the extent to which things presented as oppositional are, in fact, interdependent."[29] It is such an oppositional model that lends itself to the service of hierarchical arrangements. Hierarchical arrangements are less likely when we see sexual difference through a model of dynamic interdependence instead.

Barlas, Wadud, and other scholars of feminist tafsir have repeatedly maintained that the Qur'an recognizes sexual differences between men and women but still treats men and women as equals. As Barlas has put it, the Qur'an acknowledges sexual difference but does not promote sexual "differentiation."[30] The strength of this argument rests on the observation that treating men and women in an identical manner would result in injustice because it would fail to account for important differences between them that require different treatment.[31] The weakness of this argument, though, is that it treats sexual difference as a binary opposition—not unlike arguments for inequality based of the "undeniable" fact of how God created men and women. As Joan Scott has argued, the notion of irreducible, essential difference between the sexes easily lends itself to becoming a logical explanation for unequal treatment; the "certainty" and stability of that difference between the sexes is used to draw detrimental conclusions about essential sexual differences between men and women.[32] An insistence on difference is easily used as a biological or "natural" explanation for inequality.[33] When difference is used to justify inequality, counterarguments for equality become limited to rationales of sameness.[34] In short, equality and difference function in opposition to one another when sexual differences are treated as fixed binaries of difference.

Let me illustrate these points in more concrete terms by revisiting a common rationalization of the difference-within-equality model we have encountered in feminist tafsir. A commonly offered argument is that if men and women were put in exactly the same role of providing financially for their families, then mothers would be disadvantaged by the double burden of both nursing and wage earning since they perform a biological function that male wage earners do not. However, once it is agreed that nursing mothers require accommodations on account of this *biological* function (one that is attached to inherent and fixed biological difference), it can also be logically argued that women who are nursing *should not* work outside the home, or at the very least not hold leadership positions at work, due to their biological difference from men; mothers who demand to do so act in defiance of a natural, biological division between the sexes (i.e., God made them this way). In other words, women become defined by their individually unique sex difference (the capacity to breastfeed). Thus, in schemes of sexual difference that assume a fixed binary of biological difference between the sexes, unequal treatment may appear as the benign, logical alternative to equal treatment.

Exegetes of feminist tafsir have claimed that both identical treatment and unequal treatment are unacceptable options, but I argue that these, in fact, are often the *only* options we tend to be left with if we rely on fixed, oppositional delineations of difference. This is because such an understanding of difference easily leads to the acceptance of ideas about biologically based difference as "normative statements" or indisputable "truths ... outside human invention."[35] We observe here that oppositional difference between the sexes "draws one line of difference, invests it with biological explanations, and then treats each side of the opposition as a unitary phenomenon."[36] Such essential conceptions of sexual difference preclude viable options for a sustained equality between Muslim men and women, since meaningful equality is easily subverted under the conditions of a difference that is understood as fixed opposition. In this scheme of oppositional difference between men and women, men and women are unitary sex-based groups that are "autonomous," "self-contained," and "self-same"; difference plays out between one "individuated subject and another."[37] The assumption is that "men" and "women" are categories that are "coherent" and "self-same" within themselves and have "clearly marked boundaries" between them.[38] Within a structure of essential difference between the sexes, one sexual identity emerges by "projecting" absolute "'otherness' onto a secondary term" treated as external to itself.[39]

It is my view that a more productive understanding of equality will require a different view of sexual difference and sex. How exactly do we understand the nature of the difference between women and men that our call for equality is based upon? As Sa'diyya Shaikh has recently argued, a sustainable gender critique requires questioning fundamental assumptions about the nature of human beings; notions of the self must be engaged by feminist thinkers to prevent the ideological cooptation and undermining of feminist platforms.[40] The model of sexual difference I find most useful is one that treats sexual categories as dynamic and mutually and constitutionally interdependent. In such a model, sexual difference is based not on fixed binaries but rather on constructive, interdependent relationality. Difference does not derive from one's self-generated "uniqueness" but rather from a dynamic and relative contrast with the other.[41] Categories of male and female are relative and fluid; the two are interdependent because each requires the other, and neither exists within a fixed or static self. Man and woman are dependent on each other for their being: man cannot be man without woman, and woman cannot be woman without man. (Interestingly, this is exactly how Wadud speaks of sexual difference in *Inside the Gender Jihad*, though this conception is not consistently applied in her interpretations of Qur'anic verses.[42]) Furthermore, as the relations between men and women evolve, so do the meanings of what it means to be a woman and a man. This is, in fact, one of many reasons why a consideration of women's identities without a consideration of men's identities can be impoverished and misleading.[43]

When we think about men and women as dynamic subjects that are mutually constitutive of one another, we can begin to conceive of difference and equality through a model in which they are not opposed to one another. We are able to think about difference and equality so that "one is inscribed on the other."[44] When sexual differences are not related through binary opposition, then equality and difference are not opposed to each other. Here it is important to clarify that by arguing against essential, fixed, self-same differences between men and women, I am not advocating some form of androgyny or the erasure of difference between men and women.[45] Nor do I treat sex as an imaginary concept that makes any claims to justice for women impossible (after all, if there are no real women, then there are little grounds to seek their equality with men). There are in fact material, embodied differences between men and women, but they have a ground that is always shifting based on variant male-female relationships and historical context.[46]

Sexual difference should be viewed as dynamic in relation to at least three factors, which I discuss in turn: the specificities of situational contexts, variations that come with historical progression, and changing definitional relationships. First of all, the significance of biological differences should be treated as context-dependent; their "context must be specified" since differences are not "transcendent."[47] In some contexts, a biological difference is relevant to men's and women's capacities to perform the same tasks, but sometimes that same biological difference is irrelevant. In revisiting the issue of nursing mothers in the workplace, we may argue that when women give birth, they should be treated differently at work by being granted greater flexibility in work location and/or the distribution of work hours. A nursing woman's biological difference means that she cannot work according to the same schedule and/or in the same location, so it is relevant to her work capacity. However, when she is accommodated for this difference through location/scheduling flexibility, this difference does not necessarily change her capacity to perform the same amount and quality of work. And even if it does, it becomes irrelevant to her capacity to work when she is no longer nursing. Similarly, it is irrelevant to the work capacity of women who are not mothers (or who choose not to breastfeed their children). The consideration of when (in what contexts) sex differences should matter becomes possible only when we view sex differences as differences that are situational rather than absolute.[48] It is both the case that sex differences are relevant and that sometimes they are irrelevant. This example helps illustrate the point that a notion of fixed difference means that sex difference is *either* always relevant *or* always irrelevant, while a notion of fluid difference allows for both scenarios of relevance *and* irrelevance in different situations.[49]

To build on the same example to illustrate the second and third causes of dynamic difference (historical progression and changing definitional relationships), we can observe that contemporary technologies (e.g., formula and breast-milk pumps) now make it possible for men to "nurse" babies. (In the revelatory context of the Qur'an, we could say the parallel would have been the employment of a wet nurse, for which the Qur'an makes an allowance in verse 2:233.[50]) Here, advanced technology (a historical change) alters sex-based roles and thereby changes the relationship between men and women; in the relationship between the father and mother of a child, the mother is no longer the only party capable of nursing a child, since the father can now share in the role. A historical change and relational change means that mothers are no longer defined by the exclusive biological ability to nurse a child with breast milk, and fathers are no longer defined by their inability to perform a biological function only women can perform.

As this example illustrates, biological difference is best treated as historically fluid, relational, and contextual, rather than essential and stable. Such a conception can help us "denaturalize and expose the illusion of identity and certainty" of sexual differences that undergird common arguments for inequality.[51] Not only does this view of difference make it more difficult to divide the sexes hierarchically (since they are generative and mutually constitutive of one another), but it also allows for a scheme in which difference and equality are not opposed to one another.

One possible way to treat men and women as mutually constitutive subjects in feminist tafsir is to approach male-female relations within the broader context of human relationships of dependency.[52] Relations of dependence are not necessarily or only relations of subjugation or loss; they may also be productive of the self. The primary exemplification of this for Muslims is, of course, the divine-human relationship which produces the human being. This dynamic is captured by Amina Wadud's notion of "engaged surrender," whereby one gains one's agency precisely through one's surrender to God.[53] Through one's submission to God, the human being becomes *khalifah*, an agent responsible for enacting God's will on earth. As a mirror of this relationship of dependency on the human level, human beings rely on their relationships to others for their being. Social relations shape how one understands oneself; we become our "selves" through being in relation to another. We find that "the only way to know oneself is through a mediation that takes place outside of oneself, exterior to oneself."[54] Thus, we are "beings who are formed in relations of dependency."[55] That is, our dependency on others is productive of our being. A conception of agency based on this notion of being-through-dependency might help us disrupt the dichotomies of male control and female passivity.

As Sa'diyya Shaikh has demonstrated in her study of Ibn al-'Arabi, one way to view relations between men and women as relations of interdependence is through concepts of activity and receptivity. According to Ibn al-'Arabi's insights, "men and women are both simultaneously active and receptive" in relation to one another.[56] The performance and distribution of active and receptive roles is always shifting: "Men and women may each embody active or receptive modes, contingent on their particular relationships at a specific juncture."[57] It is not only active roles that are productive, since the "activity" of an active role is dependent on its reception. Receptivity also engenders activity and therefore takes on productive power. This productive power reveals "porous boundaries between activity and receptivity."[58] Thus, when viewed relationally, active and passive roles may potentially be performed in nonhierarchical relation to one another.[59] This nuanced view may help us problematize what Ziba Mir-Hosseini has called "formal" models of equality but without resorting to unjust models of complementarity.[60] Formal models of male-female equality often call for inclusion and equal access without accounting for the realities of male-female dependency. Reimagining difference through interdependence may allow us to move beyond the limitations of models of male-female equality based either on sameness or oppressive complementarity.

Theory and Practice

At this point I must address the very important matter of practical utility. One may duly question how my assertions could be of any benefit to those Muslim women whose primary and most urgent aim is to persuade their community leaders of the egalitarian principles of the Qur'an and to advocate for practical reform on their basis.[61] Here I refer to those Muslim women activists who are responding to very real and serious practical exigencies; those women in the trenches who—unlike those of us (myself of course included) who could be said to reside safely in the remote ivory towers of U.S. academia—do not have the luxury of living without immediate practical consequences for undercutting the advocacy of Qur'an-based gender justice. What interest could they possibly have in conceding that the Qur'anic text may not support our views of gender justice, let alone pursuing a radically different understanding of our relationship to the Qur'an's revelation and the exegetical tradition? To pose the question even more bluntly: How is mine not an elitist intellectual endeavor that is wholly insensitive, and perhaps even harmful, to the goals of Muslim women for whom the pursuit of these ideas is much more than a theoretical inquiry?

As I pointed out in the preface to this book, these questions were precisely the reason for my initial hesitation in publishing my criticisms of feminist Qur'anic interpretation. I am aware that it is one thing to test these critical views in the academy, and quite another to expect them to be useful (or perhaps I should say, not detrimental) to anyone outside the academy (that is, useful to anyone besides bigoted or sexist readers of the Qur'an intent on proving feminist tafsir wrong—yet another cause for alarm, and perhaps another good reason to stay quiet). My answer then, after a long and ambivalent struggle with these concerns, is that even when one is seeking practical change, persuasion still remains one's central goal. If the key to practical reform is convincing the powers that be of the legitimacy of our arguments, we ought not to continue to appeal to and thus reinforce the authority of a text that cannot definitively support our demands for feminist justice and the authority of an exegetical tradition that is perhaps constitutionally averse to them. So, bearing in mind those Muslim women who do the urgent and all-important work of seeking practical reform, I argue that we should stop handing over the weapons for our own argumentative demise to the vanguard of Islamic authority and allow ourselves the freedom to think in new ways about the Qur'anic text that can help us produce stronger arguments and strategies for pursuing practical victories in the long term. It is time to imagine new ways to achieve Islamically grounded justice.

A Radical Uncertainty

Pursuing the questions I have raised in this book about the Qur'an's possible incommensurability with our notions of equality and justice and the formidable obstacles of the exegetical tradition to the inclusion of feminist positions radically destabilizes the project of feminist tafsir. These questions lead us to a theological wrestling that may be deeply unsettling and even terrifying. When the certainty of our views about the Qur'an and our place in the Islamic tradition is thus shaken, what are we left with? How do we go on?

I imagine that for many Muslim women, it is their belief in the divinity of the Qur'an that so passionately motivates them to try to redeem the text from sexist interpretations in the first place. The starting point is that God is just, and that the Qur'an is the word of God, so then the Qur'an must also be just (in a way that upholds the absolute equality of men and women). But if, as it turns out, we cannot be sure that the text upholds the justice we seek, then we are left to question whether the Qur'an is really a divine text. If we do not question the divinity of the Qur'an, then we are left to question whether God is just (in a manner that upholds male-female equality). Both questions are, of course, deeply disturbing, even unbearable for some, and negative answers to them would mean the end of the faith-based endeavor of feminist tafsir. Thus, continuing to pursue feminist tafsir as Muslims means that we sustain some hope that God's justice upholds the equality of men and women and that the text is divine. Since we have also had to confront the possibility that perhaps feminist positions are at odds with structures of exegetical authority, then continuing to pursue feminist tafsir probably also means that we hold out some hope that subverting tradition does not eliminate the possibility of being persuasive or acceptable to other Muslims.

There are other questions still. What does it mean that we seek a standard of justice that is "beyond" the Qur'anic text? What does it mean to stop handing ultimate authority to the text in this particular way? Do we fear the awesome human responsibility this implies? And where does that leave us in our relationship to the text? In what way is the text still divine? And what does the answer mean about us as Muslims? What does it mean to challenge the exegetical tradition in ways that make some Muslims question our Islam? To what and whom do we belong? What does calling into question so many foundations of feminist tafsir mean for its future?

There have been times in the past when I have feared that questioning the certainty of the Qur'an's justice for women would send me headlong into an abyss of uncertainty that would inevitably result in the end of my faith and my demise as a Muslim feminist. It was unthinkable to admit that feminist exegetical thought had reached dead ends in some places. It was only after allowing myself to ask questions that were once unthinkable, reassessing many of the most basic principles of feminist exegetical thought, that I have been able to look into the abyss of uncertainty and see it as a place of life and not only death. As Catherine Keller has elegantly written, it may very well be that "the abyss, upon closer meditation, is not an empty void" but rather the site of becoming, of "our always already . . . fluidity."[62] Jumping into the abyss of uncertainty need not be a death sentence; working under the "conditions of theoretic incommensurability and radical uncertainty" can lead to the birth of new possibilities.[63] As Keller points out, we need not "plunge . . . from the absolute" into a void.[64] Embracing "an unknowing" is always a risk, as I am confronted with "a beyond that I cannot ever fully construct, author, or control," but this confrontation might also be the best way to think the unthinkable.[65] Thinking from a place of a "radical" or "critical" uncertainty may be terrifying, but it might also be revitalizing.[66] As Keller writes, when we can "accept the undecidability in our work as precisely our receptiveness to . . . the unexpected," then "it need not paralyze action. It may *free* us to make our uncertain decisions."[67] In the journey of writing this book, I have come to see uncertainty as a mercy in the face of the daunting finality of certainty and the permanence of its limits. In embracing an uncertainty about feminist tafsir, I am not confined to the choices of "all or nothing" in answer to questions about feminist justice in the Qur'an. I am free to consider new, unexpected ways of pursuing feminist justice in Islam that were previously unimaginable or impossible.

Finally, I return to the much feared question of whether it is possible for Muslim feminist exegesis of the Qur'an to survive the conclusion that our demands for gender justice may not cohere fully with the Qur'an. If I am correct that confronting the uncertainty of this leads us to pursue other paths, then we need not despair. These paths may help us continue to read the Qur'an as Muslims and as feminists dynamically, even if we come to inhabit those positions in ways that we could never have imagined before. Once we are able to view this questioning not just as the ending of something but also as the beginning of something else, not only as the closing of a door but also as the opening of another, we can forge ahead toward new possibilities.

Appendix: Select Qur'anic Verses

To serve as a reference aid for the reader, I provide translations of the Qur'anic verses most commonly cited by scholars of feminist tafsir. My translations differ on a few occasions from some translations provided elsewhere in this book; on those occassions, I have specified that I am referring to popular understandings of certain verses.

2:187 On the night of fasting, (sexually) approaching your wives is permissible for you; they are garments for you, and you are garments for them. God knows that you were betraying yourselves, and [God] turned to you and pardoned you. So now have intercourse with them, and seek what God has prescribed for you, and eat and drink until the white thread of dawn is evident from the black thread. Then complete the fast up to the night, and do not have intercourse with them when you have retreated to the mosque. These are the limits of God; do not approach them. Thus does God make evident [God's] signs to humankind, that they may be God-conscious.

2:222 They ask you about menstruation. Say: it is painful, so withdraw from women during menstruation, and do not approach them until they are clean, but when they have cleansed themselves then approach them as God has commanded you. God loves those who turn in repentance, and [God] loves those who cleanse themselves.

2:223 Your wives are (like) a field for you, so approach your field as you wish, and make provisions for yourselves and be conscious of God and be aware that you will meet [God]. And give good news to the believers.

2:228 Divorced women shall wait by themselves three menstrual periods. It is not permissible for them to conceal what God has created in their wombs if they believe in God and the Last Day. Their husbands have a better right to take them back in that time if they want reconciliation. And women have (rights) similar to those which they owe as is commonly recognized (as fair), but men have a degree over them. And God is mighty and wise.

2:282 O you who believe, when you contract a debt for a fixed period, record it in writing . . . And call upon two witnesses from among your men, but if there are not two men, then a man and two women from among whom you approve as witnesses, so that if one of the two women errs the other reminds her. [. . .]

4:1 O humankind, be conscious of your Lord, who created you from a single soul, and created from it its mate, and disseminated numerous men and women from the two. And be conscious of God, through whom you seek from one another (your rights), and kinship ties. Indeed God is watchful over you.

4:3 If you fear that you cannot act justly toward orphans, then marry the women who seem good to you—two, three, or four; but if you fear you cannot be equitable, then one, or what your right hands possess. That is more appropriate so that you do not act unjustly.

4:34 Men are the maintainers of women according to what God has favored for some of them over others and according to what they provide from their means. Righteous women are devout and guard the unseen according to what God has guarded. As for those women on whose part you fear marital discord, admonish them, abandon their beds, and strike them. But if they yield to you, then do not pursue a path against them. God is great and above all.

4:128 If a woman fears marital discord or desertion on the part of her husband, there is no fault in the two reconciling with one another. Reconciliation is best, though souls are prone to greed. If you do good and are God-conscious, God is aware of what you do.

4:129 You will not be able to act equitably toward your wives, even if you desire. But do not turn away (from a wife) entirely, so that you leave her hanging. If you make amends and are God-conscious, God is forgiving and merciful.

9:71 The male and female believers are protectors of each other. They command what is right and forbid what is wrong, practice prayer, perform almsgiving, and obey God and [God's] messenger. God will have mercy upon them. God is mighty and wise.

30:21 And among [God's] signs is that [God] created mates for you from among yourselves so that you might find rest in them. And [God] has put love and mercy between you. Indeed in that are signs for people who reflect.

33:35 Muslim men and women, believing men and women, devout men and women, sincere men and women, patient men and women, humble men and women, alms-giving men and women, fasting men and women, men and women guarding their chastity, and men and women remembering God much: for them God has made ready forgiveness and great reward.

Notes

PREFACE

1. Amina Wadud, *Qur'an and Woman* (Kuala Lumpur: Penerbit Fajar Bakti Sdn. Bhd., 1992). Later published as *Qur'an and Woman: Rereading the Sacred Text from a Woman's Perspective* (New York: Oxford University Press, 1999).
2. Published as "Mariyya the Copt: Gender, Sex and Heritage in the Legacy of Muhammad's *umm walad*," *Islam and Christian-Muslim Relations* 21.3 (July 2010).
3. Rhouni, *Secular and Islamic Feminist Critiques* 251.
4. I have discussed the issue of honoring one's intellectual genealogy while critically engaging with previous works in a roundtable piece: "Muslim Feminist Birthdays" *Journal of Feminist Studies in Religion* 27.1 (Spring 2011).
5. It is perhaps also worth mentioning that I am not afforded the luxury, as some other scholars might be, to do such work without bearing in mind its impact upon the devoutly Muslim family in which I was raised; though it may be unpopular within academia to admit openly, being a scholar does not sever these communal ties which inevitably shape our work.
6. Hammer, *American Muslim Women* 202.

INTRODUCTION

1. Hasan Mahmud 'Abd al-Latif Al-Shafi'i, "The Movement for Feminist Interpretation of the Qur'an and Religion and Its Threat to the Arabic Language and Tradition" (2010), 1, 14. http://dialogicws.files.wordpress.com/2011/06/feminist-hermeneutics_shafii.pdf.
2. Bulliet, *The Case for Islamo-Christian Civilization* 135; Taji-Farouki, Introduction, 13.
3. Hammer, *American Muslim Women* 119.
4. I am deeply indebted to Peter Wright of Colorado College (as well as to Bulliet himself) for his recommendation of Bulliet's work as a model for talking about

tradition and its subversion, a recommendation that would later inspire the title of this book.
5. Bulliet, *Islam* 186.
6. Bulliet, *Islam* 186.
7. Bulliet, *Islam* 195.
8. Bulliet, *Islam* 195.
9. Bulliet, *The Case for Islamo-Christian Civilization* 140.
10. Bulliet, *The Case for Islamo-Christian Civilization* 144, 145.
11. See also Hammer, *American Muslim Women* 219 n48.
12. Hammer, *American Muslim Women* 76.
13. For the problem of treating Muslim women as a homogenous category, see miriam cooke, "The Muslimwoman." *Contemporary Islam* 1 (2007): 139–154.
14. Laleh Bakhtiar, *The Sublime Qur'an*. See pages xliii, xlviii, and lii–lv for her views of women in the Qur'an and their impact on her translation.
15. Badran, *Feminism in Islam* 245.
16. Hammer, "Identity, Authority, and Activism" 452.
17. Abbas, "The Echo Chamber of Freedom" 184.
18. Zayn Kassam, "The Hermeneutics of Problematic Gender Verses in the Qur'an," *Postscripts* 1.1 (2005): 77–104.
19. Marcotte, "Muslim Women's Scholarship" 131–162.
20. Van Doorn-Harder, "Women Reading the Qur'an" 51–60.
21. Hammer, *American Muslim Women* 56–76; "Identity, Authority, and Activism" 443–464.
22. Hammer, *American Muslim Women* 88, 93.
23. As Sadia Abbas points out, Hassan's work began as a response to Islamic resurgence in Pakistan beginning in 1979 under the administration of General Zia-ul-Haq, a time notorious for the instantiation of Pakistan's infamous Hudud Ordinance. Abbas, "The Echo Chamber of Freedom" 172–173.
24. Gisela Webb, Introduction xiii–xiv.
25. I owe this observation and many others in this section to vital conversations with Juliane Hammer.
26. Hammer, *American Muslim Women* 93.
27. The response to this tendency is captured in Azizah al-Hibri's classic contribution to a volume typical of late 1990s U.S. feminism: "Is Western Patriarchal Feminism Good for Third World/Minority Women?" 41–46.
28. Hassan, "Jihad Fi Sabil Allah" 11–30; Al-Hibri, "Hagar on My Mind" 198–210; Wadud, "On Belonging" 253–265; Wadud, *Inside the Gender Jihad*.
29. A similar observation has made been by Juliane Hammer in *American Muslim Women*, 121.
30. *Windows of Faith: Muslim Women Scholar-Activists in North America*, ed. Gisela Webb (Syracuse: Syracuse University Press, 2000).
31. Al-Hibri, "Islamic Law" 546.

32. Wadud, *Qur'an and Woman* 71–72, 81, 92 n17, 92 n19, 92 n21, 92 n24, 92 n25, 93 n39, 93 n40. Wadud also cites al-Hibri in her endnotes for quoting a certain Hadith report. Wadud, *Qur'an and Woman* 101, 105 n13.
33. Wadud, *Qur'an and Woman* 28 n19.
34. Al-Hibri traces her use of the term to a conversation with the Grand Mufti of Lebanon in Maryland in the late 1980s. Al-Hibri, "Hagar on My Mind," 204–205; Al-Hibri, "Divine Justice 240ff; al-Hibri, "An Introduction 54; Wadud, "Foreword" 437; Wadud, *Inside the Gender Jihad* 28, 265 n20.
35. Barlas, "Amina Wadud's Hermeneutics" 97–124.
36. Hassan, "Jihad Fi Sabil Allah" 11–30.
37. Braude, "Riffat Hassan" 181. Elsewhere, Hassan notes that difficult life experiences "made me a feminist with a resolve to develop feminist theology in the framework of Islamic tradition." Hassan, "Jihad Fi Sabil Allah," 25.
38. Hassan, "Jihad Fi Sabil Allah" 23.
39. Braude, "Riffat Hassan" 183, 185.
40. Riffat Hassan, "The Issue" 68.
41. Braude, "Riffat Hassan" 182, 183.
42. Braude, "Riffat Hassan" 184–190.
43. Hassan, "The Issue" 65–82.
44. Al-Hibri, "Hagar on My Mind" 203.
45. Braude, "Azizah al–Hibri," 48–49.
46. Al-Hibri, "Hagar on My Mind" 203.
47. Al-Hibri, "Hagar on My Mind" 203.
48. Al-Hibri, "Hagar on My Mind" 200. Similar sentiments are also expressed in a short personal piece published in an anthology of North American women of Arab heritage: al-Hibri, "Tear Off Your Western Veil!" 160–164.
49. Al-Hibri employs the term "womanist" in her 1998 contribution on Islamic law to an edited volume on feminist philosophy: al-Hibri, "Islamic Law" 542.
50. Karamah, "Women's Conference in Beijing," *Karamah: Muslim Women Lawyers for Human Rights*, http://www.karamah.org/news_womens_conference.htm.
51. Karamah, "Women's Conference in Beijing."
52. Al-Hibri, "Hagar on My Mind" 203–205.
53. Al-Hibri, "A Study of Islamic Herstory" 207–219.
54. Al-Hibri, "A Study of Islamic Herstory" 208.
55. Braude, "Azizah al–Hibri," 53.
56. Al-Hibri, "Qur'anic Foundations".
57. Barlas, "Amina Wadud's Hermeneutics" 98–99.
58. Wadud, "On Belonging as a Muslim Woman."
59. Wadud, *Qur'an and Woman*.
60. Wadud, *Qur'an and Woman*, ix, xv.
61. Barlas, "Amina Wadud's Hermeneutics" 100–101; Zainah Anwar, "From Local to Global: Sisters in Islam and the Making of Musawah: A Global Movement

for Equality in the Muslim Family," *Gender and Equality in Muslim Family Law:* ed. Mir-Hosseini, et al. 109.
62. Wadud, *Qur'an and Woman* 102.
63. For a discussion of how Wadud first became interested methodology, see Wadud, "Qur'an, Gender, and Interpretive" 327–328.
64. Wadud, *Qur'an and Woman* xviii.
65. Wadud, *Inside the Gender Jihad* 79–80.
66. Haddad, Smith, and Moore, *Muslim Women in America* 157.
67. "The Qur'an Doesn't Support Patriarchy," interview by Naufil Shahrukh, ABC, *The Nation*, Pakistan, Feb. 2005.
68. Barlas, *"Believing Women."*
69. Barlas, *"Believing Women"* 19.
70. Barlas, "Globalizing Equality" 107.
71. Barlas, *"Believing Women"* 19.
72. Guardi, "Women Reading the Quran" 313.
73. Barlas, *"Believing Women"* 19, 169.
74. Shaikh, "Transforming Feminisms" 147; Shaikh, *Sufi Narratives*.
75. Shaikh, "Exegetical Violence" 49–73.
76. Shaikh, "Transforming Feminisms" 150.
77. Shaikh, "Exegetical Violence" 3, 4.
78. Kecia Ali, *Marriage and Slavery in Early Islam* (Cambridge, MA: Harvard University Press, 2010); Kecia Ali, *Imam Shafi'i: Scholar and Saint* (Oxford: Oneworld, 2011).
79. Ali, *Sexual Ethics*.
80. Plaskow, *Standing Again at Sinai* 26.

CHAPTER 1

1. Wadud, *Qur'an and Woman* xvi.
2. Von Denffer, *'Ulum al–Qur'an* 122.
3. Andrew Rippin, "Tafsir" 237.
4. Andrew Rippin, "Tafsir (a.)" Brill online, 2007; Rippin, "Tafsir" 238.
5. Gilliot, "Exegesis" Brill online, 2007.
6. Esack, *The Qur'an* 130.
7. Gilliot, "Exegesis."
8. Gilliot, "Exegesis"; Gätje, *The Qur'an and Its Exegesis* 33.
9. Gilliot, "Exegesis."
10. Gilliot, "Exegesis."
11. Gilliot, "Exegesis."
12. McAuliffe, "The Tasks" 196.
13. McAuliffe, "The Tasks" 192.
14. Mu'tazilism is a school of Islamic theology (*'ilm al–kalam*) that began in the eighth century C.E. and centralized reason and the justice of God. See

"Muʿtazila," *Encyclopaedia of Islam*, 2nd ed., Brill online, 2013, http://referenceworks.brillonline.com/entries/encyclopaedia-of-islam-2/mutazila-COM_0822.

15. Ashʿarism is the dominant school of Sunni Islamic theology (*ʿilm al-kalam*) with origins in the tenth century C.E. See "Ashʿariyya," *Encyclopedia of Islam*, 2nd ed., Brill online, 2013, http://referenceworks.brillonline.com/entries/encyclopaedia-of-islam-2/ashariyya-COM_0067.
16. McAuliffe, "The Tasks" 196.
17. McAuliffe, "The Tasks" 197.
18. McAuliffe, "The Tasks" 198.
19. McAuliffe, "The Tasks" 198.
20. Gätje, *The Qur'an and Its Exegesis* 39.
21. McAuliffe, "The Tasks" 193; Rippin, "Tafsir" 242.
22. Gätje, *The Qur'an and Its Exegesis* 32.
23. McAuliffe, "The Tasks" 184.
24. Rippin, "Tafsir" 240.
25. Esack, *The Qur'an* 131.
26. Rippin, "Tafsir (a.)."
27. Rippin, "Tafsir" 240.
28. Esack, *The Qur'an* 132.
29. Rippin, "Tafsir (a.)."
30. Taji-Farouki, Introduction, 9.
31. Kurzman, "Modernism" 456.
32. Kurzman, "Modern Thought" 468.
33. Majeed, "Modernity" 456.
34. Kurzman, "Modern Thought" 467.
35. Rippin, *Muslims* 222; Wielandt, "Exegesis."
36. Rippin, *Muslims* 220.
37. Rippin, *Muslims* 221.
38. Rippin, *Muslims* 219.
39. Rippin, *Muslims* 219; Wielandt, "Exegesis."
40. Saeed, "Fazlur Rahman" 40.
41. Saeed, "Fazlur Rahman" 45.
42. Rippin, *Muslims* 241.
43. Rippin, *Muslims* 241.
44. Majeed, "Modernity" 457; Rippin, *Muslims* 218.
45. Wielandt, "Exegesis."
46. Wielandt, "Exegesis."
47. Wielandt, "Exegesis."
48. Rippin, *Muslims* 219.
49. Wielandt, "Exegesis"; Majeed, "Modernity" 456–457.
50. Wielandt, "Exegesis."
51. Majeed, "Modernity" 456.

52. Majeed, "Modernity" 456–457.
53. Rippin, *Muslims* 221.
54. Rippin, *Muslims* 221.
55. Wielandt, "Exegesis."
56. Wielandt, "Exegesis."
57. Wielandt, "Exegesis."
58. Wielandt, "Exegesis."
59. Wielandt, "Exegesis."
60. Rahman, *Islam* 219.
61. Rippin, *Muslims* 236.
62. Rippin, *Muslims* 236.
63. Rippin, *Muslims* 222.
64. Wielandt, "Exegesis."
65. Rippin, *Muslims* 222.
66. Saeed, "Fazlur Rahman" 42–43.
67. Saeed, "Fazlur Rahman" 48.
68. Saeed, "Fazlur Rahman" 47.
69. Saeed, "Fazlur Rahman" 43. Saeed is partly quoting from Rahman.
70. Rippin, *Muslims* 243.
71. Saeed, "Fazlur Rahman" 42–43.
72. Saeed, "Fazlur Rahman" 59.
73. Saeed, "Fazlur Rahman" 59.
74. Wielandt, "Exegesis."
75. Saeed, "Fazlur Rahman" 50.
76. Saeed, "Fazlur Rahman" 47.
77. Saeed, "Fazlur Rahman" 50. Emphasis his.
78. Rahman in Rippin, *Muslims* 242.
79. Saeed, "Fazlur Rahman" 50.
80. Rahman, *Islam and Modernity* 20.
81. Rahman, *Islam and Modernity* 20.
82. Saeed, "Fazlur Rahman" 51.
83. Saeed, "Fazlur Rahman" 53.
84. Rahman in Rippin, *Muslims* 242.
85. Saeed, "Fazlur Rahman" 49–50.
86. Rahman in Saeed, "Fazlur Rahman" 51.
87. Saeed, "Fazlur Rahman" 43, 53.
88. Saeed, "Fazlur Rahman" 56.
89. Saeed, "Fazlur Rahman" 58.
90. Saeed, "Fazlur Rahman" 58.
91. Saeed, "Fazlur Rahman" 58.
92. Kurzman, "Modern Thought" 468.
93. Kurzman, "Modern Thought" 468.

94. Rippin, *Muslims* 157.
95. Taji-Farouki, Introduction 14.
96. Majeed, "Modernity" 458.
97. Taji-Farouki, Introduction 13, 14.
98. Badran, "Feminism and the Qur'an."
99. Badran, "Feminism and the Qur'an."
100. Phrase taken from Deniz Kandiyoti, "Identity and Its Discontents" 387.
101. See: Ahmed, *Women and Gender*; al-Ali, *Secularism*; Badran, *Feminists, Islam, and Nation*; and Badran, *Feminism in Islam*.
102. Badran, "Feminism and the Qur'an."
103. Badran, "Feminism and the Qur'an"; Badran, *Feminism in Islam* 324. Ruth Roded has called the Egyptian scholar 'A'ishah "'Abd al-Rahman (1913–96), often published under the pseudonym Bint al-Shati," the first Muslim woman *mufassir*; her tafsir, however, did not engage in discussions of gender or feminism. Ruth Roded, "Women and the Qur'an."
104. Badran, *Feminism in Islam* 233, 313.
105. Badran, *Feminism in Islam* 247.
106. Badran, *Feminism in Islam* 244. See also Roded, "Women and the Qur'an."
107. Tohidi, "Muslim Feminism" 113.
108. Abugideiri, "The Renewed Woman of American Islam" 5.
109. Badran, *Feminism in Islam* 331. Wadud notes, however, that "female inclusive theory" was "not developed initially as a direct consequence of already existing discourse over Qur'anic interpretation by male liberal and reformist scholars." Wadud, *Inside the Gender Jihad* 16.
110. Abugideiri, "Qur'an."
111. Abugideiri, "Qur'an."
112. Tohidi, "Muslim Feminism" 113.
113. Abugideiri, "The Renewed Woman" 13.

CHAPTER 2

1. Badran, *Feminism in Islam* 250.
2. Barlas, "Engaging " 6.
3. Badran, *Feminism in Islam* 325.
4. Barlas, "Engaging" 5, 7.
5. Here I make a number of very broad generalizations about political developments mainly in the Middle East and South Asia. A more precise and detailed history is outside the scope of this book and may be found in numerous works that have covered it extensively. Such works include *Islam, Gender, and Social Change*, ed. Yvonne Yazbeck Haddad and John L. Esposito (New York: Oxford University Press, 1998); Leila Ahmed, *Women and Gender in Islam: Historical Roots of a Modern Debate* (New Haven: Yale University Press, 1992); Nadje

al-Ali, *Secularism, Gender, and the State in the Middle East: The Egyptian Women's Movement* (Cambridge: Cambridge University Press, 2000); Margot Badran, *Feminists, Islam, and Nation: Gender and the Making of Modern Egypt* (Princeton: Princeton University Press, 1995); Margot Badran, *Feminism in Islam: Secular and Religious Convergences* (Oxford: Oneworld, 2009); *Gender and Islam in Africa: Rights, Sexuality, and Law*, ed. Margot Badran (Stanford: Stanford University Press, 2011); *Women, Islam, and the State*, ed. Deniz Kandiyoti (Philadelphia: Temple University Press, 1991); and Nilufer Gole, *The Forbidden Modern: Civilization and Veiling* (Ann Arbor: University of Michigan Press, 1996).

6. Kandiyoti, "Identity and Its Discontents" 387.
7. Ahmed, *Women and Gender* 151ff.
8. Shaikh, "Transforming Feminisms" 150.
9. Shaikh, "Transforming Feminisms" 150.
10. Kandiyoti, "Identity and Its Discontents" 387.
11. Phrase taken from Ahmed, *Women and Gender* 149.
12. cooke, "Multiple Critique" 151.
13. Badran, *Feminism in Islam* 303.
14. cooke, "Multiple Critique" 147.
15. cooke, "Multiple Critique" 147.
16. cooke, "Multiple Critique" 147.
17. Mir-Hosseini, "Beyond 'Islam' vs. 'Feminism'" 71.
18. Badran, *Feminism in Islam* 247, 324.
19. Mir-Hosseini, "Beyond 'Islam' vs. 'Feminism'"; Valentine M. Moghadam, "Islamic Feminism and its Discontents: Towards a Resolution of the Debate," *Signs: Journal of Women in Culture and Society* 27. 4 (2002): 1135–1171; cooke, "Multiple Critique"; Shaikh, "Transforming Feminisms"; Abou-Bakr, "Islamic Feminism: What's In a Name?"; Badran, *Feminism in Islam*.
20. Shaikh, "Transforming Feminisms" 155.
21. Badran, *Feminism in Islam* 327.
22. Badran, *Feminism in Islam* 246, 310, 326.
23. Badran, *Feminism in Islam* 245ff, 311ff.
24. Shaikh, "Transforming Feminisms" 155.
25. Badran, *Feminism in Islam* 243–244, 326.
26. Badran, *Feminism in Islam* 303, 325.
27. Shaikh, "Transforming Feminisms" 155.
28. Shaikh, "Transforming Feminisms" 156.
29. Shaikh, "Transforming Feminisms" 156.
30. Badran, *Feminism in Islam* 324.
31. Mir-Hosseini, "Beyond 'Islam' vs. 'Feminism'" 68.
32. Mir-Hosseini, "Beyond 'Islam' vs. 'Feminism'" 71.
33. Mir-Hosseini, "Beyond 'Islam' vs. 'Feminism'" 67.

34. Barlas, "Engaging" 2.
35. Barlas, "Engaging" 4.
36. Barlas, "Engaging" 5.
37. Barlas, "Engaging" 5.
38. Barlas, "Engaging" 5.
39. Barlas, "Engaging" 5.
40. Barlas, "Engaging" 5.
41. See Barlas, *"Believing Women"* 19; Wadud, *Inside the Gender Jihad* 79–80.
42. Ziba Mir-Hosseini has similarly stated that Muslim feminist scholars "must recognise that the legacy of colonialism and the Western hegemony does not allow any of us complete freedom of manoeuvre and analysis" in "Beyond 'Islam' vs. 'Feminism' " 72.
43. Hidayatullah, "Muslim Feminist Birthdays" 120.
44. A similar observation is made by Raja Rhouni in *Secular and Islamic Feminist Critiques* 32. Leila Ahmed makes a parallel argument about how the terms for resisting Western discourses on the veil were set by those very discourses. Ahmed, *Women and Gender* 162, 164.
45. Barlas, "Engaging" 6–7.
46. Barlas, "Women's Readings of the Qur'an," 258–259.
47. Raja Rhouni has similarly called feminism "a cluster of indispensable tools of analysis." Rhouni, *Secular and Islamic Feminist Critiques* 31.
48. Rhouni, *Secular and Islamic Feminist Critiques* 29.

CHAPTER 3

1. Trible and Russell, Introduction 25.
2. Mahmood, "Secularism" 329, 335–336.
3. Valkenberg, "Does the Concept of 'Abrahamic Religions' Have a Future?" 103.
4. Valkenberg, "Does the Concept of 'Abrahamic Religions' Have a Future?" 104.
5. Valkenberg, "Does the Concept of 'Abrahamic Religions' Have a Future?" 104.
6. Valkenberg, "Does the Concept of 'Abrahamic Religions' Have a Future?" 105.
7. Wadud, *Inside the Gender Jihad* 122.
8. Wadud, *Inside the Gender Jihad* 122.
9. Trible and Russell, Introduction 24.
10. Armstrong, Foreword, *Daughters of Abraham* xi.
11. Armstrong, Foreword, *Daughters of Abraham* xii.
12. Amy-Jill Levine, "Settling at Beer-lahai-roi" 27.
13. Harrison, "Modern Women" 158.
14. Tohidi, "Muslim Feminism" 113.
15. Clifford, *Introducing* 64, 65.
16. Clifford, *Introducing* 55.
17. Clifford, *Introducing* 56.

18. Watson, *Feminist Theology* 10.
19. Ruether, "Methodologies" 193.
20. Ruether, *Sexism and God-Talk* 31.
21. Clifford, *Introducing* 30.
22. Clifford, *Introducing* 30.
23. Ruether, *Sexism and God-Talk* 22–23.
24. Ruether, "Methodologies" 194.
25. Ruether, "Methodologies" 194.
26. Ruether, "Methodologies" 189.
27. Ruether, "Methodologies" 190.
28. Daly, *Beyond God the Father* 11–12.
29. Clifford, *Introducing* 69.
30. Clifford, *Introducing* 68.
31. Clifford, *Introducing* 70.
32. Clifford, *Introducing* 70.
33. Fiorenza, *Bread Not Stone* 5.
34. Fiorenza, *Bread Not Stone* 5.
35. Fiorenza, *But She Said* 5.
36. Clifford, *Introducing* 54.
37. Fiorenza, *Bread Not Stone* 15.
38. Plaskow, *Standing Again at Sinai* 33.
39. Plaskow, *Standing Again at Sinai* 34.
40. Watson, *Feminist Theology* 13.
41. Plaskow, "Jewish Theology" 79.
42. Clifford, *Introducing* 56.
43. Watson, Feminist Theology 13.
44. Kwok, *Introducing Asian Feminist Theology* 10.
45. Clifford, *Introducing* 79.
46. Clifford, *Introducing* 29.
47. Ruether, "Methodologies" 195.
48. Cannon, *Black Womanist Ethics*.
49. Williams, *Sisters in the Wilderness*.
50. Mitchem, *Introducing Womanist Theology* 83.
51. Mitchem, *Introducing Womanist Theology* 111.
52. Mitchem, *Introducing Womanist Theology* 47.
53. Mitchem, *Introducing Womanist Theology* 124.
54. Mitchem, *Introducing Womanist Theology* 63.
55. Isasi-Díaz, *Mujerista Theology* 92.
56. Isasi-Díaz, *Mujerista Theology* 95.
57. Isasi-Díaz, *La Lucha* 6.
58. Isasi-Díaz, *La Lucha* 6.
59. Aquino, Machado, and Rodriguez, Introduction xv.

60. Aquino, Machado, and Rodriguez, Introduction xvi.
61. Chung Hyun Kyung's *Struggling to Be the Sun Again: Introducing Asian Women's Theology* (Maryknoll, NY: Orbis, 1990).
62. Kwok, *Introducing*.
63. Kwok, *Introducing* 10.
64. Kwok, *Introducing* 9.
65. Braude, "Riffat Hassan" 183.
66. Hassan, "The Issue" 68.
67. Hassan, "Islam," 228.
68. Shaikh, "Exegetical Violence" 3.
69. Barlas, *"Believing Women"* 20; Barlas, "Women's Readings" 256.
70. Barlas, *"Believing Women"* 22–23.
71. Barlas, *"Believing Women"* 139, 223 n15.
72. Shaikh, "Exegetical Violence" 4 n17.
73. Shaikh, "Exegetical Violence" 8 n32, 13 n94.
74. Shaikh, "Knowledge" 100 n7.
75. Abugideiri, "Hagar" 84.
76. Al–Hibri, "Hagar" 198.
77. Hassan, "Islamic Hagar" 149.
78. Wadud, *Inside the Gender Jihad* 120ff.
79. Wadud, *Inside the Gender Jihad* 148, 153, 145. Wadud begins her chapter "A New Hajar Paradigm: Motherhood and Family" with the poem "The Fire of Hajar" by the Muslim American scholar, author, and poet Mohja Kahf. It is also interesting to note that the organizer of the congregational prayer led by Wadud, Asra Nomani, repeatedly invokes the figure of Hagar in her autobiographical book *Standing Alone in Mecca*, identifying with Hagar as a single mother performing the *hajj* and later founding an organization for Muslim women activists in America called "Daughters of Hajar." Nomani, *Standing Alone in Mecca*.
80. Plaskow and Christ, *Weaving the Visions*.
81. Shaikh, "A *Tafsir* of Praxis" 68 n5.
82. Wadud, *Inside the Gender Jihad* 96.
83. Wadud, *Qur'an and Woman* xv.
84. Wadud, *Inside the Gender Jihad* 96.
85. Wadud, *Inside the Gender Jihad* 7.
86. Amina Wadud, "The Authority of Experience." As I recall, being present in the audience, Wadud did not name Mary Daly in her address.
87. Wadud, *Inside the Gender Jihad* 96. Wadud is quoting Fiorenza.
88. It is important to point out that despite Wadud's use of Jewish and Christian feminist works in 2006, as late as 2000, she remained remarkably suspicious of Muslim women's use of them: "Rather than to enter into the master tool of Islam's own patriarchal intellectual development, Muslim feminists

and others tend to sidestep this task. Instead they offer second-hand versions of western Jewish and Christian feminist critique, as if these could adequately fulfill the task of building an authentic Islamic gender-inclusive reconstruction." It is not clear exactly whom Wadud is faulting here. Wadud, "Roundtable" 99.

89. Shaikh, "Exegetical Violence" 4 n14; Shaikh, "Knowledge" 100 n5.
90. Shaikh, "Exegetical Violence" 4.
91. Ruether, *Sexism and God–Talk* 53.
92. Barlas, *"Believing Women"* 94. Her reference to Ruether appears in the text on page 105, and in endnote 20 on page 224.
93. Barlas, *"Believing Women"* 106. See also her discussion on page 108.
94. Shaikh, "Exegetical Violence" 10 n45.
95. Levine, "Settling" 18–19.
96. Armstrong, Foreword, *Daughters of Abraham* xii.
97. Gross, "Feminist Theology" 63.
98. Majeed, "Womanism" 42.
99. Wadud, "Roundtable" 95.
100. Majeed, "Womanism" 42–43.
101. Wadud, "Roundtable" 95.
102. Wadud, "Roundtable" 94.
103. Rosemary Radford Ruether, ed., *Feminist Theologies: Legacy and Prospects* (Minneapolis: Fortress Press, 2007).
104. I further examine this problem in "The Qur'anic Rib-ectomy: Scriptural Purity, Imperial Dangers, and Other Obstacles to the Interfaith Engagement of Muslim Feminist Hermeneutics."
105. Roald, "Feminist" 41.
106. Roald, "Feminist" 40.
107. Roald, "Feminist" 21.
108. Roald, "Feminist" 21.
109. Wadud, *Inside the Gender Jihad* 204.
110. Wadud, *Inside the Gender Jihad* 206.
111. Hammer, "Identity" 456.
112. Hammer, "Identity" 456; Mahmood Mamdani, *Good Muslim, Bad Muslim: America, the Cold War, and the Roots of Terror* (New York: Pantheon Books, 2004).
113. Taji-Farouki, Introduction 8.
114. Manji, *The Trouble with Islam Today*.
115. Rastegar, "Managing 'American Islam'" 469.
116. Mahmood, "Secularism, Hermeneutics, and Empire" 329, 336.
117. Barlas, "Engaging" 5; Barlas, "Does the Qur'an Support Gender Equality?" 9.
118. Barlas, "Engaging" 5.

CHAPTER 4

1. Ali ibn Ahmad al-Wahidi, *Al-Wahidi's Asbab al-Nuzul*, trans. Mokrane Guezzou, ed. Yousef Meri (Amman, Jordan/Louisville, KY: Fons Vitae/Royal Aal al-Bayt Institute for Islamic Thought, 2008), x.
2. Barlas, *"Believing Women"* 50–51.
3. Stowasser, "The Qur'an and History" 35. Stowasser is quoting Rotraud Wielandt.
4. Stowasser, "The Qur'an and History" 59–60.
5. Wadud, "Qur'an, Gender, and Interpretive" 331.
6. Barlas, *"Believing Women"* 55.
7. Wadud, *Qur'an and Woman* 9. Elsewhere, Wadud similarly notes: "The expansive and eternal intent of universal guidance toward right actions, . . . revealed in the seventh-century Arabia, was . . . particularized within the parameters of the social-cultural, moral, legal, and linguistic constraints of that context." Wadud, *Inside the Gender Jihad* 213.
8. Wadud, *Qur'an and Woman* 100–101.
9. Wadud notes of her work: "My analysis tends to restrict the meaning of many passages to a particular subject, event, or context." *Qur'an and Woman* 63.
10. Rippin, "Occasions of Revelation."
11. Rippin identifies the *Kitab Asbab nuzul al-Qur'an* of Abu al-Hasan 'Ali b. Ahmad al-Wahidi al-Nisaburi (d. 468/1075) as the earliest such work that was key to the formation of the genre. Rippin, "Occasions of Revelation."
12. Rippin, "Al-Zarkashi and al-Suyuti" 250.
13. Rippin, "Al-Zarkashi and al-Suyuti" 258.
14. Rippin, "The Function" 8.
15. Von Denffer, *'Ulum al–Qur'an* 101.
16. Von Denffer, *'Ulum al–Qur'an* 101.
17. Rippin, "Al-Zarkashi and al-Suyuti" 251–252.
18. Stowasser, "The Qur'an and History" 23.
19. Rippin, "The Function of 'Asbab al-Nuzul' " 8.
20. Rippin, "Al-Zarkashi and al-Suyuti" 255.
21. Von Denffer, *'Ulum al–Qur'an* 100–101.
22. Rahman, *Islam and Modernity* 5.
23. Rahman, *Islam and Modernity* 6.
24. Rahman, *Islam and Modernity* 20.
25. Rahman offers interesting observations on the *asbab al-nuzul* genre: "The literature on the 'occasions of revelation' is often highly contradictory and chaotic. The basic reason for this state of affairs seems to be that, although most Qur'anic commentators were aware of the importance of these 'situational contexts,' either because of their historical significance or for their aid in understanding the point of certain injunctions, they never realized their full

import . . . Instead, they enunciated the principle that 'although an injunction might have been occasioned by a certain situation, it is nevertheless universal in its general application.' This principle is sound enough provided it means by an 'injunction' the value underlying that injunction and not merely its literal wording. But the value can be yielded only by understanding well not only the language, but above all the situational context of a given injunction. This, however, was not generally not done, since, as I have just said, the real significance of the 'occasions of revelation' was not realized." Rahman, *Islam and Modernity*, 17.

26. Wadud, *Qur'an and Woman* 4.
27. Wadud, *Inside the Gender Jihad* 195.
28. Wadud, *Inside the Gender Jihad* 194.
29. Wadud, *Inside the Gender Jihad* 194.
30. Wadud, *Inside the Gender Jihad* 194.
31. Wadud, *Inside the Gender Jihad* 194.
32. Wadud, *Inside the Gender Jihad* 196, 194.
33. Wadud, *Qur'an and Woman* 99.
34. Barlas, "*Believing Women*" 6.
35. Wadud, *Qur'an and Woman* 81.
36. Henceforth, verses of the Qur'an will be indicated by this notation: chapter number, followed by a colon, followed by the verse number. See appendix for full verse. Verse 4:34 is also discussed extensively in chapters 5 and 6.
37. Wadud, *Qur'an and Woman* 70. The verse most commonly associated with female shares of inheritance is 4:11. According to Azizah al-Hibri, the "Qur'an does specify that a *sister* inherits half of the amount her *brother* inherits, but also specifies that other females of different degrees of kinship may inherit more than other males." However, she points out that even in the case of siblings, the wealth inherited by a woman is hers to keep, whereas the wealth inherited by a man is used to financially support his family. Al-Hibri, "Muslim Women's Rights" 49.
38. Wadud, *Qur'an and Woman* 71.
39. Wadud, *Qur'an and Woman* 73.
40. Al-Hibri, "An Introduction" 63–64.
41. Al-Hibri, "Quranic Foundations" 19.
42. Al-Hibri, "An Introduction" 64.
43. Al-Hibri, "Deconstructing" 228. Interestingly, Riffat Hassan claims that the Qur'an is making a prescriptive, not a descriptive statement. For her, the statement about men being the *qawwamun* of women "is not a descriptive one stating that all men as a matter of fact are providing for women, since obviously there are at least some men who do not provide for women. What this sentence is stating, rather, is that men ought to have the capability to provide (since ought implies can). In other words, this statement, which almost all Muslim

societies have taken to be an actual description of men, is in fact a normative statement pertaining to the Islamic concept of division of labor in an ideal family or community structure. The fact that men are *qawwamun* does not mean that women cannot or should not provide for themselves, but simply that in view of the heavy burden that most women shoulder with regard to childbearing and rearing, they should not have the additional obligation of providing the means of living at the same time." Hassan, "Muslim Women" 55.

44. Al-Hibri, "An Introduction" 64.
45. Al-Hibri, "Qur'anic Foundations" 18.
46. See appendix for full verse. This verse is discussed again in chapter 5.
47. Hassan interprets the term *darajah* differently (without a clear rationale), though with the same argumentative effect of delimiting the context of the verse: "The 'advantage' that men have over women in this context is that women must observe a three-month period called *iddat* before remarriage, but men are exempted from this requirement. The main reason why women are subjected to this restriction is because at the time of divorce a woman may be pregnant and this fact may not become known for some time. As men cannot become pregnant, they are allowed to remarry without a waiting period." Hassan, "Muslim Women" 58.
48. Wadud, *Qur'an and Woman* 68.
49. Wadud, *Qur'an and Woman* 69. Barlas agrees that "it is clear that the 'degree' does not refer to the ontological status of men as males, or even to their rights over women; rather it is a specific reference to a husband's rights in divorce." Barlas, *"Believing Women"* 196.
50. Wadud, *Qur'an and Woman*, 80.
51. Wadud, *Qur'an and Woman* 80.
52. This verse is also discussed extensively in chapter 5.
53. The phrase "what your right hands possess" is generally understood as referring to female slaves owned by a man as his property, in accordance with the customs of many premodern Islamic societies.
54. Wadud, *Qur'an and Woman* 82 83.
55. Wadud, *Qur'an and Woman* 83. Amira al-Azhary Sonbol has attributed the verse to the period immediately following the Battle of Uhud: "The verse addresses a situation in which, due to the death of many at the battle of Uhud, the women and orphans left behind became wards of those who survived. As such, they risked having whatever property they had inherited or already owned appropriated by the new guardians." She specifies the context even further at one point, citing a Hadith report in which a man with an orphan married her and took her property even though he had no other desire for her. For Sonbol, "the verse was closely connected with a particular event; and given the details of the verse, it does not seem to have been meant to establish a general rule." Amirah al-Azhary Sonbol, "Rethinking Women and Islam" 143, 134, 137–138.

56. Barlas concurs: in this verse, "polygyny serves a very specific purpose: that of securing *justice for female orphans*." Barlas, *"Believing Women"* 190.
57. As Barlas puts it, in this verse the Qur'an "limited the number of wives men could now marry, restricted multiple marriages to orphans, and made such marriages contingent on a set of well-specified and stringent criteria." Barlas, *"Believing Women"* 191. Al-Hibri produces a congruent reading. According to her, the first part of the verse "conditions the permission upon a certain context that obtained at the time of its revelation, namely, one of justice and fairness concerning the treatment of orphaned wives." Therefore, this verse is "highly conditional and fact-specific" and thus should not be taken as a general rule. Al-Hibri, "An Introduction" 66.
58. Wadud, *Qur'an and Woman* 83.
59. Wadud, *Qur'an and Woman* 84.
60. Azizah al-Hibri offers a very similar reading of 4:3; like Wadud, she argues that this "highly conditional and fact-specific" verse "conditions the permission [for polygyny] upon a certain context . . . at the time of its revelation, namely one of justness and fairness concerning the treatment of orphaned wives." Al-Hibri, "An Introduction" 66.
61. Wadud, *Qur'an and Woman* 84.
62. This verse is discussed again in chapter 5.
63. Wadud, *Qur'an and Woman*, 85.
64. Wadud, *Qur'an and Woman* 86.
65. This is in contradiction to a number of Hadith reports, such as one cited by Riffat Hassan in which a group of women asked the Prophet, "What is deficient in our intelligence and religion?" In response the Prophet is reported to have asked, "Is not the evidence of two women equal to the witness of one man?," to which he replies himself, "This is the deficiency in your intelligence." Hassan, "An Islamic Perspective" 123.
66. Wadud, *Qur'an and Woman* 85. Wadud quotes from Fazlur Rahman's reading of this verse to substantiate her own.
67. See appendix for full verse.
68. Wadud, *Qur'an and Woman* 77.
69. Wadud, *Qur'an and Woman* 77.
70. For example, as seen in verse 44:54.
71. Wadud, *Qur'an and Woman* 55.
72. Wadud, *Qur'an and Woman* 57. Wadud observes that after the Meccan period, the phrase *hur al-'ayn* is never again repeated in the Qur'an and is replaced with a more general term: *azwaj*, meaning mates (both male and female), *Qur'an and Woman* 55.
73. The historical contextualization of Qur'anic pronouncements on women's modesty discussed in this section intersects in crucial ways with the work of Fatima Mernissi in chapter 10 of her *The Veil and the Male Elite*. Barlas does not draw directly on Mernissi, but some indirect influence is not out of the question.

74. Barlas, *"Believing Women"* 55–56.
75. Barlas, *"Believing Women"* 55.
76. Barlas, *"Believing Women"* 56.
77. In reading these verses historically, the concern is not only with the irrelevance of these particular verses today but also that their application today is counterproductive to the Qur'an's vision of sexual modesty and propriety; interpreters worry that their application now lends itself to a *Jahili* type of sexual corruption that the Qur'an sought to combat. Barlas notes, "the rule of Islam, by ordaining sexual modesty for women and men, *runs counter* to the rule of the veil, brought on by *Jahili* male promiscuity." Barlas, *"Believing Women"* 57.
78. Wadud, *Inside the Gender Jihad* 215.
79. Wadud, *Inside the Gender Jihad* 215.
80. Wadud, *Qur'an and Woman* 5.
81. Wadud, *Qur'an and Woman* 22.
82. Wadud, *Qur'an and Woman* 8.
83. Barlas, *"Believing Women"* 52.
84. Wadud, *Qur'an and Woman* 8. Wadud uses this argument again in her discussion of verse 2:228: "Each social context divides the labour between the male and the female in such a way as to allow for the optimal function of that society. The Qur'an does not divide the labour and establish a monolithic order for every social system which completely disregards the natural variations in society . . . [The Qur'an] allows and encourages each individual social context to determine its functional distinction between members, but applies a single system of equitable recompense which can be adopted in every social context." Wadud, *Qur'an and Woman* 67.
85. Wadud, *Qur'an and Woman* 8–9.
86. Barlas, *"Believing Women"* 9.
87. Barlas, *"Believing Women"* 17.
88. Shaikh, "Exegetical Violence" 59–60.
89. Shaikh, "Exegetical Violence" 58–59. Shaikh makes similar observations in another piece on domestic violence: Shaikh, "A *Tafsir* of Praxis" 70–73.
90. Shaikh, "Exegetical Violence" 72.
91. Speight, "The Function" 63–64.
92. Speight, "The Function" 64.
93. Rahman, *Islam* 64.
94. Rahman, *Islam* 64.
95. Humphreys, *Islamic History* 76.
96. Humphreys, *Islamic History* 86.
97. Rahman, *Islam* 67.
98. Rahman, *Islam* 66.
99. Afsaruddin, "'Enlightened' Interpretations" 66–67.
100. Esack, *The Qur'an* 131.
101. Rahman, *Islam* 64.

102. Rahman, *Islam* 64–65.
103. Rahman, *Islam* 65.
104. Rahman, *Islam* 65.
105. Rahman, *Islam* 66.
106. Rahman, *Islam* 67.
107. Rahman makes the observation that as a result of this dilemma, "even the thoroughgoing skeptics about the Hadith cannot resist supporting their views by [the Hadith] whenever it suits them." *Islam* 67.
108. Barlas, *"Believing Women"* 42–49, 64–68.
109. Barlas, *"Believing Women"* 44.
110. Barlas, *"Believing Women"* 52–53.
111. Barlas, *"Believing Women"* 64.
112. Hassan, "The Issue" 76.
113. Barlas, *"Believing Women"* 67.
114. Barlas, *"Believing Women"* 66.
115. Hassan, "An Islamic Perspective" 94.
116. Hassan, "The Issue" 80.
117. Wadud, *Qur'an and Woman* xvii.
118. Rahman, *Islam* 64.
119. The criticism of the authenticity of anti-women Hadith reports is developed at length by Fatima Mernissi. See especially chapters 3 and 4 of *The Veil and the Male Elite*.
120. Hassan, "The Issue" 77–80.
121. Hassan, "The Issue" 80.
122. Hassan, "An Islamic Perspective," 114, 108, 115, 123.
123. Wadud, *Inside the Gender Jihad* 202.
124. Wadud, *Inside the Gender Jihad* 202.
125. Wadud, *Inside the Gender Jihad* 202.
126. Al-Hibri, "An Islamic Perspective" 207.
127. Al-Hibri, "An Islamic Perspective" 207; al-Hibri, "Muslim Women's Rights" 60.
128. Al-Hibri, "An Islamic Perspective" 207, 211; Al-Hibri, "Muslim Women's Rights" 61.
129. Al-Hibri, "An Islamic Perspective" 210–211; Al-Hibri, "Muslim Women's Rights" 61.
130. On the matter of Hadith reports that are "positive" regarding women, Barlas notes that there are very few "misogynistic" Hadith reports in the *sahih* collections but that these are the ones with more currency than the large number of "positive" ones; they include reports that "emphasize women's full humanity; counsel husbands to deal kindly and justly with their wives; confirm the right of women to acquire knowledge; elevate mothers over fathers; proclaim that women will be in heaven, ahead, even of the Prophet; record women's attendance at prayers in the mosque during the Prophet's lifetime . . . ; and

record that the Prophet accepted the evidence of one woman over that of a man." Such reports would indeed be vastly useful toward feminist arguments; thus their appeal to women exegetes is understandable. Barlas, *"Believing Women"* 46.
131. More recently, Indonesian scholar Faqihuddin Abdul Kodir has argued that in ignoring or rejecting the Hadith, feminist scholarship has missed the opportunity for locating a paradigm of gender equality once Hadith is subject to historical contextualization; he argues that a close historical reading of the Hadith allows for the positive usage of the reports' intents and essential purposes. Faqihuddin Abdul Kodir, "Gender Equality and the Hadith of the Prophet Muhammad: Reinterpreting the Concepts of Mahram and Qiwama," *Gender and Equality in Muslim Family Law*, ed. Mir-Hosseini et al. 170, 178.
132. Shaikh, "Knowledge" 99–108.
133. Barlas, *"Believing Women,"* 67–68.
134. Wadud, *Inside the Gender Jihad* 7.

CHAPTER 5

1. Rahman, *Major Themes* xv.
2. I borrow the term intratextual from Asma Barlas and Amina Wadud. Barlas, *"Believing Women"* 16, 18; Wadud, "Towards a Qur'anic Hermeneutics" 43. The term is sometimes used synonymously with "intra-Qur'anic."
3. Mir, *Coherence in the Qur'an* 3–4.
4. This term may be used to mean the arrangement or ordering of something, particularly the composition of Arabic poetry. Wehr, *A Dictionary of Modern Written Arabic* 1147.
5. Esack, *The Qur'an* 129.
6. Saeed, *Interpreting the Qur'an* 43.
7. Ibn Taymiyyah, *Muqaddimah fi usul al-tafsir (An Introduction to the Principles of Tafseer)* 53.
8. Rahman, *Islam and Modernity* 2.
9. Mir, *Coherence* 1.
10. Rahman, *Islam and Modernity* 2.
11. Barlas, *"Believing Women"* 6.
12. Barlas, *"Believing Women"* 16, 15. Barlas quotes from Abdullah Yusuf Ali's translation of verse 3:7 and Marmaduke Pickthall's translation of verses 15:91–93 respectively. Wadud also cites as evidence verse 3:119's reference to Muslims believing in "the whole of the book." Wadud, *Qur'an and Woman* 81.
13. Wadud, "Qur'an, Gender and Interpretive" 331.
14. Wadud, "Qur'an, Gender and Interpretive" 327. Brackets indicate my clarifications of Wadud's text. See also: Wadud, "Towards" 43.
15. Wadud, *Qur'an and Woman* 2.

16. According to Rahman and Mir, this trend in Western scholarship is exhibited in the works of Montgomery Watt and Richard Bell. Rahman, *Major Themes* xiv–xv; Mir, *Coherence* 2.
17. Mir, "Unity of the Text of the Qur'an." However, in his *Coherence in the Qur'an*, Mir notes: "A few modern scholars have essayed to show the cohesion in the Qur'anic outlook, but . . . without sufficient account for the arrangement the Qur'an actually possesses." For Mir, an exception is the *Tadabbur-i Qur'an* of Hamid ad-Din 'Abd al–Hamid al–Farahi (d. 1930 C.E.), "the first thoroughgoing attempt to show that the Qur'an is marked by thematic, and also by structural, coherence." Mir, *Coherence* 4. Mir summarizes Islahi's central argument: "The Qur'an possesses unity at several levels: the verse-sequence in each sura deals with a well-defined theme in a methodical manner; the suras, as a rule, exist as pairs, the two suras of any pair being complementary to each other; and the suras are divisible into seven groups, each dealing with a master theme that is developed systematically within the suras of the group." Mir, "Unity."
18. Rippin, "Tafsir (a.)."
19. Rahman, *Major Themes* 15.
20. Rahman, *Islam and Modernity* 6.
21. Al-Hibri, "Muslim Women's Rights" 60; Cf. al-Hibri, "Quranic Foundations" 16.
22. Barlas, *"Believing Women"* 17, 16. For Barlas, "the best way to read the Qur'an is by the Qur'an." Barlas, "Does the Qur'an Support Gender Equality?" 4.
23. Wadud, *Qur'an and Woman* xii. Wadud also briefly refers to the concept of nazm in the work of Islahi. Wadud, "Towards" 44.
24. For Wadud, this holistic reading strategy—understanding "the whole text, its Weltanschauung or world-view"—constitutes one of the essential tools for interpreting any text. Wadud, *Qur'an and Woman* 3, 62.
25. Rahman, *Major Themes* 15.
26. Barlas, *"Believing Women"* 168–169. Al-Hibri also makes a number of parallel statements. She notes "the danger of separating an ayah, or part of an ayah, from its context to reach an isolated interpretation of its meaning." Al-Hibri, "An Islamic Perspective" 206. "The Qur'an is an integral whole and thus the full and proper meaning of any verse cannot be understood in isolation from other verses in the rest of the Qur'an." Al-Hibri, "Muslim Women's Rights" 60. "There is a unified worldview that permeates the Qur'an, and that makes it a seamless web of ideas, so that each verse cannot be properly understood without reference to others. In one sense, this is not a new argument, because ancient jurists have already stated that passages in the Qur'an explain each other." Al-Hibri, "Divine Justice" 238.
27. Wadud, *Qur'an and Woman* 3. Emphasis mine.
28. Barlas, *"Believing Women"* 8.
29. Portions of the Adam and Eve story appear in verses 2:35–38, 7:19–25, and 20:120–123.

30. Hassan, "Muslim Women" 47, 49. Cf. Wadud, *Qur'an and Woman* 25; Barlas, *"Believing Women"* 138–139.
31. Hassan, "Muslim Women" 49–50.
32. Hassan comments on this point: "Although the Genesis 2 account of woman's creation is accepted by virtually all Muslims, it is difficult to believe that it entered the Islamic tradition directly, for very few Muslims ever read the Bible. It is much more likely that it became a part of Muslim heritage through its assimilation in Hadith literature." Hassan, "The Issue" 75.
33. Hassan, "The Issue" 80.
34. Hassan, "Muslim Women" 54.
35. Hassan, "Muslim Women" 44.
36. See chapter 4's discussion of the Muslim feminist conundrum of disavowing problematic Hadith reports. Hassan observes that "the fact that almost all Muslims believe that the first woman (Hawwa) was created from Adam's rib shows that, in practice, the Hadith literature has displaced the teaching of the Qur'an at least insofar as the issue of woman's creation is concerned." Hassan, "The Issue" 80.
37. Hassan, "Muslim Women" 44.
38. See appendix for full verse. Hassan also points to 75: 36–39 (on the creation of male and female from a single clot) as further evidence that men and women were created from a single unit. Hassan, "The Issue" 74.
39. Wadud also translates *nafs* as "living entity." Wadud, "Qur'an, Gender and Interpretive" 326.
40. Barlas disagrees on the definition of *nafs*, rejecting the term "soul" in favor of "Self" or "Person" in order to avoid any gendered "typology of spirit, soul, and body," such as that used by early Muslim scholars to overlay "body-soul dualisms" and hierarchy onto the creation of man and woman. Barlas does not, however, develop this point further, and I am not convinced that her alternative definition has any significant bearing on the basic argument of man and woman originating from the same source. Barlas, *"Believing Women"* 133–134.
41. Hassan, "The Issue" 74; Wadud, *Qur'an and Woman* 19 20.

    To rule out the possibility of man or Adam as God's first creation at any other point in the Qur'an, Hassan also points out that the word *adam* in the Qur'an usually "functions generally as a collective noun referring to *the human* (species) rather than to a male human being." In the Qur'an, *adam* "refers, in twenty-one cases out of twenty-five, to humanity" and does not function as the proper name Adam. Hassan, "Muslim Women" 45.
42. Hassan, "The Issue" 72; Wadud, *Qur'an and Woman* 20.
43. Wadud, *Qur'an and Woman* 18–19.
44. Hassan, "The Issue" 74, 77. Cf. Barlas, *"Believing Women"* 135.
45. Wadud, *Qur'an and Woman* 26.
46. Barlas, *"Believing Women"* 140.

47. For example, Hassan, "Muslim Women" 52–53. See appendix for the text of the verse.
48. Barlas, *"Believing Women"* 143.
49. See appendix for text of the verse. Barlas, *"Believing Women"* 147–148. Cf. Hassan, "Muslim Women" 52–53; Shaikh, "A *Tafsir* of Praxis" 66.
50. Barlas, *"Believing Women"* 140.
51. Wadud, *Qur'an and Woman* 50, 51, 58.
52. Hassan, "Muslim Women" 52–53.
53. Wadud, *Qur'an and Woman* 63.
54. Barlas, *"Believing Women"* 144.
55. Wadud, *Qur'an and Woman* 50.
56. Hassan, "Muslim Women" 53–54.
57. Wadud, *Qur'an and Woman* 68–69. Elsewhere, Wadud also notes that "it is in the very nature of the text itself to encourage and implement greater experiences of equality and equity between women and men." Wadud, "Alternative Qur'anic Interpretation" 20–21.
58. Hassan, "The Issue" 80.
59. Barlas, *"Believing Women"* 17.
60. Hassan, "Muslim Women" 44.
61. Wadud, *Qur'an and Woman* 81.
62. See appendix for full verses. Sometimes also cited in conjunction with these verses is 7:189, a key portion of which reads: "It is [God] who created you from a single soul and made from it its mate so that he might find rest in her."
63. Wadud, *Qur'an and Woman* 78.
64. Al-Hibri, "An Islamic Perspective" 202; Al-Hibri, "Deconstructing" 226; Riffat Hassan also cites verse 2:187 to refer to the Qur'an's position on the mutuality and equality of men and women in marriage. Hassan, "Muslim Women" 59.
65. Barlas, *"Believing Women"* 148.
66. The relevant portion of the verse reads, "Divorce is allowable twice, then holding fast (in a manner) as is commonly recognized (as fair) or separating with charity . . ."
67. Al-Hibri, "Muslim Women's Rights" 63.
68. Al-Hibri, "An Islamic Perspective" 202–203.
69. Shaikh, "A *Tafsir* of Praxis" 67.
70. Wadud, "Qur'an, Gender and Interpretive" 334.
71. Wadud, *Qur'an and Woman* 9.
72. Wadud, *Qur'an and Woman* 82.
73. Al-Hibri, "Muslim Women's Rights" 56.
74. Al-Hibri, "Muslim Women's Rights" 56.
75. Wadud, *Qur'an and Woman* xiii.
76. Wadud, *Qur'an and Woman* xiii.
77. Wadud, *Qur'an and Woman* 81.
78. Wadud, *Qur'an and Woman* 63.

79. Wadud, "Qur'an, Gender and Interpretive" 334; *Qur'an and Woman* 63.
80. Hassan, "Muslim Women" 61–62.
81. Wadud, *Inside the Gender Jihad* 213.
82. Wadud, *Inside the Gender Jihad* 215.
83. Wadud, *Qur'an and Woman* 101.
84. Wadud, *Qur'an and Woman* xiii.
85. One rare mention is Azizah al-Hibri's brief reference to it in a discussion of Islam's adaptability to change in her early work. Al-Hibri, "A Study of Islamic Herstory" 214. Another is Barlas's mention of it in a discussion on polyvalent readings of the Qur'an. Barlas, *"Believing Women"* 36. Wadud also briefly mentions *naskh* but only as an incidental part of the history of *tafsir al-Qur'an bi-l-Qur'an*. Wadud, "Towards" 43.
86. Rippin, "Abrogation."
87. Rippin, "Abrogation."
88. Al-Hibri, "A Study of Islamic Herstory" 214.
89. Rippin, "Abrogation."
90. Renard, *Seven Doors to Islam* 3; Al-Hibri, "A Study of Islamic Herstory" 214.
91. Renard, *Seven Doors to Islam* 3.
92. Rippin, "Abrogation."
93. Burton, "Abrogation."
94. Esack, *The Qur'an* 127.
95. Esack, *The Qur'an* 127.
96. Rippin, "Abrogation."
97. Wadud points out that some Muslim countries have already begun the process of enacting reforms that "operate outside the literal content of some Qur'anic passages and make modifications on the basis of greater Qur'anic intent with respect to such issues as repudiation, polygamy, inheritance, and the rules for witnessing, etc." Wadud, *Qur'an and Woman* 82.
98. See appendix for full verse.
99. Wadud, *Qur'an and Woman* 68–69.
100. See appendix for full verse.
101. See appendix for verse.
102. Barlas, *"Believing Women"* 164.
103. Barlas, *"Believing Women"* 164.
104. See appendix for verse.
105. Barlas, *"Believing Women"* 190.
106. Al-Hibri, "An Introduction" 66.
107. See appendix for full verse.
108. Al-Hibri, "A Study of Islamic Herstory" 216; Wadud, *Qur'an and Woman* 83; Barlas, *"Believing Women"* 191.
109. Barlas, *"Believing Women"* 191; Cf. Al-Hibri, "A Study of Islamic Herstory" 216; Wadud, *Qur'an and Woman* 83.
110. Barlas, *"Believing Women"* 192.

111. Barlas, *"Believing Women"* 192.
112. Al-Hibri, "Muslim Women's Rights" 59.
113. Wadud, *Qur'an and Woman* 83. The bracketed insertions are Wadud's.
114. Al-Hibri, "Muslim Women's Rights" 58.
115. See appendix for full verse.
116. Wadud, *Qur'an and Woman* 73.
117. Barlas, *"Believing Women"* 186. Along the same lines, al-Hibri asks, "How could women be 'Awliya' of men if men are superior to women in . . . physical and intellectual strength?" Al-Hibri, "A Study of Islamic Herstory" 218.
118. Al-Hibri, "Deconstructing" 227, 228.
119. Al-Hibri, "Deconstructing" 228.
120. Al-Hibri, "Deconstructing " 226, 228.
121. See appendix for full verse.
122. Wadud, *Qur'an and Woman* 74. Cf. Ali, *Sexual Ethics* 120.
123. Wadud, *Qur'an and Woman* 74.
124. Wadud, *Qur'an and Woman* 75.
125. See appendix for full verse.
126. Al-Hibri argues that based on the Prophet's use of the phrase *"fahishah mubayyinah"* in the portion of his Farewell Address that appears to refer to 4:34 and similar language in verses 4:15 and 4:19, *nushuz* refers specifically to cases of "clear and evident adultery" or something equally egregious or disobedient toward God but not to mere "violations of the husband's whims and wishes." Al-Hibri, "An Islamic Perspective" 218–219.
127. Al-Hibri, "Muslim Women's Rights" 64–65.
128. Hassan, "An Islamic Perspective" 112.
129. Wadud, *Qur'an and Woman* 76.
130. Wadud, *Qur'an and Woman* 76.
131. Wadud, *Qur'an and Woman* 76.
132. Al-Hibri, "Muslim Women's Rights" 61–62; Al-Hibri, "An Islamic Perspective" 211–212.
133. Al-Hibri, "Muslim Women's Rights" 61.
134. Al-Hibri, "Muslim Women's Rights" 65.
135. Al-Hibri, "Muslim Women's Rights" 60.
136. Al-Hibri, "Muslim Women's Rights" 62.
137. Al-Hibri, "Muslim Women's Rights" 64–65.
138. Al-Hibri, "An Islamic Perspective" 209. Al-Hibri cites a number of juristic opinions noting that if a man strikes his wife in accordance with 4:34, the strike must be mild, not on face, and must not leave a mark. He is allowed to strike her with something like a toothbrush or handkerchief. Al-Hibri, "Muslim Women's Rights" 63–64. Barlas cites the same interpretation. Barlas, *"Believing Women"* 188.
139. Al-Hibri, "An Islamic Perspective" 204.

140. Al-Hibri, "An Islamic Perspective" 204.
141. See appendix for verse.
142. Al-Hibri, "Deconstructing Patriarchal Jurisprudence" 228.
143. Barlas, *"Believing Women"* 189. Brackets mine.
144. Wadud, *Qur'an and Woman* 76.
145. Wadud, *Inside the Gender Jihad* 199. As I will discuss later, Kecia Ali arrives at a similar conclusion on the problems of the verse itself. She notes that an intratextual treatment of references to both male and female *nushuz* does not change the fact that the verses outline different consequences for each sex in response to this behavior. She observes that "simply noting that the Qur'an treats both male and female *nushuz* as problems does not automatically absolve the Qur'an of preferring the male over the female in this respect. That is to say, the consequences for female *nushuz* . . . do not merely differ in the interpretations of the exegetes, but are clearly differentiated in the text of the Qur'an itself." Ali, *Sexual Ethics* 122.
146. Wadud, *Inside the Gender Jihad* 200.
147. Wadud, *Inside the Gender Jihad* 203.
148. Wadud, *Inside the Gender Jihad* 203.
149. Wadud, *Inside the Gender Jihad* 202–203.
150. Wadud, *Inside the Gender Jihad* 203.
151. Wadud, *Inside the Gender Jihad* 203.
152. Wadud, *Inside the Gender Jihad* 203. Brackets mine.
153. Wadud, "Qur'an, Gender and Interpretive" 332; Wadud, *Qur'an and Woman* xiii.
154. Wadud, "Qur'an, Gender and Interpretive" 333. Cf. Wadud, *Qur'an and Woman* xiv. See also Wadud's use of the metaphor of a three-tiered sculptural frieze to visualize the Qur'an's structural coherence. Wadud, "Qur'an, Gender and Interpretive" 334–335.

CHAPTER 6

1. Abou El Fadl, *Speaking in God's Name* 93.
2. I borrow this phrasing from Amina Wadud, who coins the term "the *tawhidic paradigm*" in her *Inside the Gender Jihad* 24.
3. Barlas, *"Believing Women"* 13, 96.
4. Wadud, *Inside the Gender Jihad* 28.
5. Wadud, *Inside the Gender Jihad* 13.
6. Wadud, *Inside the Gender Jihad* 13.
7. Wadud, *Inside the Gender Jihad* 13.
8. Barlas, *"Believing Women"* 96.
9. Al-Hibri, "An Introduction" 52.
10. Wadud, *Inside the Gender Jihad* 185.

11. Wadud, *Inside the Gender Jihad* 185.
12. Wadud, *Inside the Gender Jihad* 32.
13. Al-Hibri, "Divine Justice" 240.
14. Al-Hibri, "Divine Justice" 247.
15. Al-Hibri, "Divine Justice" 240–241.
16. Al-Hibri, "Divine Justice" 247.
17. Wadud, "Islam Beyond Patriarchy" 103.
18. Wadud, "Foreword" 437.
19. Al-Hibri, "An Introduction" 54.
20. See appendix for verse.
21. Al-Hibri, "An Islamic Perspective" 215.
22. Barlas, *"Believing Women"* 108.
23. Al-Hibri, "An Islamic Perspective" 214.
24. Shaikh, "Exegetical Violence" 61.
25. Shaikh, "Exegetical Violence" 61–62. In this discussion, Shaikh is responding specifically to *Al–Tafsir al–Kabir* of Fakhr al–Din al–Razi.
26. Barlas, *"Believing Women"* 106.
27. Shaikh, "Exegetical Violence" 62.
28. Barlas, *"Believing Women"* 106.
29. Shaikh, "Exegetical Violence" 62.
30. Shaikh, "Exegetical Violence" 62.
31. Shaikh, "Exegetical Violence" 71.
32. Shaikh, "Exegetical Violence" 62. Here Shaikh is quoting the term from Rosemary Ruether.
33. Wadud, *Qur'an and Woman* 55.
34. Wadud, *Qur'an and Woman* 56.
35. Hassan, "Muslim Women" 59.
36. Hassan, "Muslim Women" 59.
37. Such is also the case in readings of certain Hadith accounts. In one popular tradition discussed by Hassan, the following statement is attributed to the Prophet: "If it were permitted for one human being to bow down (*sajada*) to another I would have ordered the woman to bow down to her husband." This tradition seems to indicate that the Prophet, in contradiction to a core tenant of his divine message, wished for women to worship their husbands literally or symbolically. For Hassan, such a desire on the Prophet's part—for women to worship someone other than God, or to orient themselves toward their husbands as superior beings—would amount to his desire for Muslim women to practice *shirk*. Hassan holds that such Hadith reports "make man not only superior to a woman but virtually into her god" and worse, attribute this notion to the Prophet. She concludes that such a tradition, because its content violates the principle of tawhid, must be deemed inauthentic and thus holds no authority. Hassan, "Muslim Women" 58.

38. Barlas, "Believing Women" 15.
39. Barlas cites *Surat al-Ikhlas*, chapter 112 of the Qur'an, which she translates as: "Say: [God] is God, the One and Only; God, the Eternal, Absolute; [God] begetteth not, nor is [God] begotten; And there is none like unto [God]." Barlas, "Believing Women" 95.
40. Barlas, "Believing Women" 95.
41. Barlas, "Believing Women" 100.
42. Barlas, "Believing Women" 105.
43. Barlas, "Believing Women" 22.
44. Barlas, "Believing Women" 22. Farid Esack is suspicious of the Qur'an's own use of male-gendered pronouns (i.e., *huwa*) to refer to God, calling for attention to the "limits that this Qur'anically rooted patriarchal portrayal of the transcendent places on the development of a truly feminist theology." Esack, "Islam and Gender Justice" 195.
45. Barlas, "Believing Women" 108.
46. Barlas, "Believing Women" 106.
47. Barlas, "Believing Women" 106.
48. Barlas, "Believing Women" 51.
49. Barlas, "Believing Women" 52.
50. Amina Wadud, "Qur'an, Gender, and Interpretive" 333.
51. Abou El Fadl, *Speaking* 129.
52. Abou El Fadl, *Speaking* 141.
53. Abou El Fadl, *Speaking* 265.
54. Barlas, "Believing Women" 17. Barlas cites the Qur'anic verses 2:79 and 5:105 as evidence.
55. Wadud, "Alternative" 11.
56. Barlas, "Believing Women" 17.
57. Barlas, "Believing Women" 33.
58. Barlas, "Believing Women" 19.
59. Barlas, "Amina Wadud's" 106.
60. Barlas, "Amina Wadud's" 106. Nimat Hafez Barazangi has similarly argued that "accepting the authority of text interpreters as though their authority was as binding as the authority of the Qur'an itself" contradicts "the basic tenet of the affirmation of God's sovereignty." Barazangi, *Woman's Identity* 4.
61. See the discussion of ijtihad in chapter 1 for related information on arguments for dynamic interpretation of the Qur'an.
62. Abou El Fadl, *Speaking* 92.
63. Abou El Fadl, *Speaking* 92.
64. Abou El Fadl, *Speaking* 146.
65. Wadud, "Alternative" 17.
66. Wadud, "Qur'an, Gender, and Interpretive" 327.
67. Barlas, "Believing Women" 60.

68. Wadud, "Alternative" 20.
69. Wadud, *Inside the Gender Jihad* 192.
70. Wadud, *Qur'an and Woman* 11.
71. Wadud, *Qur'an and Woman* 11; *Inside the Gender Jihad* 196.
72. Wadud, "Qur'an, Gender, and Interpretive" 335.
73. Wadud, *Inside the Gender Jihad* 212. Wadud refers to verse 31:27 as evidence.
74. Wadud, "Qur'an, Gender, and Interpretive" 328.
75. Barlas, *"Believing Women"* 105.
76. Wadud, "Qur'an, Gender, and Interpretive" 329; Wadud, *Qur'an and Woman* xii.
77. Wadud, *Inside the Gender Jihad* 213.
78. Wadud, "Qur'an, Gender, and Interpretive" 319. Emphasis hers. Wadud is quoting Stefen Wild.
79. Barlas, *"Believing Women"* 33.
80. Wadud, *Inside the Gender Jihad* 208.
81. Wadud, *Inside the Gender Jihad* 197.
82. Barlas, *"Believing Women"* 105.
83. Wadud, *Inside the Gender Jihad* 213.
84. Wadud, *Inside the Gender Jihad* 213.
85. Wadud, *Inside the Gender Jihad* 213. Khaled Abou El Fadl makes a similar statement: "The text does not embody the full Divine Will and does not embody the full authorial intent either." Abou El Fadl, *Speaking* 128.
86. Wadud, *Inside the Gender Jihad* 214.
87. In Kecia Ali's words, the text of the Qur'an "as manifested in the earthly realm . . . is, and can only ever be, a pale shadow of the ultimately Reality." Ali, *Sexual Ethics* 134.
88. Wadud, *Inside the Gender Jihad* 196.

CHAPTER 7

1. Barlas, "Women's Readings" 268.
2. Wadud, "Alternative" 18.
3. Barlas, *"Believing Women"* 199.
4. Hassan, "Muslim Women" 55, 61; Hassan, "An Islamic Perspective" 116.
5. Al-Hibri, "An Introduction" 64; Al-Hibri, "Muslim Women's Rights" 47.
6. Wadud, *Qur'an and Woman* 102.
7. Wadud, *Inside the Gender Jihad* 28.
8. Wadud, *Inside the Gender Jihad* 155.
9. Barlas, *"Believing Women"* 145.
10. Barlas, *"Believing Women"* 165.
11. Barlas, *"Believing Women"* 165. Emphasis hers.
12. Barlas, *"Believing Women"* 129, 103.

13. Barlas, *"Believing Women"* 103. Emphasis hers.
14. Barlas, *"Believing Women"* 145.
15. Barlas, *"Believing Women"* 145. Barlas is partly quoting the work of M. Mac an Ghaill.
16. Wadud, *Qur'an and Woman* 21.
17. Wadud, *Inside the Gender Jihad* 26.
18. Wadud, *Inside the Gender Jihad* 156.
19. Margot Badran traces the origins of the term: "The term 'gender jihad' was first used by Omar Rashied, the South African struggler against multiple oppressions within the community and wider society, in the 1980s at the height of the anti-apartheid campaign that South Africans called the 'Struggle.'" Badran, *Feminism in Islam* 311. Wadud also references the same person as the originator of the term (though she refers to him as "Rashied Omar"). Wadud, *Inside the Gender Jihad*, 264 n13. Farid Esack also uses the phrase "gender jihad" as early as 1997 in the final chapter of his *Qur'an, Liberation, Pluralism* as the subtitle for a section discussing women's activism within the South African anti-apartheid struggle. Esack, *Qur'an, Liberation, and Pluralism* 239.
20. Wadud, *Qur'an and Woman* x.
21. Wadud, *Inside the Gender Jihad* 10. Before Wadud offered the mentioned definition of gender jihad in *Inside the Gender Jihad*, Hibba Abugideiri offered her own definition based on Wadud's earlier work: "Gender jihad seeks greater complementarity between the sexes, as based on the Qur'an. Gender jihad, in short, is a struggle for gender parity in Muslim society in the name of divine justice. It is a struggle to end a long-standing gender regime that has paralyzed Muslim women, preventing them from becoming Muslim leaders." Abugideiri, "Hagar" 89–90.
22. Wadud, *Inside the Gender Jihad* 47.
23. Wadud, *Inside the Gender Jihad* 10.
24. Wadud, *Qur'an and Woman* 103.
25. Wadud, *Inside the Gender Jihad* 262, 32.
26. Wadud, *Inside the Gender Jihad* 72.
27. Al-Hibri, "Islamic Law" 545.
28. Al-Hibri, "Islamic Law" 545.
29. Wadud, *Inside the Gender Jihad* 10–11.
30. Wadud, *Inside the Gender Jihad* 16.
31. Wadud, *Inside the Gender Jihad* 36.
32. Barbara Stowasser makes an interesting observation on this topic but without further elaboration: "The Qur'an does not associate its principle of equal human dignity and worthiness with notions such as absolute and individual social, political, or economic equality. That is, the Qur'an legislates equality in terms not comparable to the natural law concept of 'human rights' that Western political theory derived from . . . eighteenth-century Europe and America."

Barbara Freyer Stowasser, "Women and Citizenship in the Qur'an," *Women, the Family, and Divorce Laws in Islamic History*, ed. Amira El-Azhary Sonbol (Syracuse: Syracuse University Press, 1996) 33.

33. Qudsia Mirza, "Islamic Feminism" 31.
34. Wadud notes that though "at the time of revelation, gender was not a category of thought" and the "absence of such a category of thought was not sexist at the time of revelation," such an oversight "*is* palpably so today." Wadud, *Inside the Gender Jihad* 205. Emphasis mine.
35. Ali, "Timeless Texts" 98.
36. Mir-Hosseini, "Islam and Gender Justice" 87.
37. Leo, "Islamic Female Sexuality" 131, 139.
38. Ali, *Sexual Ethics* 154. Barlas poses a similar question: "Whose perspective and definition are we to apply if we are to determine if [the Qur'an's] teachings are ethical and egalitarian—those of the Qur'an itself or of (Muslim and Western) patriarchies, feminists, or some combination? This is a critical question since different perspectives yield different assessments." Barlas, *"Believing Women"* 169.
39. Ali, *Sexual Ethics* 133. Similarly, Qudsia Mirza observes: "Feminist writers have not addressed the question of when, and to what extent, the idea of sexual difference is acceptable within scripture." Mirza, "Islamic Feminism" 31.
40. Barlas, *"Believing Women"* 206.
41. Al-Hibri, "Muslim Women's Rights" 40 n12.
42. Hassan, "An Islamic Perspective" 94. Emphasis hers.
43. Hassan, "An Islamic Perspective" 103.
44. Hassan, "An Islamic Perspective" 94.
45. Hassan, "Islam" 240.
46. Hassan, "Muslim Women" 60.
47. Barlas, *"Believing Women"* 205.
48. Barlas, *"Believing Women"* 206. Emphasis mine.
49. Barlas, *"Believing Women"* 199. Azizah al-Hibri attributes anti-women readings of the Qur'an to "misunderstanding or misapplication of the Qur'anic text resulting from cultural distortions or patriarchal bias." Al-Hibri, "Muslim Women's Rights" 40.
50. Barlas, *"Believing Women"* 205–206.
51. Ali, *Sexual Ethics* 131.
52. Ali, *Sexual Ethics* 128.
53. See appendix for full verses.
54. Ali, *Sexual Ethics* 128.
55. Ali, *Sexual Ethics* 131.
56. Ali, *Sexual Ethics* 113, 128.
57. Ali, *Sexual Ethics* 129.

58. Ali, *Sexual Ethics* 128.
59. Ali, *Sexual Ethics* 130.
60. Ali, *Sexual Ethics* 131.
61. Ali, *Sexual Ethics* 112.
62. See appendix for these verses.
63. Ali, "Timeless Texts" 90. See also Ali, *Sexual Ethics* 128.
64. Ali, *Sexual Ethics* 152.
65. Ali, *Sexual Ethics* 131.
66. Wadud agrees that the Qur'an "promotes male sexuality in particular" in verses 4:3, 2:223 and verses about heavenly companions. Wadud, *Inside the Gender Jihad* 192–193.
67. Ali, *Sexual Ethics* 131–132.
68. Ali, "Timeless Texts" 90.
69. Ali, *Sexual Ethics* 153.
70. Ali, *Sexual Ethics* 153–154.
71. Ali, "Timeless Texts" 98.
72. See appendix for verse.
73. See the work of Ayesha S. Chaudhry for a detailed analysis of the history of interpretations of verse 4:34: Chaudhry, "The Problems of Conscience"; and Chaudhry, *Domestic Violence*.
74. Al-Hibri, "Muslim Women's Rights" 55–56.
75. Al-Hibri, "Muslim Women's Rights" 65.
76. Al-Hibri, "Muslim Women's Rights" 60.
77. Al-Hibri, "An Introduction" 55.
78. Al-Hibri, "An Introduction" 55.
79. Esack, "Islam" 202.
80. Wadud, *Inside the Gender Jihad* 188.
81. Wadud, *Inside the Gender Jihad* 192.
82. Wadud, *Inside the Gender Jihad* 199. Emphasis mine.
83. Wadud, *Inside the Gender Jihad* 200.
84. Wadud, *Inside the Gender Jihad* 203.
85. Wadud, *Inside the Gender Jihad* 203. Brackets mine.
86. Wadud, *Inside the Gender Jihad* 204.
87. Silvers, "'In the Book'" 173.
88. Silvers, "'In the Book'" 173.
89. Ali, *Sexual Ethics* 132.
90. Esack, "Islam" 190–191.
91. Wadud, *Inside the Gender Jihad* 200.
92. Wadud, *Inside the Gender Jihad* 192. Wadud notes elsewhere: "Muslims seem to lack faith in the possibility that the Qur'anic whole could yield something greater than its parts." Wadud, "Towards" 44.
93. Wadud, *Inside the Gender Jihad* 212.

94. Wadud, *Inside the Gender Jihad* 212. One is reminded of Muhammad 'Abduh's conjecture that the existence of some seemingly contradictory verses is likely an intentional characteristic of the Qur'anic text, since "any ambiguity which exists in the Qur'an . . . is there for a reason: in order to divert attention away from the material world toward the spiritual." Thus, he argues, some passages of the Qur'an may appear deliberately as such in order to perform this special function. Rippin, *Muslims* 222.
95. Wadud, *Inside the Gender Jihad* 212–213.
96. Wadud, *Inside the Gender Jihad* 214.
97. Wadud, *Inside the Gender Jihad* 204.
98. Wadud, *Inside the Gender Jihad* 203. Emphasis hers.
99. Wadud, *Inside the Gender Jihad* 204.
100. Wadud, *Inside the Gender Jihad* 204.
101. Wadud, *Inside the Gender Jihad* 191.
102. Wadud, *Inside the Gender Jihad* 204.
103. Wadud, *Inside the Gender Jihad* 200.
104. Wadud, *Inside the Gender Jihad* 192.
105. Wadud, *Inside the Gender Jihad* 205.
106. Abou El Fadl, *Speaking* 93.
107. Abou El Fadl, *Speaking* 93–94.
108. Abou El Fadl, *Speaking* 94.
109. Abou El Fadl, *Speaking* 94.
110. Abou El Fadl, *Speaking* 94.
111. Abou El Fadl, *Speaking* 94.
112. Wadud, *Inside the Gender Jihad* 191.
113. Wadud, *Inside the Gender Jihad* 201.
114. Ali, *Sexual Ethics* 150.
115. Wadud, *Inside the Gender Jihad* 192.
116. Wadud, *Inside the Gender Jihad* 197.
117. Silvers, "'In the Book'" 173.
118. Silvers, "'In the Book'" 172.
119. Silvers, "'In the Book'" 177. Emphasis mine.
120. Silvers, "'In the Book'" 172.
121. Silvers, "'In the Book'" 172.
122. Silvers, "'In the Book'" 172
123. Silvers, "'In the Book'" 172 Emphasis hers.
124. Silvers, "'In the Book'" 177.
125. Silvers, "'In the Book'" 177. Emphasis hers.
126. Silvers, "'In the Book'" 175.
127. Ali, *Sexual Ethics* 133.
128. Anwar, "Muslim Feminist" 59.

129. Ali, *Sexual Ethics* 153. Emphasis hers.
130. Rhouni, *Secular and Islamic Feminist Critiques* 272.
131. Mirza, "Islamic Feminism" 31.
132. Moosa, "The Debts" 123, 124.
133. Moosa, "The Debts" 124.
134. Madigan, "Themes and Topics" 79.
135. Abou El Fadl, *Speaking* 142.
136. Abou El Fadl, *Speaking* 163–164.
137. Abou El Fadl, *Speaking* 142.
138. Phrase taken from Madigan, "Themes and Topics" 79. Wadud states: "I accept that even my own reading is dwarfed by my context in history as well as by human incompetence and lack of understanding. This acceptance frees me from defending any understanding I develop or meaning I find as the *only* right understanding." Wadud, *Inside the Gender Jihad* 197.
139. Ali, *Sexual Ethics* 153.
140. Ali, *Sexual Ethics* 133.
141. Ali, *Sexual Ethics* 156. Ali points out another serious consequence of such claims: the suppression of "interpretive leeway" and multiple interpretations that results from claiming that one's position, even if it is "feminist," is what "Islam" or "the Qur'an says." Ali, *Sexual Ethics* 110.
142. Badran, *Feminism in Islam* 323.
143. Badran, *Feminism in Islam* 324.
144. Badran, *Feminism in Islam* 325.
145. Rhouni, *Secular and Islamic Feminist Critiques* 35, 34.
146. Rhouni, *Secular and Islamic Feminist Critiques* 254.
147. Ali, *Sexual Ethics* 156; Rhouni, *Secular and Islamic Feminist Critiques* 272.
148. Rhouni, *Secular and Islamic Feminist Critiques* 14.
149. Abu Zayd, "Rethinking the Quran" 11.
150. Abu Zayd, *Reformation of Islamic Thought* 98.
151. Rhouni, *Secular and Islamic Feminist Critiques* 252.
152. As Mirza puts it: "The question for scholars and activists is how are we to influence those in power—the ulama, mosque leaders, politicians, and the whole gamut of religious and political authority—so that theoretical improvements are implemented into legal and political rights that effect real change in the material reality of women's lives." Mirza "Islamic Feminism" 31.
153. Ali, "Paradigms and Pragmatism" 27.
154. Ali, "Paradigms and Pragmatism" 27. Mirza concurs: "The need to put forward a . . . position located within an Islamic framework may be necessary from a strategic perspective . . . The more radical proposals offered by Islamic feminists remain outside the mainstream of legal thought and peripheral to the centres of power." Mirza, "Islamic Feminism" 31.

CHAPTER 8

1. Wadud, "What's Interpretation Got to Do With It" 93.
2. Rhouni, *Secular and Islamic Feminist Critiques* 254.
3. Hassan, "Muslim Women" 60.
4. Barlas, *"Believing Women"* 11, 17, 21, 24.
5. Al-Hibri, "Muslim Women's Rights" 40; Wadud *Qur'an and Woman* xxii, 2–3.
6. Ali, *Sexual Ethics* 153.
7. Wadud, *Inside the Gender Jihad* 6.
8. Wadud, *Inside the Gender Jihad* 18.
9. Janet Halley, *Split Decisions: How and Why to Take a Break from Feminism* (Princeton: Princeton University Press, 2006), 273.
10. Phrasing taken from Halley, *Split Decisions* 319.
11. Chaudhry, *Domestic Violence* 98–99, 200–203; Chaudhry, "Wife-Beating" 10, 413.
12. Barlas, *"Believing Women"* 11, 17.
13. Barlas, *"Believing Women"* 14.
14. In her dissertation, Karen Bauer has made a similar observation about premodern exegesis (rather than the Qur'an itself). Bauer, "Room for Interpretation" 182.
15. Barlas, "Does the Qur'an Support Gender Equality?" 2. Her emphasis.
16. Barlas, "Does the Qur'an Support Gender Equality?" 2.
17. Mir-Hosseini et al., eds., *Gender and Equality in Muslim Family Law*.
18. Ali, *Sexual Ethics* 133.
19. Bauer, "The Male Is Not Like the Female" 639.
20. Barlas, *"Believing Women"* 172, 201; Wadud, *Qur'an and Woman*, 8.
21. Wadud, *Qur'an and Woman* 21.
22. Wadud, *Qur'an and Woman* 8.
23. Wadud, *Qur'an and Woman* 104.
24. Barlas, *"Believing Women"* 165.
25. Barlas, *"Believing Women"* 165, 166.
26. Barlas, *"Believing Women"* 130, 165.
27. Barlas, "Does the Qur'an Support Gender Equality?" 6.
28. Barlas, *"Believing Women"* 179. Her emphasis.
29. See appendix for verse.
30. Barlas, *"Believing Women"* 186.
31. Barlas, *"Believing Women"* 187.
32. Barlas, *"Believing Women"* 187.
33. Wadud, *Qur'an and Woman* 73.
34. Wadud, *Qur'an and Woman* 65.
35. Wadud, *Qur'an and Woman* 65.
36. Wadud, *Qur'an and Woman* 64.
37. Wadud, *Qur'an and Woman* 73.
38. Wadud, *Qur'an and Woman* 73–74.

39. Wadud, *Qur'an and Woman* 73.
40. Wadud, *Qur'an and Woman* 65.
41. Wadud, *Qur'an and Woman* 102.
42. Wadud, *Qur'an and Woman* 67.
43. Wadud, *Qur'an and Woman* 102.
44. Barlas, *"Believing Women"* 187.
45. Wadud, *Qur'an and Woman* 102.
46. Wadud, *Qur'an and Woman* 102.
47. Al-Hibri, "Quranic Foundations" 19.
48. Abdallah Adhami, "Women, Society, and Human Nature," *ChaiPod with Brother Dash*, talk show recording, sakeenah.org.
49. Abdallah Adhami, "The Nature of Women," lecture recording, sakeenah.org.
50. Abdallah Adhami, "Women, Islam, and ControVERSEy," *ChaiPod with Brother Dash*, talk show recording, sakeenah.org.
51. Adhami, "Women, Society, and Human Nature"; Adhami, "Women, Islam, and ControVERSEy."
52. Adhami, "Women, Society, and Human Nature."
53. Adhami, "The Nature of Women."
54. Adhami, "Women, Society, and Human Nature."
55. Adhami, "The Nature of Women."
56. Rebecca Merrill Groothuis, *Good News for Women: A Biblical Picture of Gender Equality* (Grand Rapids, MI: Baker Books, 1997), 54.
57. Groothuis, *Good News* 54.
58. Ali, *Sexual Ethics* 132.
59. Refer to appendix for the text of key verses discussed here.
60. Ali, *Sexual Ethics* 130, 129.
61. Ali, *Sexual Ethics* 129.
62. Barlas, *"Believing Women"* 12.
63. Barlas, *"Believing Women"* 14.
64. Wadud, *Inside the Gender Jihad* 96.
65. Barlas, *"Believing Women"* 11, 204.
66. Wadud, "Islam Beyond Patriarchy" 102.
67. Wadud, *Inside the Gender Jihad* 131.
68. In later work, Wadud places even more emphasis on the concept of reciprocity, making it a conceptual focus and referring to it as mu'awadhah. Wadud, "Islam Beyond Patriarchy" 102–107.
69. Barlas, *"Believing Women"* 162.
70. Barlas, *"Believing Women"* 163–164.
71. Barlas, *"Believing Women"* 164. She goes on to claim based on a verse about female slaves and a verse about inheriting women as part of an estate that the "Qur'an imputes a will to women in matters of sexual access and choice and it also mandates that men respect its expression." Barlas, *"Believing Women"* 164–165.

72. Barlas, "Believing Women" 165.
73. Wadud, Inside the Gender Jihad 199, 192–193, 238.
74. Wadud, Inside the Gender Jihad 238.
75. Wadud, Inside the Gender Jihad 193, 195, 197.
76. Wadud, Inside the Gender Jihad 197.
77. Wadud, Inside the Gender Jihad 239.
78. Barlas, "Believing Women" 189. The term *sukun* connotes rest and tranquility.
79. Barlas, "Believing Women" 188.
80. Wadud, Inside the Gender Jihad 203.
81. Wadud "Islam Beyond Patriarchy" 106–107.
82. Wadud, Inside the Gender Jihad 22.
83. See, for example, works within the extensive field of the study of love, gender, and sexuality in Greek and Roman antiquity. One general reference source is Marilyn B. Skinner, *Sexuality in Greek and Roman Culture* (Malden, MA: Blackwell, 2005).
84. Laura Luitje, Response to Asma Barlas, "Muslim Women and Sexual Oppression: Reading Liberation from the Qur'an," *Macalester International* 10 (2001): 152.
85. Barlas, "Believing Women" 204.
86. Chaudhry, *Domestic Violence*.
87. The phrase is taken from Barlas, "Believing Women" 184, where she makes this argument. Another clear example of this argument is found in the work al-Hibri, who also argues against interpretations of *qiwamah* in verse 4:34 as a domineering role by referring to the Qur'an's consistency and the kindness and gentleness of the male-female relationship. Al-Hibri, "Quranic Foundations" 16.
88. Wadud, "Islam Beyond Patriarchy" 102.
89. Barlas, "Believing Women" 134, 189, 162, 165.
90. Well-known examples include Umm Salamah in possible relation to verses 33:35, 3:195, or 4:32 (discussed below), and Khawlah bint Tha'labah in relation to verse 58:1
91. Wadud, Inside the Gender Jihad 239.
92. Barlas, "Believing Women" 145.
93. Wadud, Inside the Gender Jihad 30.
94. Wadud, Inside the Gender Jihad 168.
95. Wadud, "Islam Beyond Patriarchy" 108.
96. Wadud, Inside the Gender Jihad 31.
97. I would like to recognize the students of my Islamic Feminist Ethics classes at University of San Francisco since 2008 for continually posing the question to me of why sexist male interpreters did not understand that they were committing *shirk*. It was the freshness of their insight as newcomers to the topic that first inspired me to try to pursue the answer to this question with more rigor.

Notes to Pages 169–177

98. Quotations taken from Chaudhry, "Wife-Beating" 418. See also Bauer, "Room for Interpretation" 150–151; Chaudhry, *Domestic Violence* 40–50.
99. Barlas, *"Believing Women"* 172.
100. Wadud, *Qur'an and Woman* 37.
101. Wadud, *Inside the Gender Jihad* 28–29.
102. Wadud, "Islam Beyond Patriarchy" 102.
103. Rebecca Merrill Groothuis "'Equal in Being, Unequal in Role': Exploring the Logic of Woman's Subordination," *Discovering Biblical Equality: Complementarity without Hierarchy*, ed. Ronald W. Pierce and Rebecca Merrill Groothuis (Downers Grove, IL: InterVarsity Press, 2004) 316.
104. Groothuis, "'Equal in Being'" 316–317.
105. Groothuis, "'Equal in Being'" 318.
106. Groothuis, "'Equal in Being'" 320.
107. Wadud, *Inside the Gender Jihad* 204. Emphasis hers.
108. Rhouni, *Secular and Islamic Feminist Critiques* 214–215, 234–235.
109. Ali, "Paradigms and Pragmatism" 27.
110. Anwar, "Muslim Feminist Discourses" 59. My emphasis.
111. Anwar, "Muslim Feminist Discourses" 59.
112. Ali, "Timeless Texts" 96.
113. Wadud, *Inside the Gender Jihad* 212–213.
114. Wadud, *Qur'an and Woman* 77–78, 81.
115. Wadud, *Inside the Gender Jihad* 195.
116. Wadud, *Inside the Gender Jihad* 191.
117. Ali, "Timeless Texts" 92.
118. This position has a precedent in Muʻtazilite positions on the justice of God, though a full discussion of parallels to Muʻtazilite thought is beyond the scope of this book.
119. Wadud, "Qur'an, Gender, and Interpretive" 328–329.
120. Wadud, *Inside the Gender Jihad* 213.
121. Rhouni, *Secular and Islamic Feminist Critiques* 269.
122. Abu Zayd, "The Qur'an: God and Man in Communication," http://www.let.leidenuniv.nl/forum/01_1/onderzoek/lecture.pdf, 5.
123. Abu Zayd, "The Nexus of Theory and Practice" 155.
124. Abu Zayd, "The Nexus of Theory and Practice" 162.
125. The application of Abu Zayd's approach would need to be refined, however. In one of his last published writings on the topic of women in the Qur'an, Abu Zayd ends up universalizing verses of the "ethical-spiritual" domain while deciding that those of the societal domain are dictated by the Qur'an's dialogue with the audience of revelation. As I have argued, verses of both kinds cannot be separated so easily from each other, and such a move may still reinforce the authority of the Qur'an in debilitating ways. Nasr Abu Zayd, "The Status of Women between the Qur'an and *Fiqh*," *Gender and Equality in Muslim Family Law*, ed. Mir-Hosseini, et al. 164.

CHAPTER 9

1. Michel Foucault, *The History of Sexuality*, vol. 2: *The Use of Pleasure*, trans. Robert Hurley (New York: Vintage, 1985), 7. It was Janet Halley's book *Split Decisions* that drew my attention to this elegant passage from Foucault's work, which encapsulates my embrace of rethinking feminist exegesis of the Qur'an. The courageous spirit of Halley's book *Split Decisions* has inspired many of my observations in this chapter, indebting me to her as well as my colleague Taymiya Zaman, who directed me to the book. Halley, *Split Decisions*.
2. Catherine Keller, "The Apophasis of Gender: A Fourfold Unsaying of Feminist Theology," *Journal of the American Academy of Religion* 76.4 (2008): 916.
3. Bulliet, *The Case for Islamo-Christian Civilization* 140.
4. Bulliet, *The Case for Islamo-Christian Civilization* 140.
5. Muhammad Qasim Zaman, *The Ulama in Contemporary Islam: Custodians of Change* (Princeton: Princeton University Press, 2002) 3, 6, 10.
6. Chaudhry, "The Ethics of Marital Discipline" 128.
7. Hammer, *American Muslim Women* 119.
8. For example, Barlas makes reference to Umm Salamah to argue that the Qur'an directly addresses women in response to her questioning. Barlas, "Women's Readings of the Qur'an" 255.
9. Umar F. Abd-Allah, "Creativity, Innovation, and Heresy in Islam," *Voices of Islam*, vol. 5, ed. Vincent Cornell (Westport, CT: Prager, 2007) 5.
10. Bauer, "Room for Interpretation" 185.
11. Wright, "Modern Qur'anic Hermeneutics" 41–43, 55, 87, 89, 97.
12. Adis Duderija, *Constructing* 73–74, 131.
13. Wright, "Modern Qur'anic Hermeneutics" 89, 106, 117; Duderija, *Constructing* 131.
14. Barlas, *"Believing Women"* 24.
15. Barlas, *"Believing Women"* 79.
16. Barlas, *"Believing Women"* 81. For her discussion of the accumulative nature of Islamic tradition, see *"Believing Women"* 76ff.
17. It is for this reason that I tend to disagree with Karen Bauer's observation that premodern exegetes "perhaps . . . tacitly acknowledged" that exegesis is a "subjective and time-bounded" endeavor. Given that they did not share our concept of historicity it is unlikely that they could "implicitly acknowledge that different times, and different customs, will bring about different recommendations for the behavior of the sexes." Their differences of opinion with their predecessors would probably not have been rationalized from an awareness of the *historicity* of their view or those of their predecessors. Bauer "Room for Interpretation" 194.
18. A concrete illustration of this is found in the rationale put forward by Ingrid Mattson, the first female president of the Islamic Society of North America,

for women's leadership. See Ingrid Mattson, "Can a Woman be an Imam? Debating Form and Function in Muslim Women's Leadership," http://www.onbeing.org/program/new-voice-islam/feature/can-woman-be-imam-debating-form-and-function-muslim-womens. For a nuanced discussion of Mattson and Muslim women's leadership roles, see: Ayubi, "'Alimah to Imamah."

19. Phrase taken from Halley, *Split Decisions* 149.
20. Barlas *"Believing Women"* 130–131.
21. Judith Butler, *Gender Trouble: Feminism and the Subversion of Identity*, 10th anniversary ed. (New York: Routledge, 1999) 11.
22. Butler, *Gender Trouble* 11.
23. Joan Scott, *The Fantasy of Feminist History* (Durham, NC: Duke University Press, 2011) 7.
24. Linda Martin Alcoff, *Visible Identities: Race, Gender, and the Self* (New York: Oxford University Press, 2006) 157.
25. Alcoff, *Visible Identities* 156.
26. Barlas, *"Believing Women"* 130, 129, 136.
27. Wadud, *Qur'an and Woman* 21.
28. Barlas, *"Believing Women"* 135.
29. Joan W. Scott, "Deconstructing Equality-Versus-Difference: Or, the Uses of Poststructuralist Theory for Feminism," *Feminist Studies* 14.1 (1988): 37.
30. Barlas, *"Believing Women"* 133, 165.
31. Anver Emon has identified this as "the paradox of equality." Anver M. Emon, "The Paradox of Equality and the Politics of Difference: Gender Equality, Islamic Law and the Modern Muslim State," *Gender and Equality*, ed. Mir-Hosseini, et al. 237, 244.
32. Scott, "Deconstructing" 43.
33. Anver Emon has made a parallel observation. Emon, "The Paradox of Equality" 238–242.
34. Scott, "Deconstructing" 38.
35. Scott, "Deconstructing" 46, 35.
36. Scott, "Deconstructing" 46.
37. Teresa L Ebert, "The 'Difference' of Postmodern Feminism," *College English* 53.8 (1991): 892.
38. Ebert, "The 'Difference'" 892.
39. Ebert, "The 'Difference'" 893.
40. Shaikh, *Sufi Narratives* 222–223, 225.
41. Ebert, "The 'Difference'" 892.
42. Wadud, *Inside the Gender Jihad* 29, 30, 33.
43. A new study on masculinity in the Qur'an is a first step towards a corrective: De Sondy, *The Crisis of Islamic Masculinities*.

44. Ebert "The 'Difference'" 891.
45. This is what Abdullah Adhami thinks feminists are trying to achieve; according to him, women in the West attempt to shed their femininity in the effort to gain the respect given to men. He does not seem to understand that what many feminists seek is not the eradication of femininity but rather its destabilization from a singular fixity.
46. Alcoff, *Visible* 176.
47. Scott, "Deconstructing" 44. Anver Emon has drawn related conclusions. Emon, "The Paradox of Equality" 239–254.
48. Joan C. Williams, "Dissolving the Sameness/Difference Debate: A Post-Modern Path beyond Essentialism in Feminist and Critical Race Theory" *Duke Law Journal* 1991. 2 (1991): 308.
49. Williams "Dissolving the Sameness" 309–310.
50. Wadud *Qur'an and Woman* 90.
51. Ebert "The 'Difference'" 896; Scott, "Deconstructing" 46.
52. Some key questions about the kind of equality sought by Muslim women in relation to male authority have recently been asked by Ziba Mir-Hosseini; she raises the question of whether *qiwamah* may have "positive" aspects. Ziba Mir-Hosseini, "Justice, Equality and Muslim Family Laws: New Ideas, New Prospects," *Gender and Equality in Muslim Family Law*, ed. Mir-Hosseini et al. 26–27.
53. Wadud, *Inside the Gender Jihad* 23.
54. Judith Butler, *Giving an Account of Oneself* (New York: Fordham University Press, 2005) 28.
55. Butler, *Giving* 20.
56. Shaikh *Sufi Narratives* 131.
57. Shaikh *Sufi Narratives* 157.
58. Shaikh *Sufi Narratives* 159.
59. Shaikh *Sufi Narratives* 160.
60. Mir-Hosseini, "Justice, Equality and Muslim Family Laws" 27.
61. See for instance the work of the Malaysian NGO Sisters in Islam, particularly their Musawah project. Musawah's "Framework for Action" is available at http://www.musawah.org/about-musawah/framework-action. An excellent examination of the relationship between the conclusions of feminist tafsir and NGO work is found in Marwa Sharafeldin, "Egyptian Women's Rights NGOs: Personal Status Law Reform between Islamic and International Human Rights Law," *Gender and Equality in Muslim Family Law*, ed. Mir-Hosseini et al. 57–80.
62. Catherine Keller, "Returning God: The Gift of Feminist Theology," *Feminism, Sexuality, and the Return of Religion*, ed. Linda Martin Alcoff and John D. Caputo (Bloomington: Indiana University Press, 2011) 61–62.

63. Halley, *Split Decisions* 279. I have borrowed the phrase "radical uncertainty" from Halley.
64. Keller "Apophasis" 925.
65. Keller "Apophasis" 925.
66. Halley *Split Decisions* 279; Keller "Apophasis" 927.
67. Keller, "Returning God" 68.

Bibliography

Abbas, Sadia. "The Echo Chamber of Freedom: The Muslim Woman and the Pretext of Agency." *boundary 2*. 40 (2013): 155–189.

Abou El Fadl, Khaled. *Speaking in God's Name: Islamic Law, Authority and Women*. Oxford: Oneworld, 2001.

Abou-Bakr, Omaima. "Islamic Feminism: What's in a Name?" *Middle East Women's Studies Review* 15.4 (2001): 1–4.

Abrahamov, Binyamin. "Theology." *The Blackwell Companion to the Qur'an*. Ed. Andrew Rippin. Malden, MA: Blackwell, 2006. 420–433.

Abu Zayd, Nasr. "From Revelation to Interpretation: Nasr Hamid Abu Zayd and the Literary Study of the Qur'an." *Modern Muslim Intellectual and the Qur'an*. Ed. Suha Taji-Farouki. New York: Oxford University Press, 2006.

———. "The Nexus of Theory and Practice." *The New Voices of Islam: Rethinking Politics and Modernity*. Ed. Mehran Kamrava. Berkeley: University of California Press, 2006.

———. "The Qur'an: God and Man in Communication." Unpublished paper. http://www.let.leidenuniv.nl/forum/01_1/onderzoek/lecture.pdf.

Abugideiri, Hibba. "Hagar: A Historical Model for 'Gender Jihad.'" *Daughters of Abraham: Feminist Thought in Judaism, Christianity, and Islam*. Ed. Yvonne Yazbeck Haddad and John L. Esposito. Gainesville: University Press of Florida, 2001. 81–107.

———. "Qur'an: Modern Interpretations, Euro-American Languages." *Encyclopedia of Women and Islamic Cultures*. Ed. Suad Joseph. 2006–2009. Brill online. Dec. 6, 2007. http://www.brillonline.nl/subscriber/entry?entry=ewic_COM-0608.

———. "The Renewed Woman of American Islam: Shifting Lenses Toward 'Gender Jihad?'" *The Muslim World* 91.1–2 (2001): 1–18.

Afsaruddin, Asma. "Enlightened Interpretations of the Hadith Literature." *Islam and Enlightenment: New Issues*. Ed. Erik Borgman and Pim Valkenberg. *Concilium* 2005, no. 5. Maryknoll, NY: Orbis, 2005. 61–70.

Ahmed, Leila. *Women and Gender in Islam: Historical Roots of a Modern Debate*. New Haven: Yale University Press, 1992.

Ali, Abdullah Yusuf. *The Holy Qur'an: Text, Translation, and Commentary.* 4th ed. Brentwood, MD: Amana Corp., 1989.

Al-Ali, Nadje. *Secularism, Gender, and the State in the Middle East: The Egyptian Women's Movement.* Cambridge: Cambridge University Press, 2000.

Ali, Kecia. "Paradigms and Pragmatism in Muslim Women's Reformist Thinking." Middle East Program Occasional Papers Series, Woodrow Wilson International Center for Scholars, Spring 2009, 26–27. http://www.wilsoncenter.org/sites/default/files/reformistwomenthinkers.pdf.

———. *Sexual Ethics and Islam: Feminist Reflections on Qur'an, Hadith, and Jurisprudence.* Oxford: Oneworld, 2006.

———. "Timeless Texts and Modern Morals: Challenges in Islamic Sexual Ethics." *New Directions in Islamic Thought: Exploring Reform and Muslim Tradition.* Ed. Kari Vogt, Lena Larsen, and Christian Moe. New York: I.B. Tauris, 2009. 89–99.

Anwar, Ghazala. "Muslim Feminist Discourses." *Feminist Theology in Different Contexts.* Ed. Elisabeth Schüssler Fiorenza and M. Shawn Copeland. *Concilium* 1996, no. 1. Maryknoll, NY: Orbis, 1996. 55–61.

Aquino, Maria Pilar, Daisy L. Machado, and Jeanette Rodriguez. Introduction. *A Reader in Latina Feminist Theology: Religion and Justice.* Ed. Aquino, Machado, and Rodriguez. Austin: University of Texas Press, 2002. xiii–xx.

Armstrong, Karen. Foreword. *Daughters of Abraham: Feminist Thought in Judaism, Christianity, and Islam.* Ed. Yvonne Yazbeck Haddad and John L. Esposito. Gainesville: University Press of Florida, 2001. vii–xiii.

Ayubi, Zahra M. "'*Alimah* to *Imamah*: Muslim Women's Approaches to Religious Leadership and Authority in the American Context." M.A. thesis. University of North Carolina, Chapel Hill, 2010.

Badran, Margot. "Feminism and the Qur'an." *Encyclopedia of the Qur'an.* Ed. Jane Dammen McAuliffe. 2001–2006. Brill online. May 8, 2009. http://www.brillonline.nl/subscriber/entry?entry=q3_COM-00065.

———. *Feminism in Islam: Secular and Religious Convergences.* Oxford: Oneworld, 2009.

———. *Feminists, Islam, and Nation: Gender and the Making of Modern Egypt.* Princeton: Princeton University Press, 1995.

———. "Toward Islamic Feminisms: A Look at the Middle East." *Hermeneutics and Honor: Negotiating Female "Public" Space in Islamic/ate Societies.* Ed. Asma Afsaruddin. Cambridge: Harvard University Press, 1999. 159–188.

Bakhtiar, Laleh. *The Sublime Qur'an.* Trans. Laleh Bakhtiar. Chicago: Kazi, 2007.

Barazangi, Nimat Hafez. *Woman's Identity and the Quran: A New Reading.* Gainesville: University Press of Florida, 2004.

Barlas, Asma. "Amina Wadud's Hermeneutics of the Qur'an: Women Rereading Sacred Texts." *Modern Muslim Intellectuals and the Qur'an.* Ed. Suha Taji-Farouki. Oxford: Oxford University Press, 2006. 97–124.

———. "Believing Women" in Islam: Unreading Patriarchal Interpretations of the Qur'an. Austin: University of Texas Press, 2002.

———. "Does the Qur'an Support Gender Equality? Or, Do I Have the Autonomy to Answer this Question?" Keynote address. Workshop on Islam and Autonomy at University of Groningen. Nov. 24, 2006.

———. "Engaging Feminism: Provincializing Feminism as a Master Narrative." Paper presented at Tempere Peace Research Institute. Finland. Aug. 31, 2007. http://www.asmabarlas.com/TALKS /Finland_07.pdf.

———. "Globalizing Equality: Muslim Women, Theology, and Feminism." *On Shifting Ground: Muslim Women in the Global Era*. Ed. Fereshteh Nouraie-Simone. New York: Feminist Press at the City University of New York, 2005. 91–110.

———. *Re-understanding Islam: A Double Critique*. Amersterdam: Royal van Gourcum, 2008.

———. "Women's Readings of the Qur'an." *The Cambridge Companion to the Qur'an*. Ed. Jane McAuliffe. New York: Cambridge University Press, 2006. 255–271.

Bauer, Karen A. "The Male Is Not Like the Female (Q 3:36): The Question of Gender Egalitarianism in the Qur'an." *Religion Compass* 3/4 (2009): 637–654.

———. "Room for Interpretation: Qur'anic Exegesis and Gender." Ph.D. diss. Princeton University, 2008.

Bennett, Clinton. *Muslims and Modernity: An Introduction to the Issues and Debates*. New York: Continuum, 2005.

Braude, Ann. "Azizah al-Hibri." *Transforming the Faiths of Our Fathers: Women Who Changed American Religion*. Ed. Ann Braude. New York: Palgrave Macmillan, 2004. 47–54.

———. "Riffat Hassan." *Transforming the Faiths of Our Fathers: Women Who Changed American Religion*. Ed. Ann Braude. New York: Palgrave Macmillan, 2004. 173–197.

Brock, Rita Nakashima. "Pacific, Asian, and North American Asian Women's Theologies." *Feminist Theologies: Legacy and Prospects*. Ed. Rosemary Radford Ruether. Minneapolis: Fortress Press, 2007. 45–54.

Brown, Daniel. *A New Introduction to Islam*. Malden, MA: Blackwell, 2004.

Bulliet, Richard W. *The Case for Islamo-Christian Civilization*. New York: Columbia University Press, 2004.

———. *Islam: The View from the Edge*. New York: Columbia University Press, 1994.

Burton, John. "Abrogation." *Encyclopaedia of the Qur'an*. Ed. Jane Dammen McAuliffe. 2001–2006. Brill online. July 12, 2009. http://www.brillonline.nl/subscriber/entry?entry=q3_COM-00002.

Cannon, Katie G. *Black Womanist Ethics*. Atlanta: Scholars Press, 1988.

Chaudhry, Ayesha S. *Domestic Violence and the Islamic Tradition: Ethics, Law, and the Muslim Discourse on Gender*. New York: Oxford University Press, 2013.

———. "The Ethics of Marital Discipline in Premodern Qur'anic Exegesis." *Journal of the Society of Christian Ethics* 30.2 (2010): 123–130.

Chaudhry, Ayesha S. "The Problems of Conscience and Hermeneutics: A Few Contemporary Approaches." *Comparative Islamic Studies* 2.2 (2006): 157–170.

———. "Wife-Beating in the Pre-Modern Islamic Tradition: An Inter-Disciplinary Study of Ḥadīth, Qur'anic Exegesis and Islamic Jurisprudence." Ph.D. diss. New York University, 2009.

Chittick, William C. "Worship." *The Cambridge Companion to Classical Islamic Theology.* Ed. Tim Winter. Cambridge: Cambridge University Press, 2008. 218–236.

Clifford, Anne M. *Introducing Feminist Theology.* Maryknoll, NY: Orbis Books, 2001.

cooke, miriam. "Multiple Critique: Islamic Feminist Rhetorical Strategies." *Postcolonialism, Feminism, and Religious Discourse.* Ed. Laura E. Donaldson and Kwok Pui-Lan. New York: Routledge, 2002. 142–160.

———. "The Muslimwoman." *Contemporary Islam* 1 (2007): 139–154.

Daly, Mary. *Beyond God the Father: Toward a Philosophy of Women's Liberation.* Boston: Beacon Press, 1973.

De Sondy, Amanullah. *The Crisis of Islamic Masculinities.* New York: Bloomsbury, 2013.

Duderija, Adis. *Constructing a Religiously Ideal "Believer" and "Woman" in Islam: Neo-traditional Salafi and Progressive Muslims' Methods of Interpretation.* New York: Palgrave, 2011.

Esack, Farid. "Islam and Gender Justice: Beyond Simplistic Apologia." *What Men Owe to Women: Men's Voices from World Religions.* Ed. John C. Raines and Daniel C. Maguire. Albany: State University of New York Press, 2001. 187–210.

———. *The Qur'an: A User's Guide.* Oxford: Oneworld, 2005.

———. *Qur'an, Liberation, and Pluralism: An Islamic Perspective on Interreligious Solidarity against Oppression.* Oxford: Oneworld, 1997.

Esack, Farid, and Sarah Chiddy, eds. *Islam and AIDS: Between Scorn, Pity and Justice.* Oxford: Oneworld, 2009.

Esposito, John L. *Islam: The Straight Path.* New York: Oxford University Press, 1991.

Fiorenza, Elisabeth Schüssler. *Bread Not Stone: The Challenge of Feminist Biblical Interpretation.* Boston: Beacon Press, 1995.

———. *But She Said: Feminist Practices of Biblical Interpretation.* Boston: Beacon Press, 1992.

Gätje, Helmut. *The Qur'an and Its Exegesis: Selected Texts with Classical and Modern Muslim Interpretations.* Trans. Alford T. Welch. Oxford: Oneworld, 1996.

Gilliot, Claude. "Exegesis of the Qur'an: Classical and Medieval." *Encyclopedia of the Qur'an.* Ed. Jane Dammen McAuliffe. 2001–2006. Brill online. June 11, 2007. http://www.brillonline.nl/subscriber/entry?entry=q3_COM-00058.

Gross, Rita M. "Feminist Theology as a Theology of Religions." *The Cambridge Companion to Feminist Theology.* Ed. Susan Frank Parsons. Cambridge: Cambridge University Press, 2002. 60–78.

Guardi, Jolanda. "Women Reading the Quran: Religious Discourse and Islam." *Hawwa* 2.3 (2004): 301–315. Haddad, Yvonne Yazbeck, Jane I. Smith, and Kathleen

M. Moore. *Muslim Women in America: The Challenge of Islamic Identity Today*. New York: Oxford University Press, 2006.

Hammer, Juliane. *American Muslim Women, Religious Authority, and Activism: More Than a Prayer*. Austin: University of Texas Press, 2012.

———. "Identity, Authority, and Activism: American Muslim Women Approach the Qur'an." *The Muslim World* 98 (2008): 443–464.

Harrison, Victoria S. "Deconstructing Patriarchal Jurisprudence in Islamic Law: A Faithful Approach." *Global Critical Race Feminism: An International Reader*. Ed. Adrien Katherine Wing. New York: New York University Press, 2000. 221–233.

———. "Modern Women, Traditional Abrahamic Religions and Interpreting Sacred Texts." *Feminist Theology* 15.2 (2007): 145–159.

Hassan, Riffat. "Divine Justice and the Human Order: An Islamic Perspective." *Humanity before God: Contemporary Faces of Jewish, Christian, and Islamic Ethics*. Ed. William Schweiker, Michael A. Johnson, and Kevin Jung. Minneapolis: Fortress Press, 2006. 238–255.

———. "Hagar on My Mind." *Philosophy, Feminism, and Faith*. Ed. Ruth E. Groenhout and Marya Bower. Bloomington: Indiana University Press, 2003. 198–210.

———. "An Introduction to Muslim Women's Rights." *Windows of Faith: Muslim Women Scholar-Activists in North America*. Ed. Gisela Webb. Syracuse: Syracuse University Press, 2000. 51–71.

———. "Is Western Patriarchal Feminism Good for Third World/Minority Women?" *Is Multiculturalism Bad for Women?* by Susan Moller Okin et al. Eds. Joshua Cohen, Matthew Howard, and Martha C. Nussbaum. Princeton: Princeton University Press, 1999. 41–46.

———. "Islam." *Her Voice, Her Faith: Women Speak on World Religions*. Ed. Arvind Sharma and Katherine K.Young. Boulder: Westview Press, 2003. 215–242.

———. "Islamic Hagar and Her Family." *Hagar, Sarah, and their Children: Jewish, Christian, and Muslim Perspectives*. Ed. Phyllis Trible and Letty M. Russell. Louisville: Westminster John Knox Press, 2006. 149–167.

———. "Islamic Law." *A Companion to Feminist Philosophy*. Ed. Alison M. Jaggar and Iris Marion Young. Malden, MA: Blackwell, 1998. 541–549.

———. "An Islamic Perspective." *Women, Religion, and Sexuality: Studies on the Impact of Religious Teachings on Women*. Ed. Jeanne Becher. Philadelphia: Trinity Press International, 1990. 93–128.

———. "An Islamic Perspective on Domestic Violence." *Fordham International Law Journal* 27.1 (2003): 195–219.

———. "The Issue of Woman-Man Equality in the Islamic Tradition." *Women's and Men's Liberation: Testimonies of Spirit*. Ed. Leonard Grob, Riffat Hassan, and Haim Gordon. New York: Greenwood Press, 1991. 65–82.

———. "'Jihad Fi Sabil Allah': A Woman's Faith Journey from Struggle to Struggle to Struggle." *Women's and Men's Libertaion: Testimonies of Spirit*. Ed. Leonard Gobb, Riffat Hassan, and Haim Gordon. New York: Greenwood Press, 1991. 11–30.

Hassan, Riffat. "Muslim Women and Post-Patriarchal Islam." *After Patriarchy: Feminist Transformations of the World Religions.* Ed. Paula M. Cooey, William R. Eakin, and Jay B. McDaniel. Maryknoll, NY: Orbis Books, 1991. 39–64.

———. "Muslim Women's Rights in the Global Village: Challenges and Opportunities." *Journal of Law and Religion* 15.37 (2000–2001): 37–66.

———. "Qur'anic Foundations of the Rights of Muslim Women in the Twenty-First Century." *Women in Indonesian Society: Access, Empowerment, and Opportunity.* Ed. Atho Mudzhar et al. Yogyakarta, Indonesia: Sunan Kalijaga Press, 2002. 3–26.

———. "A Study of Islamic Herstory: Or How Did We Ever Get into This Mess?" *Women's Studies International Forum* 5.2 (1982): 207–219.

———. "Tear Off Your Western Veil!" *Food for Our Grandmothers: Writings by Arab-American and Arab-Canadian Feminists.* Ed. Joanna Kadi. Cambridge, MA: South End Press, 1994. 160–164.

———. *Women's Rights and Islam: From the I.C.P.D. to Beijing.* Self-published. Louisville, KY, 1999.

Hidayatullah, Aysha A. "Mariyya the Copt: Gender, Sex and Heritage in the Legacy of Muhammad's *umm walad.*" *Islam and Christian-Muslim Relations* 21.3 (July 2010): 221–243.

———. "Muslim Feminist Birthdays." *Journal of Feminist Studies in Religion* 27.1 (2011): 119–122.

———. "The Qur'anic Rib-ectomy: Scriptural Purity, Imperial Dangers, and Other Obstacles to the Interfaith Engagement of Muslim Feminist Hermeneutics." *Women and Interreligious Dialogue.* Ed. Catherine Cornille and Jillian Maxey (Eugene: Wipf & Stock, 2013).

Humphreys, R. Stephen. *Islamic History.* Princeton: Princeton University Press, 1991.

Ibn Kathir, Isma'il ibn 'Umar. *Tafsir Ibn Kathir.* 10 vols. Riyadh: Darussalam, 2003.

Ibn Taymiyyah, Shaykh-ul-Islaam. *Muqaddimah fi usul al-tafsir (An Introduction to the Principles of Tafseer).* Trans. Muhammad 'Abdul Haq Ansari. Birmingham, United Kingdom: Al-Hidaayah, 1993.

Isasi-Diaz, Ada Maria. *La Lucha Continues: Mujerista Theology.* Maryknoll, NY: Orbis, 2004.

———. *Mujerista Theology: A Theology for the Twenty-First Century.* Maryknoll, NY: Orbis, 1996.

Kandiyoti, Deniz. "Identity and Its Discontents: Women and the Nation." *Colonial Discourse and Post-Colonial Theory: A Reader.* Ed. Patrick Williams and Laura Chrisman. New York: Columbia University Press, 1994. 376–391.

Karam, Azza M. *Muslim Feminists in Western Academia: Questions of Power, Matters of Necessity. Islam in the Era of Globalization: Muslim Attitudes Toward Modernity and Identity.* Ed. Johan H. Meuleman. New York: Routledge Curzon, 2002. 171–188.

Karamah. "Women's Conference in Beijing." *Karamah: Muslim Women Lawyers for Human Rights.* July 2, 2009. http://www.karamah.org/news_womens_conference.htm.

Karim, Jamillah A. *American Muslim Women: Negotiating Race, Class, and Gender within the Ummah*. New York: New York University Press, 2009.

Khadduri, Majid. *The Islamic Conception of Justice*. Baltimore: Johns Hopkins University Press, 1984.

Kugle, Scott Siraj al-Haqq. "Sexual Diversity in Islam." *Voices of Islam*. Vol. 5. Gen. ed. Vincent J. Cornell. Vol. ed. Omid Safi. Westport, CT: Praeger, 2007. 131–167.

———. "Sexuality, Diversity and Ethics in the Agenda of Progressive Muslims." *Progressive Muslims: On Justice, Gender, and Pluralism*. Ed. Omid Safi. Oxford: Oneworld, 2003. 190–234.

Kugle, Scott Siraj al-Haqq, and Sarah Chiddy. "AIDS, Muslims, and Homosexuality." *Islam and AIDS: Between Scorn, Pity and Justice*. Ed. Farid Esack and Sarah Chiddy. Oxford: Oneworld, 2009. 137–153.

Kurzman, Charles. "Modern Thought." *Encyclopedia of Islam and the Muslim World*. Ed. Richard C. Martin. New York: Thomson/Gale, 2004. 467–472.

———. "Modernism." *Encyclopedia of Islam and the Muslim World*. Ed. Richard C. Martin. New York: Thomson/Gale, 2004. 456.

Kwok, Pui-lan. *Introducing Asian Feminist Theology*. Cleveland: Pilgrim Press, 2000.

Leaman, Oliver, and Sajjad Rizvi. "The Developed Kalam Tradition." *The Cambridge Companion to Classical Islamic Theology*. Ed. Tim Winter. Cambridge: Cambridge University Press, 2008. 77–96.

Leo, Elizabeth Shlala. "Islamic Female Sexuality and Gender in Modern Feminist Interpretation." *Islam and Muslim-Christian Relations* 16.2 (2005): 129–140.

Levine, Amy-Jill. "Settling at Beer-lahai-roi." *Daughters of Abraham: Feminist Thought in Judaism, Christianity, and Islam*. Ed. Yvonne Yazbeck Haddad and John L. Esposito. Gainesville: University of Press of Florida, 2001. 12–34.

Madigan, Daniel A. "Revelation and Inspiration." *Encyclopaedia of the Qur'an*. Ed. Jane Dammen McAuliffe. 2001–2006. Brill online. 21 July 21, 2009. http://www.brillonline.nl/subscriber/entry?entry=q3_COM-00174.

———. "Themes and Topics." *The Cambridge Companion to the Qur'an*. Ed. Jane Dammen McAuliffe. New York: Cambridge University Press, 2006. 79–95.

Al-Mahalli, Jalal al-Din Muhammad ibn Ahmad, and Jalal al-Din al-Suyuti. *Tafsir al-Jalalayn*. Trans. Feras Hamza. Louisville, KY: Fons Vitae, 2008.

Mahmood, Saba. *Politics of Piety: The Islamic Revival and the Feminist Subject*. Princeton: Princeton University Press, 2005.

———. "Secularism, Hermeneutics, and Empire: The Politics of Islamic Reformation," *Public Culture* 18.2 (2006).

Majeed, Debra Mubashshir. "Womanism Encounters Islam: A Muslim Scholar Considers the Efficacy of a Method Rooted in the Academy and the Church." *Deeper Shades of Purple: Womanism in Religion and Society*. Ed. Stacey M. Floyd-Thomas. New York: New York University Press, 2006. 38–53.

Majeed, Javed. "Modernity." *Encyclopedia of Islam and the Muslim World*. Ed. Richard C. Martin. New York: Thomson/Gale, 2004. 456–458.

Manji, Irshad. *The Trouble with Islam Today: A Muslim's Call for Reform in Her Faith*. New York: St. Martin's Griffin, 2003.

Marcotte, Roxanne D. "Muslim Women's Scholarship and the New Gender Jihad." *Women and Islam*. Ed. Zayn Kassam. Santa Barbara, CA: ABC-CLIO, 2010. 131–162.

Martin, Richard C., Mark R. Woodward, and Dwi S. Atmaja. *Defenders of Reason in Islam: Mu'tazilism from Medieval School to Modern Symbol*. Oxford: Oneworld, 1997.

Maududi, S. Abul A'la. *The Meaning of the Qur'an*. 10 vols. Lahore: Islamic Publications, 1988.

McAuliffe, Jane Dammen. "The Tasks and Traditions of Interpretation." *The Cambridge Companion to the Qur'an*. Ed. Jane Dammen McAuliffe. New York: Cambridge University Press, 2006. 181–210.

McCloud, Aminah Beverly. *African American Islam*. New York: Routledge, 1995.

———. "Islam in the African American Experience." *Voices of Islam*. Vol. 5. Gen. ed. Vincent J. Cornell. Vol. ed. Omid Safi. Westport, CT: Praeger, 2007. 69–83.

———. *Transnational Muslims in American Society*. Gainesville: University Press of Florida, 2006.

McGrath, Alister E. *Christian Theology: An Introduction*. Malden, MA: Blackwell, 2007.

Mernissi, Fatima. *Beyond the Veil: Male-Female Dynamics in Modern Muslim Society*. Cambridge, MA: Schenkman, 1975.

———. *The Veil and the Male Elite: A Feminist Interpretation of Women's Rights in Islam*. Trans. Mary Jo Lakeland. Cambridge, MA: Perseus Books 1991.

Michot, Yahya. "Revelation." *The Cambridge Companion to Classical Islamic Theology*. Ed. Tim Winter. Cambridge: Cambridge University Press, 2008. 180–196.

Mir, Mustansir. *Coherence in the Qur'an: A Study of Islahi's Concept of Nazm in Tadabbur-i Qur'an*. Indianapolis: American Trust, 1986.

———. "Unity of the Text of the Qur'an." *Encyclopaedia of the Qur'an*. Ed. Jane Dammen McAuliffe. 2001–2006. Brill online. June 3, 2008. http://www.encislam.brill.nl.proxy.library.ucsb.edu:2048/subscriber/entry?entry=q3_SIM-00437.

Mir-Hosseini, Ziba. "Beyond 'Islam' vs. 'Feminism.'" *IDS Bulletin* 42.1(2011): 67–77.

———. "Islam and Gender Justice." *Voices of Islam*. Vol. 5. Gen. ed. Vincent J. Cornell. Vol. ed. Omid Safi. Westport, CT: Praeger, 2007. 85–113.

———. "Justice, Equality and Muslim Family Laws: New Ideas, New Prospects." *Gender and Equality in Muslim Family Law: Justice and Ethics in the Islamic Legal Tradition*. Ed. Ziba Mir-Hosseini, Kari Vogt, Lena Larsen, and Christian Moe. London: I.B. Tauris, 2013. 26–27.

Mir-Hosseini, Ziba, Kari Vogt, Lena Larsen, and Christian Moe, eds. *Gender and Equality in Muslim Family Law: Justice and Ethics in the Islamic Legal Tradition*. London: I.B. Tauris, 2013.

Mirza, Qudsia. "Islamic Feminism and Gender Equality." · *ISIM Review* 21 (2008): 30–31.

———. *Islamic Law and Feminism*. London: Routledge Cavendish, 2006.

Mitchem, Stephanie Y. *Introducing Womanist Theology*. Maryknoll: Orbis, 2002.

Moosa, Ebrahim. "The Debts and Burdens of Critical Islam." *Progressive Muslims: On Justice, Gender, and Pluralism*. Ed. Omid Safi. Oxford: Oneworld, 2003. 111–127.

Mubarak, Hadia. "Breaking the Interpretive Monopoly: A Re-Examination of Verse 4:34." *Hawwa* 2.3 (2004): 261–289.

Murata, Sachiko and William C. Chittick. *The Vision of Islam*. St. Paul, MN: Paragon House, 1994.

Naghibi, Nima. "Women's Studies/Gender Studies." *Encyclopedia of Women and Islamic Cultures*. Ed. Suad Joseph. 2006–2009. Brill online. May 11, 2009. http://www.brillonline.nl/subscriber/entry?entry=ewic_COM-0063.

Nomani, Asra. *Standing Alone in Mecca: An American Woman's Struggle for the Soul of Islam*. San Francisco: HarperSanFrancisco, 2005.

Plaskow, Judith. "Christian Feminism and Anti-Judaism." *The Coming of Lilith: Essays on Feminism, Judaism, and Sexual Ethics, 1972–2003*. Ed. Judith Plaskow and Donna Berman. Boston: Beacon Press, 2005. 89–93.

———. "Jewish Theology in Feminist Perspective." *The Coming of Lilith: Essays on Feminism, Judaism, and Sexual Ethics, 1972–2003*. Ed. Judith Plaskow and Donna Berman. Boston: Beacon Press, 2005. 65–80.

———. *Standing Again at Sinai: Judaism from a Feminist Perspective*. New York: Harper San Francisco, 1990.

Plaskow, Judith, and Carol P. Christ. *Weaving the Visions: New Patterns in Feminist Spirituality*. San Francisco: Harper and Row, 1989.

Qutb, Sayyid. *In the Shade of the Qur'an*. Trans. M.A. Salahi and A.A. Shamis. 18 vols. Leicester, U.K.: Islamic Foundation, 2009.

Rahman, Fazlur. *Islam*. 2nd ed. Chicago: University of Chicago Press, 2002.

———. *Islam and Modernity: Transformation of an Intellectual Tradition*. Chicago: University of Chicago Press, 1984.

———. *Major Themes of the Qur'an*. Minneapolis: Bibliotheca Islamica, 1980.

Rastegar, Mitra. "Managing 'American Islam': Secularism, Patriotism and the Gender Litmus Test." *International Feminist Journal of Politics* 10.4 (2008) 455–474.

Renard, John. *Seven Doors to Islam: Spirituality and the Religious Life of Muslims*. Berkeley: University of California Press, 1996.

Rhouni, Raja. *Secular and Islamic Feminist Critiques in the Work of Fatima Mernissi*. Boston: Brill, 2010.

Rippin, Andrew. "Abrogation." *Encyclopaedia of Islam*. 3rd ed. Ed. Gudrun Krämer, Denis Matringe, John Nawas, and Everett Rowson. 2007. Brill online. July 12, 2009. http://www.brillonline.nl/subscriber/entry?entry=ei3_COM-0104.

———. "The Function of 'Asbab al-Nuzul' in Qur'anic Exegesis." *Bulletin of the School of Oriental and African Studies* 51.1 (20.

———. *Muslims: Their Religious Beliefs and Practices*. New York: Routledge, 2001.

———. "Occasions of Revelation." *Encyclopedia of the Qur'an*. Ed. Jane Dammen McAuliffe. 2001–2006. Brill online. Dec. 6, 2007. http://www.brillonline.nl/subscriber/entry?entry=q3_SIM-00305.

———. *The Qur'an and Its Interpretive Tradition*. Aldershot, U.K.: Ashgate, 2001.

Rippin, Andrew. "Tafsir." *The Encyclopedia of Religion*. Ed. Mircea Eliade. New York: Collier Macmillan, 1987. 236–244.

———. "Tafsir. (a.)." *Encyclopaedia of Islam*. 2nd ed. Ed. P. Bearman, Th. Bianquis, C. E. Bosworth, E. van Donzel, and W.P. Heinrichs. 2006. Brill online. Feb. 16, 2009. http://www.brillonline.nl/subscriber/entry? entry= islam_SIM-7294.

———. "Al-Zarkashi and al-Suyuti on the 'Occasion of Revelation' Material." *The Qur'an and Its Interpretive Tradition*. Aldershot: Ashgate, 2001 243–258.

Roald, Anne Sofie, "Feminist Reinterpretation of Islamic Sources: Muslim Feminist Theology in the Light of the Christian Tradition of Feminist Thought." *Women and Islamization: Contemporary Dimensions of Discourse on Gender Relations*. Ed. Karin Ask and Marit Tjomsland. Oxford: Berg, 1998. 17–44.

Roded, Ruth. "Women and the Qur'an." *Encyclopedia of the Qur'an*. Ed. Jane Dammen McAuliffe. 2001–2006. Brill online. May 8, 2009 http://www.brillonline.nl/subscriber/entry?entry=q3_COM-00220.

Rouse, Caroyln Moxley. *Engaged Surrender: African American Women and Islam*. Berkeley: University of California Press, 2004.

Ruether, Rosemary Radford. *Feminist Theologies: Legacy and Prospects*. Minneapolis: Fortress Press, 2007.

———. "Methodologies in Women's Studies and Feminist Theology." *Methodology in Religious Studies: The Interface with Women's Studies*. Ed. Arvind Sharma. Albany: SUNY Press, 2002. 179–206.

———. *Sexism and God-Talk: Toward a Feminist Theology*. Boston: Beacon Press, 1983.

Saeed, Abdullah. "Fazlur Rahman: A Framework for Interpreting the Ethico-Legal Content of the Qur'an." *Modern Muslim Intellectuals and the Qur'an*. Ed. Suha Taji-Farouki. Oxford: Oxford University Press, 2006. 37–66.

———. *Interpreting the Qur'an: Towards a Contemporary Approach*. New York: Routledge, 2006.

Schmidtke, Sabine. "Mu'tazila." *Encyclopaedia of the Qur'an*. Ed. Jane Dammen McAuliffe. 2001–2006. Brill online. Apr. 3, 2009. http://www.brillonline.nl/subscriber/entry?entry=q3_COM-00127.

Schüssler Fiorenza, Elisabeth. *Bread Not Stone: The Challenge of Feminist Biblical Interpretation*. Boston: Beacon Press, 1995.

———. *But She Said: Feminist Practices of Biblical Interpretation*. Boston: Beacon Press, 1992.

al-Shafi'i, Hasan Mahmud 'Abd al-Latif. "The Movement for Feminist Interpretation of the Qur'an and Religion and its Threat to the Arabic Language and Tradition." 2010. http://dialogicws.files.wordpress.com/2011/06/feminist-hermeneutics_shafii.pdf.

Shaikh, Sa'diyya. "Exegetical Violence: *Nushuz* in Qur'anic Gender Ideology." *Journal for Islamic Studies* 17 (1997): 49–73.

———. "Family Planning, Contraception, and Abortion in Islam: Undertaking *Khilafah*." *Sacred Rights: The Case for Contraception and Abortion in World Religions*. Ed. Daniel C. Maguire. Oxford: Oxford University Press, 2003. 105–128.

———. "Knowledge, Women, and Gender in the Hadith: A Feminist Interpretation." *Islam and Muslim-Christian Relations* 15.1 (2004): 99–108.

———. *Sufi Narratives of Intimacy: Ibn 'Arabi, Gender, and Sexuality*. Chapel Hill: University of North Carolina Press, 2012.

———. "A *Tafsir* of Praxis: Gender, Marital Violence, and Resistance in a South African Muslim Community." *Violence against Women in Contemporary World Religions: Roots and Cures*. Ed. Sa'diyya Shaikh and Dan Maguire. Cleveland: Pilgrim Press, 2007. 66–89.

———. "Transforming Feminisms: Islam, Women, and Gender Justice." *Progressive Muslims: On Justice, Gender, and Pluralism*. Ed. Omid Safi. Oxford: Oneworld, 2003. 147–162.

Silvers, Laury. "'In the Book We Have Left Out Nothing': The Ethical Problem of the Existence of Verse 4:34 in the Qur'an." *Comparative Islamic Studies* 2.2 (2006): 171–180.

Sonbol, Amirah El-Azhary. "Rethinking Women and Islam." *Daughters of Abraham: Feminist Thought in Judaism, Christianity, and Islam*. Ed. Yvonne Yazbeck Haddad and John L. Esposito. Gainesville: University Press of Florida, 2001. 108–146.

———. *Women, the Family, and Divorce Laws in Islamic History*. Syracuse: Syracuse University Press, 1996.

Soroush, Abdulkarim. *The Expansion of Prophetic Experience: Essays on History, Contingency and Plurality in Religion*. Trans. Nilou Mobasser. Boston: Brill, 2009.

Speight, R. Marston. "The Function of Hadith as Commentary on the Qur'an, as Seen in the Six Authoritative Collections." *Approaches to the History of the Interpretation of the Qur'an*. Ed. Andrew Rippin. Oxford: Clarendon Press, 1988. 63–81.

Stowasser, Barbara Freyer. "Gender Issues and Contemporary Qur'an Interpretation." *Islam, Gender, and Social Change*. Ed. Yvonne Yazbeck Haddad and John L. Esposito. New York: Oxford University Press, 1998. 30–44.

———. "The Qur'an and History." *Beyond the Exotic: Women's Histories in Islamic Societies*. Ed. Amira el-Azhary Sonbol. Syracuse: Syracuse University Press, 2005. 15–36.

———. "Women and Citizenship in the Qur'an." *Women, the Family, and Divorce Laws in Islamic History*. Ed. Amira El-Azhary Sonbol. Syracuse: Syracuse University Press, 1996. 23–38.

Al-Tabari, Abu Ja'far Muhammad ibn Jarir. *The History of al-Tabari*. Vol. 17: *The First Civil War*. Trans. G.R. Hawting. Albany: SUNY Press, 1996.

Taji-Farouki, Suha. Introduction. *Modern Muslim Intellectuals and the Qur'an*. Ed. Taji-Farouki. Oxford: Oxford University Press, 2006. 1–36.

Tohidi, Nayereh. "Muslim Feminism and Islamic Reformation: The Case of Iran." *Feminist Theologies: Legacy and Prospect*. Ed. Rosemary Radford Ruether. Minneapolis, MN: Fortress Press, 2007. 93–116.

Tracy, David. "Comparative Theology." *The Encyclopedia of Religion*. Ed. Mircea Eliade. New York: Collier Macmillan, 1987. 446–455.

Trible, Phyllis, and Russell, Letty M. "Unto the Thousandth Generation." *Hagar, Sarah, and their Children: Jewish, Christian, and Muslim Perspectives*. Ed. Trible and Russell. Louisville: Westminster John Knox Press, 2006. 1–32.

Valkenberg, Pim. "Does the Concept of 'Abrahamic Religions' Have a Future?" *Islam and Enlightenment: New Issues*. Ed. Erik Borgman and Pim Valkenberg. *Concilium* 2005, no. 5. Maryknoll, NY: Orbis, 2005, 103–111.

Van Doorn-Harder, Nelly. "Women Reading the Qur'an." *Concilium: Islam and Enlightenment, New Issues*. Ed. Erik Borgman and Pim Valkenberg. 5(2005): 51–60.

Van Ess, Josef. "Verbal Inspiration? Language and Revelation in Classical Islamic Theology." *The Qur'an as Text*. Ed. Stefan Wild. New York: Brill, 1996.

Von Denffer, Ahmad. *'Ulum al-Qur'an: An Introduction to the Sciences of the Qur'an*. Leicester: Islamic Foundation, 1994.

Wadud, Amina. "Alternative Qur'anic Interpretation and the Status of Muslim Women." *Windows of Faith: Muslim Women Scholar-Activists in North America*. Ed. Gisela Webb. Syracuse: Syracuse University Press, 2000. 3–21.

―――. "American Muslim Identity: Race and Ethnicity in Progressive Islam." *Progressive Muslims: On Justice, Gender, and Pluralism*. Ed. Omid Safi. Oxford: Oneworld, 2003. 270–285.

―――. "The Authority of Experience." Keynote address. Muslim Women and the Challenge of Authority Conference. Boston University. Mar. 31, 2012.

―――. "Foreword: Engaging *Tawhid* in Islam and Feminisms." *International Feminist Journal of Politics* 10.4 (2008): 435–438.

―――. *Inside the Gender Jihad: Women's Reform in Islam*. Oxford: Oneworld, 2006.

―――. "Islam Beyond Patriarchy Through Gender Inclusive Analysis." *Wanted: Equality and Justice in the Muslim Family*. Ed. Zainah Anwar. Petaling Jaya, Malaysia: Musawah/Sisters in Islam, 2009.

―――. "On Belonging as a Muslim Woman." *My Soul is a Witness: African-American Women's Spirituality*. Ed. Gloria Wade-Gayles. Boston: Beacon Press, 1995. 253–265.

―――. *Qur'an and Woman: Rereading the Sacred Text from a Woman's Perspective*. New York: Oxford University Press, 1999.

―――. "Qur'an, Gender, and Interpretive Possibilities." *Hawwa* 2.3 (2004): 316–336.

―――. "Roundtable Discussion: Feminist Theology and Religious Diversity." *Journal of Feminist Studies in Religion* 16.2 (2000): 90–100.

―――. "Towards a Qur'anic Hermeneutics of Social Justice: Race, Class, and Gender." *Journal of Law and Religion* 12.1 (1995–1996): 37–50.

―――. "What's Interpretation Got To Do With It: The Relationship between Theory and Practice in Islamic Gender Reform." *Islamic Family Law and Justice for Muslim Women*. Ed. Hjh Nik Noriani Nik Badlishah. Kuala Lumpur, Malaysia: Sisters in Islam, 2003. 83–94.

Watson, Natalie K. *Feminist Theology*. Grand Rapids: William B. Eerdmans, 2003.

Webb, Gisela. Introduction. *Windows of Faith: Muslim Women Scholar-Activists in North America*. Ed. Webb. Syracuse: Syracuse University Press, 2000. xi–xix.

Wehr, Hans. *A Dictionary of Modern Written Arabic.* Ed. J. Milton Cowan. 4th ed. Ithaca, NY: Spoken Language Services, 1994.

Wielandt, Rotraud "Exegesis of the Qur'an: Early Modern and Contemporary." *Encyclopedia of the Qur'an.* Ed. Jane Dammen McAuliffe. 2001–2006. Brill online. Dec. 7, 2007 http://www.brillonline.nl/subscriber/entry?entry=q3_COM-00059.

Williams, Delores S. *Sisters in the Wilderness: The Challenge of Womanist God-Talk.* Maryknoll, NY: Orbis Books, 1993.

Winter, Tim. Introduction. *The Cambridge Companion to Classical Islamic Theology.* Cambridge: Cambridge University Press, 2008. 1–18.

Wright, Peter Matthews. "Modern Qur'anic Hermeneutics." Ph.D. diss. University of North Carolina, Chapel Hill, 2008.

Index

'Abd Allah ibn 'Abbas, 24
'Abduh, Muhammad, 28, 34, 230n94
'Abrahamic' faiths, 47–48
Abou El Fadl, Khaled, 110, 116–117, 118, 140, 142, 226n85
Abugideiri, Hibba, 36
Abu Zayd, Nasr, 144, 176–177, 235n125
Adam and Eve, 11, 50, 90–91
agency, 36, 99, 134, 140, 153, 161, 163, 167, 191
   human agency, 117, 140–141, 181
   khilafah, 140, 191
   moral agency, 4, 92, 95, 112
Ahmad Khan, Sayyid, 28, 98
Ahmed, Leila, vii, 5, 34, 38
Ali, Kecia, viii, 7, 8, 10, 16, 131, 135, 140, 141, 143, 146, 148, 149, 160, 161, 166, 174, 175, 223n145, 226n87
androcentrism, 18, 44, 49, 50–52, 55, 120, 126, 133–135, 145, 178, 179, 184–185
Anwar, Ghazala, 5
Aquino, Maria Pilar, 53
asbab al-nuzul, see sabab al-nuzul
awliya', 92, 95, 102, 161, 222n117
azwaj, see zawj

Badran, Margot, 6, 34, 37, 39, 40, 143
Barlas, Asma, viii, 7, 8, 10, 14–15, 37, 55–57, 62, 66–67, 71, 79, 86, 88, 89, 90, 95, 110, 114, 116–117, 119–122, 125–127, 132, 134, 137, 148, 152, 154, 163–164, 166, 168, 183, 186–187, 213n49, 214nn56–57, 215n77, 216n130, 218n22, 219n40, 225n39, 228n38, 233n71, 236n8
   relationship with feminism, 41–44
   on the Hadith, 83–84
   on moral agency of men and women, 92–94
   on polygyny, 100–102
   on Qur'anic exegesis, 80
   on *shirk*, 111–113, 115
   reading of verse 2:223, 100
   reading of verse 4:34, 102, 106, 155–156, 165
   reading of verse 9:71, 95, 100
   reading of verse 33:59, 77–78
bid'ah, 28, 179, 180
Bulliet, Richard, 3, 179

Cannon, Katie, 52
Chaudhry, Ayesha, 151, 166, 169, 179, 229n73
conscientious pause, 140
Chung, Hyun Kyung, 53

Daly, Mary 50, 55, 56, 209n86
daraba, 104–108, 120, 135–141, 165–167

engaged surrender, 191
exegetical authority, 178–185, 194
   challenges to, 2, 33–34
   cumulative authority of, 26–27, 44, 79, 184
exegesis, *see* tafsir
equality
   in relation to biological difference, 129, 156, 188, 190–191
   in relation to concept of difference, 157–159, 167, 169, 186–189
   as egalitarian, 90, 93, 128, 132, 133, 135, 138, 141–152, 159, 164–167, 172, 192, 228n38
   in male-female relations, 34–35, 90, 94, 95, 112, 126–132, 135, 151–153, 157–160, 164–180, 184–185, 190–192, 193, 234n87
   meaning of, 129–133, 142–145, 146–154, 157–169, 172–175
   in moral potential, 92–94, 158, 161, 170–172
   as relating to commensurability between mutuality and hierarchy, 152, 159–167, 170
   problems raised by premodern conceptions of, 131, 151, 153, 165–166, 169, 180–184, 213n53, 236n17
Equality Principle, 95, 103
Esack, Farid, 27, 137, 225n44, 227n19

faddala, 71, 72, 73, 156, 162
fallibility, 51, 116, 117
Al-Faruqi, Isma'il Raji, 98
feminism
   in relation to colonial and neocolonial power, 2, 4, 28, 34, 38–43, 52, 61, 207n42
   terminological contestations, 37–45
feminist theology
   Asian and Asian-American, 53–54
   Christian, 48–51, 52
   Jewish, 48–51, 52
   tensions between Jewish, Christian and Muslim, 57–60
   Latina and Chicana, 53
   Womanist, 52–53
Fiorenza, Elisabeth Schüssler, 51, 55, 56

gender justice, 40, 128–130, 146, 150–151, 192–193, 195
gender mainstreaming, 129
God-Talk, 49, 53, 56, 126
gradualism, 95–96, 101, 105, 136
Groothuis, Rebecca, 158

Hadith, 9, 16, 24, 25, 27, 30, 33, 55, 81–86, 91, 126, 132, 180, 213n55, 214n65, 216n107, 216n109, 216–217nn130–131, 219n32, 219n36, 224n37
Hagar, 9, 47–48, 55, 57–59, 209n79
Hajar, *see* Hagar
Hammer, Juliane, x, 2–3, 4, 6, 7, 60, 179, 200n29
Hassan, Riffat, vii, viii, 7, 8, 9, 10–11, 54, 55, 85, 94, 97, 104, 115, 137, 148, 155, 200n23, 201n37, 212–213n43, 213n47, 214n65, 219n32, 219n36, 219n38, 219n41, 220n64, 224n37
   on equal creation, 90–93
   on the Hadith, 83–84, 132
   reading of verse 4:34, 104–105
hermeneutics, 15, 16, 31, 46, 51, 56, 89, 126, 144
Al-Hibri, Azizah, vii, viii, 7–10, 11–13, 55, 89, 96, 112, 113, 127, 130, 136, 137, 146, 155, 157, 201n34, 212n37, 214n57, 218n26, 222n117, 228n49
   on Iblisi logic, 112
   on polygyny, 100–101
   on Qur'anic philosophy of gradualism, 96

reading of verse 4:3, 100, 214n60
reading of verse 4:34, 73, 85,
    102–106, 214n60, 222n126,
    222n138, 234n87
reading of verse 30:21, 95
historicity, 30, 66, 79, 82–83, 144, 151,
    172, 183, 184, 236n17
    shift in understanding of time and
        history, 181–184
horizontal reciprocity 113, 128, 168, 170
human creation, 90–93

ijtihad, 12, 33, 35, 39, 113, 126
'ilm al-kalam, 31, 60, 121, 202n14, 203n15
Iblisi logic, *see* satanic logic
Ibn 'Abd al-Wahhab, Muhammad, 33
Ibn al-'Arabi, Muhyi al-Din, 26, 141
Ibn Kathir, 'Imad al-Din Abi al-Fida', 25
Ibn Taymiyah, Taqi al-Din Ahmad, 25,
    33, 34, 87
Isasi-Diaz, Ada Maria, 53
Islamic authority, *see* Authority
isra'iliyat, 24, 25, 30, 59, 91
istikbar, 113, 171

justice
    notions of, 145, 149, 151, 153–154, 174

Al-Kashani, 'Abd al-Razzaq, 26
khalifah, *see* agency
khilafah, *see* agency
Kwok, Pui-lan, 53
kyriarchy, 51, 56

liberation theology, 52

Al-Mahalli, Jalal al-Din, 25
marital harmony, 94–95, 106, 107
Mernissi, Fatima, viii, 5, 142, 214n73,
    216n119,
Mir-Hosseini, Ziba, 5, 39, 41, 131, 192,
    207n42, 238n52

Mirza, Qudsia, 131, 142, 228n39,
    231nn152–154
'moderate' islam, 60–61
modernist
    interpretations of Qur'an, 27–31,
        33–36
Moosa, Ebrahim, 142
mutashabihat, 24, 26
Mu'tazilite, 25, 121, 181, 235n118

nafs, 90–94, 99, 112, 160, 170,
    219nn39–40
naskh, 97–99, 221n85
nazm, 87–89
nushuz, 80, 103–104, 113, 135, 162,
    222n126, 223n145

patriarchy, 40, 49–50, 55–56, 58, 71, 96,
    126, 131, 133–134, 143, 163–166, 172
Plaskow, Judith, 19, 51, 55
power, 4, 6, 33, 38, 43, 44–45, 51, 56, 67,
    71, 74, 78, 127–128, 133–134, 148,
    157–159, 164, 167, 169, 180, 185,
    186, 192, 231nn152–154

qanitat, 103–104, 113, 162
qawwam, *see qawwamun*
qawwamun, 71–74, 102–103, 155–159,
    162, 167, 171, 212–213n43, 234n87,
    238n52
qiwamah, *see qawwamun*
Al-Qummi, 'Ali ibn Ibrahim, 25
Qur'anic verses
    atomistic treatment of, 87–90
    descriptive vs. prescriptive, 65, 70–71,
        135, 175
    universal vs. particular, 65–67, 70–71,
        74, 175
    2:48, 93
    2:106, 97
    2:187, 94–95, 101, 133–135, 161, 197,
        220n64

Qur'anic verses (*continued*)
  2:222, 161, 164
  2:222–223, 133–134, 161
  2:223, 99–100, 134–135, 161, 164, 197, 229n66
  2:228, 74, 99–100, 162, 197, 215n84
  2:229, 95
  2:233, 191
  2:282, 76, 99–100, 198
  3:25, 93
  3:161, 93
  3:195, 93, 161, 180, 234n90
  4:1, 91, 103, 160, 198
  4:3, 74–75, 100–102, 164, 229n66
  4:24, 163
  4:32, 180, 234n90
  4:34, 9, 71, 73–76, 85, 100, 102–109, 113–114, 120, 135–141, 155, 158, 162, 164, 165, 167, 176, 180, 198
  4:110–112, 93
  4:124, 93, 161
  4:128, 104, 198
  4:129, 101, 198
  6:164, 93
  9:71, 92, 94–95, 100, 102, 135, 161, 198
  9:72, 161
  10:30, 93
  14:51, 93
  16:58–59, 161
  16:97, 93
  16:111, 93
  23:6, 163
  30:21, 94–95, 101, 103, 106, 135, 161, 198
  33:35, 92, 104, 161, 180, 198, 234n90
  33:59, 77–78
  36:55–56, 114
  37:21–22, 114
  38:44, 106
  40:40, 161
  45:21–22, 93
  52:20, 164
  55:72, 164
  56:22, 164
  70:30, 163
  81:8, 161
  82:19, 93
  87:6–7, 97
Al-Qurtubi, Abu 'Abd Allah, 25

Rahman, Fazlur, 28, 31–33, 69, 82–83, 87, 88, 89, 90, 182, 211–212n25, 216n107
Rhouni, Raja, viii, 44, 142, 143–145, 146, 176, 207n47
Rippin, Andrew, 27, 68, 98, 211n11
Ruether, Rosemary, 49, 55–57, 59

satanic logic, 9, 112, 113
sabab al-nuzul, 16, 26, 65, 67–69, 71, 180, 182
  perspective of Fazlur Rahman, 211–212n25
Scott, Joan, 186, 187
secondary creation (of woman), 91
sexual difference, 18, 127, 131, 151, 154, 168, 178, 186–191, 228n39
shirk, 111, 112–116, 121, 159, 160, 164, 171, 183–184, 224n37, 234n97
Shaikh, Sa'diyya, viii, 7, 10, 15–16, 39, 40, 54, 55, 56, 57, 80, 86, 95, 189, 191
  reading of verse 4:34, 114
Silvers, Laury, 138, 141
Sonbol, Amira, 5, 213n55
Al-Suyuti, Jalal al-Din, 25, 68, 69
sukun, 106, 165, 234n78

Al-Tabari, Abu Ja'far Muhammad, 25
Al-Tabarsi, Abu 'Ali al-Fadl, 25
tafdil, *see faddala*
tafsir,
  emergence of feminist tafsir, 35–36

types and development of, 23–35
al-tafsir bi-l-ma'thur, 24, 82,
al-tafsir bi-l-ra'y, 24, 25, 27
al-tafsir bi-l-riwayah, 24, 25, 27
al-Qur'an bi-l-Qur'an, 87–88
taklif, 73, 157
taqwa, 92, 93, 112, 160, 168, 170
ta'wil, 25, 26, 29
tawhid, 16–18, 89, 110, 112–121, 168, 169, 170, 183, 224n37
tilth, 99, 134
Trible, Phyllis, 46, 48, 50
Al-Tusi, Abu Ja'far, 25
Al-Tustari, Sahl ibn 'Abd Allah, 26

Umm Salamah, 180, 234n90, 236n8

verticality
of relations, 160, 168

Wadud, Amina, vii, viii, 7, 8, 9, 10, 13–14, 23, 42, 47, 55–56, 58, 60, 67, 70, 71, 77, 86, 88, 89, 90, 91, 92, 93, 94, 97, 99, 100, 101, 102, 114, 117, 119, 121, 122, 130, 133, 134, 146, 148, 154–157, 163–164, 169, 173, 175–177, 186, 187, 189, 191, 205n109, 209n79, 209–210n88, 211nn7–9, 214n72, 218nn23–24, 219n39, 220n57, 221n97, 223n154, 227n19, 228n34, 229n66, 229n92, 231n138, 233n68
on equality of men and women, 126–129
on the Hadith, 84
on tawhid and *shirk*, 108–113
on Qur'an addressing men, 78
on Qur'anic exegesis, 79–80
on Qur'an's gradual approach toward social change, 96
on saying 'no' to verse 4:34, 138–140
reading of verse 2:228, 74, 215n84
reading of verse 2:282, 76
reading of verse 4:3, 75
reading of verse 4:34, 71–72, 76, 85, 104–109, 120, 135, 137, 141, 165–167
reading of verse 30:21 and 2:187, 95
on verticality and horizontality of relations, 168–169
Al-Wahidi, 'Ali ibn Ahmad, 65, 211n11
Williams, Delores, 52
Wright, Peter, 181, 199n4

Zain al-Din, Nazira, 35
Al-Zamakhshari, Abu al-Qasim Mahmud, 25
zawj, 91–92, 114, 214n72

Printed in Great Britain
by Amazon